"More Than Just A Name"

Incorporating
The Bridlington Roll of Honour
for the Second World War

by
Frank Bull, Chris Bonnett and Steve Adamson.

Dedication

This book is dedicated to all those people who lost their lives in the Second World War and whose names appear on various Bridlington memorials and Rolls of Honour.

1st Edition 2015
© Frank Bull, Chris Bonnett, and Steve Adamson 2015 (Authors).
ISBN 978-1-326-45420-3

All rights reserved.
No part of this publication may be reproduced, stored in a retrieval system or transmitted in any form or by any means, electronic or mechanical, photocopying, recording or otherwise, without the permission of the copyright holders.

Published by Lodge Books

Cover: Poppy Crosses In Wellington Gardens on Remembrance Sunday 2013 (F. Bull)

Acknowledgements

Sincere thanks are due to all the many individuals who provided information during our research into the Bridlington Roll of Honour for the Second World War, particularly Sarah Hutchinson and the staff at Bridlington Local Studies Library who gave immeasurable help and assistance with their records and provided photographs of the War Damage, local historian David Mooney and family historians Judith Bull and Peter Chapman. Special thanks are due to Maria Mascarenhas of Luis Photos, Main Street, Gibraltar, (www.luisphotosgibraltar.com) for supplying most of the ship photographs used in the book. Thanks are also due to the Schroder family archive for permission to reproduce the photograph of Erich Schmidt and to Bridlington School for allowing us to use their photographs of the pupil and all the 'Old Boys' who were killed in WW2. Other images used are either from the authors' own collections, provided by relatives of the people named in the Roll of Honour, or in the public domain. Various internet organisations provided information including Ancestry.com, Findmypast.co.uk, Wikipedia, uboat.net, Aircrew Remembered and the Commonwealth War Graves Commission (CWGC).

Bibliography

The Annals of Bridlington (1867 – 1942).
The Bridlington Free Press and Chronicle newspapers, (Indexed news cuttings, articles and reports in Bridlington Library).
The Commonwealth War Graves Register and Website (cwgc.org).
The Bridlington School Roll of Honour.
The Treasure House, Beverley, (Bridlington files on the War Memorial).
The East Yorkshire Family History Society MI's for Bridlington.
The Burton Agnes Disaster by Richard Jones.
Air War over East Yorkshire in WW2 by Paul Bright.
The Bomber Command War Diaries: An Operational Reference Book 1939-1945 by Martin Middlebrook and Chris Everitt.

Introduction

The book records all the WW2 names on the Bridlington War Memorial (Cenotaph), St Mary (The Priory) Parish Church Roll of Honour, Bridlington School Roll of Honour, Christ Church Roll of Honour, Bridlington Trinity AFC Roll of Honour, NALGO Roll of Honour and the WW2 War Dead Burials in Bridlington Cemetery.

The same names appear on several memorials, The War Memorial and Priory names in particular are almost a complete match. Although these various sources have some discrepancies in their spelling and initials which we have tried to clarify. In addition names have been checked against the Commonwealth War Graves Register (CWGC) for Civilian and Service War Dead.

Not all of these deaths were military in nature and not all military casualties were killed in action because Government policy decreed that anyone in the Armed Forces or Merchant Navy who died from any cause while on active service, or after being on active service, could be counted as a war fatality. When the Second World War broke out in September 1939, there was no national mass movement to volunteer for the Armed Forces, as there had been in 1914, and the majority of those who were in the Services between 1939 and 1945 were conscripts.

We have used 'typical' Family History resources such as the census and birth, marriage and death records in order to give as much background as possible to the names on the Roll of Honour. Unfortunately these sources are not infallible and we apologise if mistakes have been made.

The Bridlington School Roll of Honour is repeated in full even though some pupils were not residents of Bridlington itself but they were all 'Bridlington Old Boys'. Likewise with the civilians, not all lived in Bridlington but they unfortunately died here as did the German Air Crews and the Polish Servicemen. Also included are the German PoWs and their guards who died in the Burton Agnes accident.

Contents

Front Sheet.. i
Dedication... ii
Acknowledgements iii
Introduction.. iv
Contents (this page) v

1 Bridlington WW2 Memorials
   - Bridlington War Memorial.. 1
   - Priory Church Roll of Honour 6
   - Bridlington School Roll of Honour 11
   - Christ Church Roll of Honour 14
   - Trinity AFC Memorial.. 16
   - NALGO Memorial 17
   - Burma Star and Dunkirk Veterans Memorials............................. 18

2 The Air raids on Bridlington.. 19

3 Allied and German Deaths
   - German Aircrew buried in Bridlington Cemetery....................... 25
   - Polish Soldiers buried in Bridlington Cemetery 26
   - The Burton Agnes Accident 27
   - Bridlington Cemetery.. 31

4 The Bridlington Roll of Honour for the Second World War 33
   (A to Z listing of names and details)

Appendix 309

Index 315

1
Bridlington WW2 Memorials

Bridlington War Memorial

Bridlington War Memorial was erected in Wellington Gardens, at the junction of Quay Road and Wellington Road, in 1921. The War Memorial is a 'Cenotaph' style monument, stands 22 feet high and is made from Darley Dale stone. The architect of the memorial was Ernest Theakston, F.R.I.B.A., and the sculptor was S Nicholson Babb, R.B.S. The War Memorial was unveiled by Captain. S.H. Radcliffe. C.M.G., R.N. at 3 o'clock on Sunday the 10th July 1921.

Bridlington War Memorial (F Bull)

The four sided monument was initially erected in honour of those men of Bridlington who lost their lives in the First World War. The upper part of the Monument is formed to suggest a stone tomb or sarcophagus, on top of which is a bronze lamp or brazier representing the flames of eternal life. The two main faces contain the name tablets for those who fell in WW1.

Victory Face, (shown left). The name tablet on this face is surmounted by a small shield showing the arms of Bridlington, above this is a large bronze depicting the winged figure of 'Victory gently laying laurel wreaths on two fallen warriors'

Winged figure of Victory (F Bull)

Seaway Face, (shown right). The name tablet on this face is surmounted by a small shield showing the arms of Yorkshire, above this is a second large bronze figure depicting 'The men who kept the seaway' in honour of British seamen and sailors who fell in WW1.

The men who kept the seaway (F Bull)

The World War Two Tablets

Surprisingly, the adding of additional name tablets to the sides of the existing war memorial was not the first choice of a memorial to honour those men and women of Bridlington who fell in WW2. Discussions on a suitable memorial began in June 1946 when the Town Clerk raised the matter in council and it was decided to ask the residents for their ideas on what form such a memorial should take. The closing date for suggestions was 30th September 1946 and a special committee would be formed to consider the suggestions and report on the best one received.

The special committee, named the War Memorial Committee reported in October 1947 that the best suggestions were (1) A rest home for old people and (2) A cultural centre for meetings & lectures etc. It was noted that funding for either could not be met by voluntary contributions and would have to be met through the rates. The matter was deferred until the end of the current financial year. The report was finally adopted in 1948 but action was again deferred for financial reasons.

In 1949 it was agreed that 26 old people's bungalows being built at Bessingby estate would be named 'Remembrance Court' and this would comply with suggestion (1). It was not until September 1949 that the Committee was asked to consider the addition of new bronze tablets to the existing WW1 War Memorial in Wellington Gardens. This was agreed and an appeal in the local papers asked for names and information on Name, Rank, Service No., Date and Circumstances of Death, and Bridlington Address before Enlistment, to be sent to the Town Clerk.

The names on the Priory Church WW2 Memorial Screens and other WW2 memorials were also consulted. Two of the main criteria seemed to be a 'Bridlington residency' at some time and verifiable details of service. After all the required information was obtained, two new tablets containing 210 names were manufactured and added to the existing WW1 memorial.

The two new tablets were unveiled by the Mayor, Alderman R. Maw, during the Remembrance service at the Bridlington War Memorial on Saturday morning, the 11th November 1950. The service was conducted by the Mayor's chaplain the Rev. A. H. Hawkins, who dedicated the tablets. The Rev. G. W. Elliot, president of the Bridlington Free Church Council, gave the scripture reading and the Rector of Bridlington, Canon J. W. Lamb, pronounced the benediction.

In addition to the new tablets the inscriptions on the top of the two main faces were amended to include the dates 1939-1945 as shown below.

1914-1919 TO OUR MEN WHO GAVE THEIR LIVES FOR FREEDOM **1939-1945**	1914-1919 TO OUR MEN WHO KEPT THE SEAWAY **1939-1945**
The Victory Face inscription	The Seaway Face inscription

The Second World War Name tablets

The two Second World War Name tablets are installed on each side face, just above the base, as shown in the left and right pictures.

A to J Tablet (F Bull)   J to W Tablet (F Bull)

The 210 names on the tablets are arranged in alphabetical order by Surname and Christian name initials only.

The following two pages repeat the list of names as they are displayed on each tablet on the Bridlington War Memorial.

TABLET 1 (A to J)

ALLBUT J F B	DRISCOLL J F	HOBSON J D
ABELL E R	DUNKERLEY E	HODGSON A W
ALLAN W S	EARNSHAW D	HOGARTH K H
ALTHAM E J T	ELLIS F G	HOGGARD T C
ANDERSON A M	ELLIS F	HOLDEN G
ANDERSON A W	EMMERSON W	HOLMES A
ARKSEY S K	FEATHERSTONE F	HOPE F W
ARMITAGE E L	FIRMAN J G	HORNBY T
ASTON D W	FLETCHER C H	HOUGHTON J D
ATKINSON J J	FLOWER F	HOWES W H
AYRE E	FORBES A E	HYLAND M
BAILEY V T	FORSTER L A	IRELAND G
BAKER H	FOSTER E	JACKSON W
BARNBY R V	FOWLER N C	JEFF J
BARRON L A	FREEMAN D	
BARRON W F	FREEMAN W	
BATTYE L	FRIEND H L	
BEECROFT G	FUSSEY G	
BROWN C E	GANT J L	
BURGESS J W	GARRETT R	
BUTCHER J A	GEE A	
CAPPLEMAN D	GEE F H	
CARTER G	GIBB G R	
CARTER C H [1]	GIBSON R E	
CAWKHILL W [2]	GILMOUR W	
CHATTERTON E G	GILSON J W	
CHEETHAM A F	GIOVETTI P A	
CHEETHAM F A	GLAZIER B F [4]	
CHIVERS F	GLEDHILL S	Notes:
CLARK G E	GLENVILLE P	[1] Should be CARTER R N
CLARK R E	GOW C H	[2] Should be CAWKILL
CLARK J	GOW I M	[3] Should be COLMAN
CLARKSON A	GRAINGER G K	[4] Should be GLAZIER F B
CLAXTON L	GRAY C	
COATES W N	GRAY D A	
COLE K G.	GREENSIDES A S	
COLEMAN R W [3]	GREGORY F W	
CONSTABLE A R	GUTHERLESS E V	
COOPER K G	HANTON L S	
COPSEY F	HARDEN G J	
CORNELL G	HAWKINS R K	
CORNELL S	HAWKSWORTH R	
DARWEN G G	HEBDON D	
DOBSON G	HERMON H C	
DOWSE L	HILLS C	
DOWSE W L	HINCHLIFFE D A	

TABLET 2 (J to W)

JEFF R V	RIPLEY R J	WHITMAN G H
JEFFREY A	ROBSON J H	WIKNER E B
JORDAN A	ROBSON N C	WILBOURNE C
JORDAN M	ROGERS H D	WILKINSON P
JORDAN R H	ROMYN R H	WILLBOURNE J T
KENNY W	SAMPSON J	WILLIAMSON A
KIRBY A W	SANDERSON G	WILSON H L
LAMMING M R	SANGWIN K	WILSON H
LEASON James W	SAWDEN C	WILSON S
LEASON John W	SAWDON J B	WITTY B B
LEDDY J P	SHAW E	WITTY G G
LINSLEY J W	SHAW J J	WOODCOCK J W
LISTER B J D	SHIPPEY H	
LONGDEN G H	SIMPSON B	
LYTH S	SIMPSON N	
MARTINDALE F	SIMPSON S	
MARTINDALE P D	SLAUGHTER H J	
McALLISTER J	SMITH R	
McKIRDY D	SPEAR B	
MEGSON G	STOREY G A	
MILLARD J W	STURGEON E	
MILNER C	TAYLOR E	
MITCHELL H	TEMPLE C H	
MORRIS J	TEMPLE E W	
MURRAY R	THACKERAY E D	
NEAL A L	THOMAS R	
NEW K E	THOMPSON A	
NEWTON J	THOMPSON S W	
NEWTON T A	THWAITES E A	
NICHOLSON A A	TURNER P E	
NICHOLSON B	TWIDDY D F	
NICHOLSON P J	UNDERWOOD E R	
NIXON S W	USHER G F	
ORUM S N	WADE H T	
PARISH E G	WAINWRIGHT C H	
PARKIN E	WAINWRIGHT G E	
PARKINSON W	WAITES A G	
PERKINS P G	WAITES W	
PINDER H	WALKER B	
POLLARD F H	WARD R	
POTTER D K	WATSON D G	
POWLS F	WATSON J W	
PURDON J K	WEBB M G	
PURDON P D K	WHITAKER H	
RENNOLDSON T	WHITTAKER E	
RILEY N	WHITE W	

St Mary (The Priory) Parish Church Memorials

Bridlington Priory was founded around 1113 as an Augustinian monastery. Over the centuries, the Priory has known good and bad times as a wealthy pilgrimage centre in the middle ages, as a semi-ruin when Henry VIII destroyed the monastery, as a flourishing parish church after Victorian restoration. Since Mediaeval times worship has been enhanced by an unbroken musical tradition which continues to this day with its traditional robed choir and world famous organ.

The Priory (F Bull)

There are three WW2 memorials in the Priory, one is dedicated to Squadron Leader 'Ginger' Lacey, another is for the 23rd Hussars and the third is the Bridlington Roll of Honour for WW2.

'Ginger' Lacey
This memorial consists of a wooden plaque, as shown on the right, and reads:-

>Squadron Leader
>J. H. 'Ginger' Lacey
>DFM and Bar
>Croix de Guerre 1917 – 1989

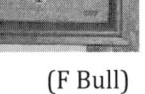

(F Bull)

'Ginger' Lacey was one of the highest scoring NCO pilots of the Battle of Britain.

The 23rd Hussars
This memorial consists of a large carved wooden panel recording the names of 40 members of 'C' Squadron of the 23rd Hussars who lost their lives in the six months after the D-Day landings. Another six small panels record the names of members of 'A' and 'B' Squadrons of the 23rd Hussars who also lost their lives in WW2.

The 23rd Hussars association with Bridlington began when they were based in Bridlington in 1944 while training for the invasion in Normandy. Equipped with Sherman tanks they were part of the 29th Armoured Brigade of the 11th (The Black Bull) Armoured Division. After the war ended the 'C' Squadron memorial was carved by German Craftsmen and placed in the 23rd Hussars chapel in Germany.

The 23rd Hussars Memorial Screen (F Bull)

When the 23rd Hussars were disbanded at the end of January1946, the memorial was presented to the Rector of the Priory by Major L. G. Haggar. It is believed that only one Bridlington resident, Trooper Ronald Henry Jordan, was killed while serving with the 23rd Hussars. His name is not included on the memorial screen.

The Bridlington Priory Roll of Honour for WW2.
This memorial consists of a large wooden screen containing a total of nine panels on which are carved the names of over 200 Bridlington people who lost their lives during the Second World War. This memorial was carved by Mr H Thomson of Kilburn, well known as the 'Mouse man' for incorporating small mice in his work.

In January 1948, General Sir Montague Stopford, GOC Northern Command, unveiled the 23rd Hussars Screen and the Priory Roll of Honour Screen. Both memorials were then dedicated by the Bishop of Hull the Rt. Rev. H. T. Vodden. The Mayor of Bridlington, Councillor F. F. Millner, asked the Rector, Canon J. W. Lamb to accept the Priory Roll of

Honour Screen on behalf of the citizens of Bridlington. A further fourteen names were later added to the Priory Roll of Honour Screen and the unveiling and dedication of the additional names took place during the morning service by Major General J. Y. Whitfield, chief of staff, Northern Command, and the Rector (Canon J. W. Lamb). After the unveiling ceremony, two minutes' silence was observed and the Last Post and Reveille were sounded. Part of the screen is shown right and unlike the War Memorial, the names include the Christian name(s) rather than just the initials. They start in alphabetical order of Surname from A to Z and are then followed by 14 additional names from A to Z. Our research indicates that at least two of the names are corrections, not additions, i.e. Beecroft for Beechcroft and Willbourn for Willbourne.

Bridlington Roll of Honour Screen (F Bull)

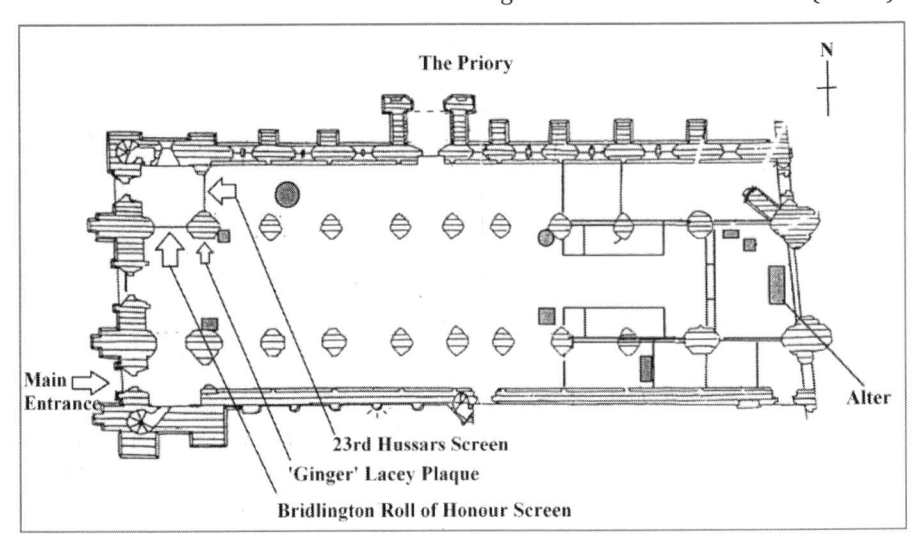

Location of WW2 Memorials in the Priory

The following 2 pages repeat the list of names as they are displayed on the Priory Roll of Honour panels for WW2. The numbers in bold text are the panel numbers.

Bridlington WW2 Memorials

1 EDWIN ABELL
WILLIAM S ALLAN
EDWIN J ALTHAM
ANNIE M ANDERSON
ALFRED W ANDERSON
SIDNEY K ARKSEY
ERIC L ARMITAGE
DEREK W ASTON
JOHN J ATKINSON
EDWARD AYRE
VINCENT T BAILEY
RICHARD V BARNBY
LOUIS BARRON
WALTER F BARRON
GEORGE BEECHCROFT[1]
CHARLES E BROWN
JOHN W BURGESS
JAMES A.BUTCHER
DEREK CAPPLEMAN
GEORGE CARTER
RAYMOND CARTER
WILLIAM CAWKHILL[2]
ELSIE G CHATTERTON
ARNOLD F CHEETHAM

2 FRANK A CHEETHAM
FRANK CHIVERS
GEORGE E CLARK
JOHN CLARK
ARTHUR CLARKSON
LEONARD CLAXTON
WILLIAM N COATES
KENNETH G COLE
ROBERT W.COLEMAN[3]
ARTHUR R CONSTABLE
KENNETH G COOPER
FREDERICK COPSEY
GEORGE CORNELL
SYDNEY CORNELL
GEOFFREY G DARWEN
GEOFFREY DOBSON
LEONARD DOWSE
WILFRED L DOWSE
JOHN F DRISCOLL
ERIC DUNKERLEY
DENIS EARNSHAW
GEORGE EDWARDS
FRANCIS G ELLIS
FRED ELLIS

3 FRANK FEATHERSTONE
CHARLES H FLETCHER
FRED FLOWER
ALEX E FORBES
THOMAS A FORSTER
HARRY FOSTER
NORMAN C FOWLER
DAVID FREEMAN
WARD FREEMAN
HARRY L FRIEND
GILBERT FUSSEY
JOHN L GANT
CHARLES H GARRETT[4]
ARTHUR GEE
FREDERICK H GEE
GEOFFREY R GIBB
RONALD E GIBSON
WILLIAM GILMOUR
JOHN W GILSON
BRIAN F GLAZIER[5]
SYDNEY GLEDHILL
PATRICK GLENVILLE
CHARLES H GOW
IAN M GOW

4 GEORGE K GRAINGER
CYRIL GRAY
DAVID A GRAY
ALAN S GREENSIDES
F W GREGORY
ERNEST V GUTHERLESS
LUCAS S HANTON
GEORGE J HARDEN
ROBERT K HAWKINS
RICHARD HAWKSWORTH
DONOVAN HEBDON
HERBERT C HERMON
CYRIL HILLS
DENIS A HINCHLIFFE
J D HOBSON
ALBERT W HODGSON
GERTRUDE HOLDEN
KENNETH H HOGARTH
WILLIAM H HOWES
DONALD HOUGHTON
TREVOR HORNBY
FREDERICK W HOPE
ARTHUR HOLMES
TOM C HOGGARD

5 MOLLY HYLAND
GEORGE IRELAND
WILLIAM JACKSON
JOHN JEFF
R V JEFF
ALFRED JEFFREY
ARTHUR JORDAN
MARK JORDAN
RONALD H JORDAN
WILLIAM KENNY
ARTHUR W KIRBY
MALCOLM R LAMMING
JAMES W LEASON
JOHN W LEASON
JOSEPH P LEDDY
JOHN W LINSLEY
BRIAN J LISTER
GEORGE H LONGDEN
SIDNEY LYTH
FRANK MARTINDALE
PETER D MARTINDALE
GEORGE MEGSON
JAMES McALLISTER
DAVID McKIRDY

6 JOHN W MILLARD
HAROLD MITCHELL
ROBERT MURRAY
ALBERT L NEAL
KENNETH E NEW
JANE NEWTON
THOMAS A NEWTON
AGNES A NICHOLSON
BEN NICHOLSON
PATRICK J NICHOLSON
STANLEY W NIXON
S N ORUM
EDWARD G PARISH
EVELYN PARKIN
WILLIAM PARKINSON
PERCIVAL G PERKINS
HARRY PINDER
FRANCIS H POLLARD
DENIS K POTTER
FRANK POWLS
JOHN K PURDON
PETER D PURDON
EDWARD REDDING
NORAH RILEY

More Than Just A Name

7 RICHARD J RIPLEY	8 EDWARD W TEMPLE	9 CYRIL WILLBOURNE
JOHN H ROBSON	EDWARD D THACKERAY	HARRY L WILSON
NORMAN C ROBSON	RONALD THOMAS	HENRY WILSON
PERCY ROGERS	ARTHUR THOMPSON	STANLEY WILSON
HAROLD D ROGERS	STANLEY W THOMPSON	PETER WILKINSON
RONALD ROMYN	ERIC THWAITES	ARTHUR WILLIAMSON
JOSEPH SAMPSON	PETER E TURNER	BASIL B WITTY
GERALD SANDERSON	ERNEST R UNDERWOOD	GEORGE G WITTY
GERALD SANGWIN	GEOFFREY F USHER	JOHN W WOODCOCK
CHARLES SAWDEN	HECTOR T WADE	
JOHN B SAWDON	CHARLES H WAINWRIGHT	JOHN ALLBUTT
ESTHER SHAW	GERTRUDE E WAINWRIGHT	HARRY BAKER
JOHN J SHAW	ALLEN G WAITES	LESLIE BATTYE
HARRY SHIPPEY	WALTER WAITES	GEORGE BEECROFT
BERNARD SIMPSON	BERNARD WALKER	ROBERT CLARK
NORMAN SIMPSON	RONALD WARD	WILLIAM EMMERSON
STANLEY SIMPSON	DOROTHY G WATSON	JAMES FIRMAN
HENRY J SLAUGHTER	JAMES W WATSON	RAYMOND GARRETT
ROBERT SMITH	MAURICE G WEBB	PIETRO GIOVETTI
BETTY SPEAR	HAROLD WHITAKER	JACK MORRIS
GEORGE A STOREY	WILLIAM WHITE	THOMAS RENNOLDSON
EARNEST STURGEON	GEORGE H WHITMAN	DONALD TWIDDY
ERIC TAYLOR	EDITH WHITTAKER	CYRIL WILLBOURN
CHARLES H TEMPLE	ERIC B WIKNER	JESSIE WILLBOURN

Notes
[1] GEORGE BEECHCROFT on panel 1 was corrected to GEORGE BEECROFT on panel 9
[2] WILLIAM CAWKHILL on Panel 1 should be spelt WILLIAM CAWKILL
[3] ROBERT W COLEMAN on Panel 2 should be spelt ROBERT W COLMAN
[4] CHARLES H GARRETT on Panel 2 was corrected to RAYMOND GARRETT on Panel 9
[5] BRIAN F GLAZIER on Panel 3 is FRANCIS BRIAN GLAZIER (see his individual page).

Bridlington School
Roll of Honour for the Second World War

Bridlington School was founded in September 1899 although it can trace its origins further back to a Bridlington School founded in 1447 by King Henry VI. In 1975 the local LEA changed the school to a comprehensive and it retained its girls' and boys' boarding house until the 1990s. It no longer has a boarding house.

The school motto is "Vitai Lampada Tradunt," taken from the Roman poet and philosopher Lucretius' and directly translates as "They Hand on the Torch of Life."

In 1949 a booklet was published which commemorated the School's Golden Jubilee and included in it were the Rolls of Honour of the First and Second World Wars. The second list was presumably used to provide the names that were inscribed on the plaque in the School's Second World War Memorial Garden which was dedicated on 22nd July 1951.

The same list was used as the starting point for the compilation of the Roll of Honour by M. J. Stewart, a reference copy of which is held in the local studies department of Bridlington Library.

The Roll of Honour booklet contains the names of 94 Old Boys and one Bridlington School pupil who died in WW2. The names are recorded in the order of armed forces precedence as it existed during the Second World War, beginning with the Royal Navy, followed by the British Army in the order of the seniority of units. The Royal Air Force comes next, with front line squadrons listed in numerical order. These are followed by training and miscellaneous units. Merchant Navy casualties are listed in chronological order, as are civilians.

Every man and boy in the Roll of Honour received an obituary in The Bridlingtonian, although some accounts were brief. For many of the Old Boys who lived in Bridlington, Driffield or Beverley there was an announcement in the press.

At the time when the Second World War broke out, Bridlington School was a fee paying day grammar school for boys which also had a boarding department.

Bridlington School in 1899 (Bridlington Free Press)

The Memorial Chairs

At the beginning of the 1932 Summer Term Mr. Wilfrid Parkinson MA commenced duties as the third Headmaster of Bridlington School. The Bridlingtonian of July 1932 reported that the Assembly Hall was to be redecorated and the Headmaster wished for the hall to be furnished in a more dignified manner and an appeal was made for donations towards the cost of new oak chairs.

The chairs were called Memorial Chairs and Old Boys could purchase a chair in memory of their time at the School, and also relatives could donate a chair as a memorial to deceased Old Boys. A small bronze name plaque was affixed to the rear of the chair and when the scheme started, the cost of a chair and plaque was 27s 6d (£1. 37p).

There are no Memorial Chairs in Bridlington School and enquiries as to what happened to them have been unsuccessful. It is believed that they were possibly disposed of in the 1970's when they would be 40years old and probably worn out.

The following page lists the Surnames and Christian names of Bridlington School Old Boys whose names appear on the School Roll of Honour for World War 2. These names are shown in alphabetical order and not in the order of armed forces precedence as they appear in the original Bridlington School Roll of Honour.

The names in bold letters are those pupils and 'Old Boys' that appear on the Bridlington War Memorial and/or the Priory Roll of Honour.

ABELL Edwin Raymond
AKESTER Alfred Harold
ALLAN William Stewart
ANDREWS John Norman
ARMITAGE Eric Leonard
ASTON Derek Wilson
ATHRON Thomas Sydney
BAILEY Vincent Thomas
BARNBY Richard Vivian
BREMNER Alexander
CAMPBELL Malcolm Anderson
CHEETHAM Arnold Foster
CHEETHAM Frank Alan
CLARK George Ellis
CLARK Robert Ernest
COOPER John Dawson
COOPER Kenneth George
DACRE Arthur Kenneth
DOBSON Geoffrey
DUNKERLEY Eric
DYNES George Charles
EARNSHAW Dennis
ELLIS Fred
ELLIS Francis Gordon
ELLIS John MM
ELLISON John
GARBETT Leslie Percival
G1BB Geoffrey Robinson
GLENVILLE Patrick
GREENSIDES Alan Swann
HARRISON Alan Bruce DSO
HARTLEY Harold Edward
HAWKINS Robert Kemplay
HERMON Herbert Cecil
HINCHLIFFE Denis Aubrey
HOGARTH Kenneth Herbert
HOGGARD William Henry
HOLMES Arthur
HORNBY Aubrey Trevor
HORSAMAN Granville
JAMES Frank Stanley
JULIAN John Philip Reginald
KELLY Vincent
LAFON Christian Roger Michel
LAMMING Malcolm Redfearn
LINDSAY Graham Douglas
LISTER Brian John Barnett
LOCKWOOD Charles Hellawell

LUMB Arthur
MARTINDALE Peter Drake
MASSEY Louis Patrick DFC & Bar
MAXWELL Stanley Maxwell
MILLARD John Wilfred
MILLS James Francis Dawson
MOLLETT Richard Douglas
NAYLOR Claude Lambert
NEAL Albert Leslie
NEEDLER George Stephenson
NEWTON Thomas Arthur AFM
NICHOLSON Ben
NICHOLSON Patrick James
OXTOBY John Martin
PEACE Eric Henry
PEXTON Harold Cass DFC
PURDON John Kirkwood
PURDON Peter David Kirkwood
ROBINSON Joseph
ROBSON John Henry DFC
ROGERS Harold Dennis
ROUNDING John Raymond
ROWLEY Joseph Peter
RUSSELL Frank Lincoln
SANDERSON Gerald
SANGWIN Keith
SAWDON John Bennett
SMITH Bryan Arnold OBE (Mil)
SMITH Malcolm Boston
SMITH Paul Boston
STOREY George Alexander
THACKERAY Edward Derek
THOMAS Ronald
TOWSE Christopher Danby DFM
TRUELOVE Arthur
USHER Geoffrey Frederick MM
WADSWORTH Philip
WALKER Colin Malcolm
WARDILL Wilfrid George
WHITTAKER Arthur John
WIKNER Eric
WILLBOURN Cyril
WILLIS Harry
WILSON Stanley
WITTY George Greenley
WOOD Harry Gilboy
WRIGHT Frank

Christ Church Roll of Honour

Christ Church in Bridlington was built in 1841 by Gilbert Scott, the architect of St Pancras Station in London, as a 'Chapel of Ease', It became a parish church in its own right in 1871 and to mark the occasion a chancel and steeple were added to the building.

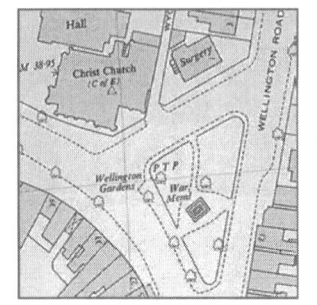

Christ Church is situated on the corner of Quay Road and Wellington Road and overlooks Wellington Gardens and the Bridlington War Memorial as shown on the map (left).

The Roll of Honour Plaques

There are two 'Roll of Honour' plaques dedicated to parishioners who died in WW1 and WW2.

The plaques consist of marble panels inset into the left hand wall just inside the main entrance to the church.

The Roll of Honour plaques are situated above each other with the top plaque dedicated to the First World War and the plaque below it is dedicated to the Second World War.

Christ Church Bridlington   (F Bull)

The Dedication of the Second World War plaque took place on the 23rd October 1946 and the plaque cost £500. Most of the twenty eight names are believed to be former members of the Christ Church Company of the Church Lads Brigade. In November 1947 wreaths were laid at the memorial Plaque and the names of the fallen were read out by the Vicar after which the 'Last Post' and 'Reveille' were sounded.

The Second World War plaque is shown below and contains twenty eight names, carved in pairs and reading from left to right. The initial letters of each name were originally gilded, which has now worn off a little but is still quite readable.

The Second World War Plaque (F Bull)

TRANSCRIPT
1939 - 1945

KENNETH ARKSEY, LESLIE BATTYE,
LEONARD DOWSE, WILFRED LAWRENCE DOWSE,
CHARLES HENRY FLETCHER, WARD FREEMAN,
WILLIAM GILMOUR, PIETRO ALFREDO GIOVETTI,
FREDERICK GILBERT, DENIS AUBREY HINCHLIFFE,
ROBERT KEMPLAY HAWKINS, ARTHUR HOLMES,
JOSEPH PATRICK LEDDY, CHARLES MILNER,
JACK MORRIS, ALBERT LESLIE NEAL,
HARRY PINDER, NORMAN ROBSON.
HARRY SHIPPEY, BERNARD SIMPSON
DONALD TWIDDY, HARRY WALKER,
MAURICE WEBB, PETER WILKINSON,
ARTHUR WILLIAMSON, HARRY WILSON,
HENRY WILSON, DAVID ANTHONY GRAY (*Civilian*)

Note:
Only Frederick Gilbert and Harry Walker do not appear on the Bridlington War Memorial or the Priory Roll of Honour.

The Trinity United AFC Memorial

The Trinity Amateur Football Club (AFC) memorial in Wellington Gardens commemorates those Trinity AFC footballers who lost their lives in the Second World War.

Trinity AFC memorial (F Bull)   Trinity AFC memorial plaque (F Bull)

The six names shown on the plaque are:-

Lt. J. F. B. ALLBUT. R.E.
FL/OFF. A. F. CHEETHAM. R.A.F.
SGT. F. A. CHEETHAM. R.A.F.
F/SGT. G. K. GRAINGER. R.A.F.
TPR. R. H. JORDAN. R.T.R.
L/CPL. H. MITCHELL. D.L.I.

Note:
All these six names appear on the Bridlington War Memorial and the Priory Roll of Honour.

The NALGO Memorial in the Town Hall

During the War Memorial Committee discussions in March 1949, representatives of the National Association of Local Government Officers (NALGO), asked permission to place a commemorative memorial in the Town Hall in honour of their members killed in WW2. This was agreed and when completed the memorial recorded the names of NALGO members from both World Wars.

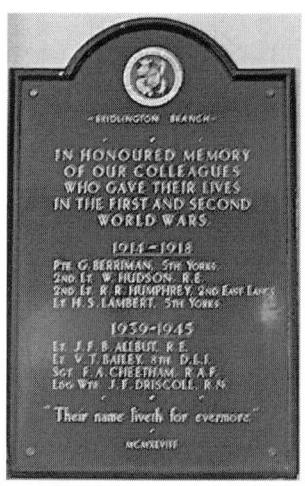

The NALGO Memorial (F Bull)

The memorial was unveiled on the 19 November 1948 by former Town Clerk G. Melvin and dedicated by Canon J. W. Lamb. The memorial is currently situated in the main entrance in Bridlington Town Hall.

The four names shown from the Second World War are:-

Lt. J. F. B. ALLBUT. R.E.

Lt. V. T. BAILEY. 8th D.L.I.

Sgt. F. A. CHEETHAM. R.A.F.

Ldg. Wtr. J. F. DRISCOLL. R.N.

Note:
All these four names appear on the Bridlington War Memorial and the Priory Roll of Honour.

Burma Star and Dunkirk Veterans Memorials

There are two more memorials in Wellington Gardens, namely the Burma Star Association memorial and the Bridlington Dunkirk Veterans Association Memorial.

The Burma Star Association was officially founded on the 26 February 1951 to promote the comradeship experienced in the bitter fighting in the jungles of Burma, and to set up a welfare organisation so that members and widows in need can be given poverty assistance in times of ill-health or other debilitating circumstances.

The Burma Star Association memorial (F Bull)

The Bridlington Dunkirk Veterans Association memorial celebrates the 50th Anniversary of the evacuation from Dunkirk and the beaches stretching 10 miles eastwards from the entrance to Dunkirk harbour of the 338,000 troops that reached safety in England between 26 May and 4 June 1940. The aim of the association is to assist all needy members and their families and to foster the spirit of comradeship which existed on and off the Dunkirk beaches in 1940.

The memorial was originally carved by Bridlington Stonemason David Mooney and was refurbished by him in July 2015.

The Bridlington Dunkirk Veterans Association memorial (D Mooney)

There are no names inscribed upon the Burma Star Association memorial and the Bridlington Dunkirk Veterans Association memorial.

2
The Air raids on Bridlington

The first civilian deaths in East Yorkshire as a result of a German air raid occurred on Thursday 11th July 1940 when Bridlington was attacked. The attackers were the bombers of Luftwaffe Kampfgeschwarder (Bomber wing) KG30 'Adler'(Eagle).

KG30 had formed in Germany in December 1939 and took part in the air battles for the occupation of Denmark, Norway and France. By 1940 KG30 had an establishment of over 90 Junkers Ju88A bombers based at Alborg-West in Denmark. KG30 bombers carried out most, if not all, of the air raids on Bridlington.

Although Bridlington suffered numerous air raids not all of them caused fatalities. The air raids began with a 'hit and run' daylight raid in July 1940 followed by a mass daylight raid in August but then reverted to 'hit and run' daylight raids by single aircraft and finally night raids. These changes in tactics were due in no small part to the gathering strength of the fighter defences of East Yorkshire and by the end of 1942 raids on Bridlington had largely ceased. The following paragraphs give the date and details of those air raids on Bridlington that resulted in the deaths of its citizens. All pictures are from Bridlington Local Studies Library.

11th July 1940.

The air raid sirens sounded over the town at 1100 hours on the 11th July 1940 and five minutes later a lone Ju88 of KG 30 on a hit and run raid, dropped a stick of five high explosive bombs between Bridlington Railway Station and Hilderthorpe Road. The railway station goods yard was damaged and a number of ammunition wagons set alight. Hilderthorpe Road was devastated and four civilians, Mabel Potter, Agnes Nicholson, Charles and Gertrude Wainwright were killed outright and Clara Hildrew was fatally injured and died later in hospital. Gunner Percy Rogers was killed and twelve people were seriously injured.

Hilderthorpe Road.

15th August 1940.

In the morning of the 15th August 1940 the radar operators at Staxton Wold picked up a large number of aircraft approaching the Yorkshire coast from the North Sea. The Spitfires of 616 Squadron together with the Hurricanes of 73 Squadron (A flight) at Leconfield and the Blenheims of 219 Squadron at Leeming were scrambled to intercept the raiders in the vicinity of Flamborough Head. The 50+ Ju88's of KG30 were intercepted and combat extended over Filey Bay and Bridlington Bay.

The attackers split up, the main body headed for its primary target of RAF Driffield and the other aircraft headed for Scarborough and Bridlington.

At Bridlington, four HE bombs were dropped over the Byass Avenue - St Alban Road area and caused considerable damage to property. One bomb ruptured a gas main but luckily no fires ensued. People had remarkable escapes but unfortunately one civilian, Norah Riley of 37 St Cuthbert Road, was killed.

St Cuthbert Road

At RAF Driffield, Bridlington serviceman LAC Kenneth Eric New serving with 77 Bomber Sqn was among those killed. The RAF shot down several of the raiders and many others were badly damaged. 3 aircraft came down in East Yorkshire, one of which, Ju88A coded 4D+DR of 7/KG30 came down near Bridlington Reservoir. Some of the German airmen killed in this raid were buried in Bridlington Cemetery.

Wreckage of a Ju88 being inspected by the RAF

20th August 1940.

On the 20 August 1940 a lone Ju88 of KG 30 dropped four 250 kg HE bombs one of which hit the G.P.O, killed Alfred William Anderson and trapped eleven other people in the collapsed building. The people trapped were brought out alive thanks to the efforts of the ARP rescue party under its leader Tom Alderson. The other three bombs caused damage to the surrounding area but did not cause any more fatalities.

The G.P.O. in Quay Road

21st August 1940.

At 15.30 hours on Wednesday the 21 August 1940, a lone bomber, almost certainly a Ju88 of KG30, made an attack on the harbour but missed and the four high explosive 250kg bombs landed in the town. One bomb made a direct hit on the Britannia Hotel in Prince Street. Half of the hotel was destroyed and 25 year old Esther Shaw, who was working there as a hotel maid, was killed. A soldier unnamed at the time but now known to have been Edmund Reginald Beecroft, was also killed. The other three bombs caused considerable damage to surrounding property and it was fortunate that no one else was killed.

The Britannia Hotel

23rd August 1940.

On Friday, 23rd August 1940, a lone Ju88 of KG30 made a low level attack on Bridlington Harbour dropping four high explosive bombs. The first bomb struck the 68grt pleasure boat *New Royal Sovereign* and blew her to pieces, luckily no crew were on board.. The second bomb dropped on the jetty, failed to explode and ricocheted through the bottom of the coble *Blue Jacket*.

 The third bomb completely wrecked Foley's Cafe and Restaurant at 13 Prince Street next to the harbour and damaged Woolworths next door. Five people were trapped under wreckage in the cellar at Foley's of which three, Evelyn Parkin (nee Foley) daughter of the owner, Betty Spear, a waitress and James Watson, a RAF officer on leave, were killed instantly. Evelyn's husband Walter Parkin and James' wife Dorothy Watson were brought out alive after five hours work by the rescue parties, but unfortunately Dorothy Watson, who ran the Cafe, died later in hospital.

Foley's Cafe and Restaurant

The fourth bomb demolished the Cock & Lion public house in Prince Street.

15th February 1941.

Early on Saturday morning a lone enemy aircraft dropped a stick of bombs on the town. Shops and houses were damaged and bombs fell on a showroom and the sorting office of the temporary GPO. One couple, Edith and George Whittaker of Victoria Road had a remarkable escape when a bomb hit their house. They were sleeping in the front downstairs room at the time and after the bomb struck this was the only room left standing! Several people were injured and taken to hospital and although there were no fatalities, Edith Whittaker never fully recovered from the shock of seeing her house destroyed and she died on the 12 April 1941.

10th April 1941.

Bridlington was attacked on the 10th April when 75 incendiary and 20 high explosive bombs were dropped on the town between 03.10 and 22.12 hrs. Many houses and commercial properties were damaged in the central area and as far out as Sewerby.

Percy George Perkins of 25 Hamilton Road was killed when his house was destroyed and two year old baby David Anthony Gray was killed in New Burlington Road. Over the town 12 people were seriously injured and 16 made homeless by this raid.

Hamilton Road

The Air Raids on Bridlington

18th June 1941.
At 2.06 am in the early hours of Wednesday the 18 June 1941 an enemy aircraft dropped two 1,000 kg parachute mines on Bridlington. One mine exploded on St Anne's Convalescent Home which was destroyed together with several surrounding houses. The second mine dropped in Lamplugh Road at the corner with Eight Avenue. About 13 houses were completely destroyed and many others damaged beyond repair. 20 people were trapped under the wreckage of which 13 were rescued suffering from various injuries and the other 7 were killed. Those killed, all civilians, were William Stewart Allen, Annie Maria Anderson, Elsie Gertrude Chatterton, Thomas Atkin Forster, Gertrude Holden, Jane Newton and John William Woodcock.

The Avenues

11th July 1941.
On the 11 July 1941 two 'C' type mines were dropped on a paddock at the rear of Elma Avenue and on Bessingby Road at its corner with St. Johns Avenue. Both mines caused extensive damage to property some of which were beyond repair. 4 people were hospitalized and about 40 treated for their injuries. Although no one was fatally injured at the time, Thomas Braithwaite of Elma Avenue was one of those injured and eventually died of his injuries on the 25 July 1943 age 64.

Elma Avenue

17th July 1941.
At 24 minutes past midnight on Thursday morning the 17th July 1941 a German aircraft dropped four HE's bombs which exploded along the Promenade in Bridlington completely destroying the properties at 101, 103, 105 and 107 the Promenade. Adjoining properties were badly damaged, utility supplies were disrupted and a gas main caught fire. Several people were trapped in collapsed buildings until they were rescued by the ARP rescue teams.

The houses hit were occupied by the RAF and at Numbers 103 and 105 twenty two airmen had a miraculous escape. Two airmen and one civilian were killed, George Ireland who lived at 105 the Promenade, Aircraftman Edward Redding and Aircraftman George Edwards. Seven Airmen and six civilians were made homeless.

The Promenade after the raid

This was the last air raid on Bridlington in which people were killed but a further air raid took place on Flamborough on the 12th September 1941 and killed Peter Jameson, the only civilian death occurring at Flamborough as a result of an air raid.

12th September 1941
Peter Jameson was born in 1876 and was brought up in Flamborough by his uncle Thomas Jameson. Peter was a fisherman like his uncle and was well liked in Flamborough village. He never married, lived alone and spent little, thus leading to rumours that he had money stashed away - though none was ever found.

65 year old Peter Jameson died on the 12 September 1941 when a German aircraft dropped HE bombs that entirely demolished No's 7, 8 and 9 Stylefield Road (Council Houses), Flamborough. Peter's house (No 8) received a direct hit and Peter and his dog died instantly.

Peter Jameson was buried in the same grave as his uncle (Thomas Jameson, grave ref 1128) at Flamborough Cemetery on the 16 September 1941, burial ref 1177. Peter is also commemorated on the Commonwealth War Graves Commission Website (Civilian War Dead) and in Flamborough Church. As a resident of Flamborough not Bridlington he is not recorded on the Bridlington War Memorial or the Priory Roll of Honour.

3
Allied and German Deaths

German Aircrew buried at Bridlington Cemetery

Fw Georg Henneske. (wireless operator)
Buried 19th August 1940, grave reference W230*.
Georg was fatally injured when Ju88A coded 4D+DR of 7/KG30 was shot down and crashed near Bridlington Reservoir on the 15th August 1940.

Uffz Severin Kursch (wireless operator}
Buried 19th August 1940, grave reference W239*
Fw Robert Pohl (Observer)
Buried 19th August 1940, grave reference W248*
Fw Robert Bihr (Pilot)
Uffz Arnulf Neumeyer (Air Gunner)
Buried together 19th August 1940, grave reference W257*
These four men were the crew of Ju88A coded 4D+?M of 4/KG30 that was shot down and crashed near Auburn Farm, Fraisthorpe on the 15th August 1940.

Lt Helmut Sinz 534/2/A/4 (age 24) grave reference W258
Fw Harald Beuting 73175/8 (age 25) grave reference W240
Uffz Wilhelm Quodt 62748/A/54 (no age given) grave reference W231
Fw Otto Donder 53557/8 (age 30) grave reference W249
All buried on the 14th July 1941
These four men were the crew of Ju88A coded M2+CL of 4/Kg106 that along with two other aircraft was on an anti-shipping patrol between Whitby and the Farne Islands, The three aircraft became 'lost' and all crashed. This aircraft crashed at Speeton on 9th July 1941 and disintegrated killing all the crew.

Note*
All the German aircrew buried in Bridlington Cemetery were transferred to the Deutschen Soldatenfriedhof (German War Memorial) at Cannock Chase in Staffordshire in June 1962.

Polish Soldiers buried in Bridlington Cemetery

The following four Polish soldiers were killed in 1944 and are buried in Bridlington Cemetery.

Strz (Rifleman) **Aleksander Zdunek** Grave Reference W50.
2 P Panc, (2nd Armoured Regiment) Polish Army. (See note 1).
Service Number 22340/AP. Died 11 May 1944, age 39 at home address. Address 20 Clarence Road Bridlington.

Kpl (Corporal) **Josef Kwiecinski** Grave Reference W41
10 Komp Zaop (10th Supply Company), Polish Army. Service Number 5196/92/1. Died 17 May 1944, age 31 by accident at Cardigan Road (Coroner's Inquest). Address 'Cliffhome' Marine Drive Bridlington.

Kpl (Corporal) **Mieczyslaw Koscielniak** Grave Reference W51
Komp Warszt (Workshop Company), Polish Army.
Service Number 3289 Died 29 June 1944 age 28 at home address (Coroner's Inquest). Address York Road Bridlington,

Drag (Dragoon) **Jan Lesniak** Grave Reference W59
10 P. Drag (10th Dragoons), Polish Army. (See note 1).
Service Number 29296 Died 19 July 1944, age 39 at the Polish Barracks. Address Polish Barracks Rudston,

Note 1: The 2nd Armoured Regiment and the 10th Dragoons were part of 10th Polish Armoured Cavalry Brigade, 1st Polish Armoured Division. Units of the 1st Polish Armoured Division arrived in Bridlington in 1944 for training for the Normandy landings.

Polish Sherman Tank in Bridlington
(Bridlington Local Studies Library)

Several other armoured units trained in Bridlington including the 3rd Royal Tank Regiment (3RTR), the 23rd Hussars and the Guards Armoured Division. While at Bridlington the Guards Armoured Division was inspected by the King and Queen and the two Princesses.

It is not believed that anyone from these units was fatally injured during their training in Bridlington.

The Burton Agnes Accident

On the 17th September 1947 arrangements had been made for 50 prisoners-of-war from No. 250 P.O.W. Camp at Rudston, who had been helping with the harvest, to return to No. 139 camp at Billington, Durham. They were to travel by train from Burton Agnes and a lorry was detailed to carry their baggage to the station. The lorry made its first trip soon after 5.00 am, it then returned to the camp, took a batch of prisoners to the station, returned to the camp again and was making its third trip with the rest of the prisoners when a terrible accident occurred. The lorry crashed through the 'closed' level crossing gates and was struck on the bonnet by an LNER express train which crushed the lorry against the gate and dragged it down the track, reducing it to scrap metal in the process. The three occupants of the driving cab, Staff Sergeant Wadey, Sergeant Cramer and Hans Graf, a prisoner, were killed instantly along with six prisoners in the back of the lorry. A further three prisoners from the lorry died later in hospital.

The subsequent Inquiry revealed that James Wadey, an interpreter, whose duty it was to be present when the prisoners and their baggage left the camp, was driving at the time, though Hans Graf was the authorised driver allocated to the lorry. Roland Cramer was in charge of the escort party. Warrant Officer (Class 1) Lee, the Transport Officer at No. 250 P.O.W. Camp, stated that Wadey had no authority to drive the lorry and that there was no reason why he should have been doing so. He was in possession of a military licence to drive motor cycles only, and Mr. Lee had never heard of him driving a lorry previously, though one of the prisoners said he had known him do so occasionally.

According to the evidence of Private Adams, one of the escort who saw the accident, and of two prisoners, Hoermann and Reichenbach, who were already at the station, and of two prisoners, Schlupper and Jungblut, who were travelling in the lorry, Wadey went to the station in the lorry on each of its three trips. Graf drove it on the first trip, with the baggage party. He also drove as far as the station on the second trip, when Wadey and Adams travelled in the driving cab with him, but after Adams and the prisoners had alighted Wadey changed places with Graf, drove back to the camp, and again to the station on the third trip.

Schlupper and Jungblut said that Wadey drove unusually fast on the way from the camp, and that the prisoners were thrown about when rounding bends in a way which caused comment; they remembered no sensation of braking just before the accident. Adams and Reichenbach watched the lorry approaching the station, unexpectedly fast, and said that it hardly slowed down at all as it reached the gates, which it hit at 15-20 m.p.h. according to the former. Adams, Schlupper, Hoermann and Reichenbach all remembered hearing its engine racing at the last moment, as if the driver was changing into a lower gear.

The accident was also witnessed at close range by a motor cyclist, Stanley Mackenzie, who has 20 years' driving experience and is now employed driving a similar type of lorry for the R.A.F. He was waiting at the crossing, on the west side of the line, with his machine in the middle of the road, a yard or two from the gates. He did not see or hear the lorry approach, and his attention was first drawn to it by the sound of its engine racing, as it passed on the near side of his machine and forced its way through the gates, there was no skidding or sound of a brake application so far as he could remember. He was sure that the lorry was struck by the train immediately it came to a stand, foul of the nearer track. Evidence substantially to the same effect was given by Porter John, who had a good view of the accident from the porters' room close to the crossing where he was engaged on clerical work, and by Signalman Gray whose attention was attracted by the noise of the lorry breaking through the gates. He had closed them across the road seven minutes earlier, at 6.35 a.m., for the passage of an up train, and had not reopened them subsequently, for when it passed his box the Hull to Bridlington train was already approaching.

Further evidence was given that the pedal arrangement and spacing on the lorry was such that a driver unfamiliar with the vehicle could let his right foot slip from the brake to the accelerator or press the brake and the accelerator at the same time.

The conclusion of the inquiry was that the accident was caused by the careless handling of the lorry by an unauthorised and apparently inexperienced driver, namely Staff Sergeant Wadey.

The bodies of the two guards, Staff Sergeant James Joseph Wadey, age 28 of the Royal Artillery and Sergeant Roland Montague Cramer, age 21 of the Bedfordshire and Hertfordshire Regiment, were buried in their home city of London. They are both recorded on the Commonwealth War Graves Commission Website.

Allied and German Deaths

The bodies of the ten Germans were buried in Bridlington Cemetery on the 22nd September 1947, several hundred prisoners of war and a large attendance of residents of Bridlington and from the neighbouring district formed a congregation of over a thousand at the funeral. Each coffin was borne by four prisoners of war, with another prisoner following behind carrying a wreath. They passed through two lines of prisoners as they entered the cemetery grounds. Other prisoners were assembled on three sides of the ten separate graves in which their comrades were to be buried.

In addition to the wreath carried by a prisoner behind each coffin, there were many more wreaths and bunches of flowers carried by Germans. Many of the floral tributes had been made by the Germans from collections of wild flowers. The service was conducted in German by Dr. J Rieger, (Dean of London Lutheran Churches in England), Padre F. Gebhardt (Protestant padre), and Padre Spuelbeck (Roman Catholic padre). Father O'Corboy, Roman Catholic priest at Bridlington, also took part and an expression of sympathy was voiced by the Rev. N. A. Vesey (vicar of Christ Church).

The Mayor and Mayoress (Councillor F. F. Millner and Mrs. Millner) were present, together with Lieut. Col. J. L. G, Marjoricbanks Egerton (commandant 250 P.O.W. Camp), Major Covenay (commandant 139 P.O.W, Camp), Captain H. C. Holmes (commandant of the P.O.W. Camp at Rudston), and R.S.M.. Small (Rudston Camp). Inspector H. H. Walker represented the Police.

The German Prisoners of War who died in the accident were:-

Name	Age	Bridlington Grave Reference*
Burghard Fischer	20	W194*
Hans Ulrich Graf	19	W213*
Albert Gronen	23	W221*
Paul Halsig	24	W203*
Heinz Krause	24	W222*
Gerhard Petry	21	W212*
Walter Prager	26	W185*
Bruno Przywarra	25	W195*
Erich Schmidt	25	W204*
Hermann Schone	25	W186*

Before the coffins were lowered into the graves Handel's Largo was played by the German prisoner-of war orchestra from 250 camp at Malton. A. choir from 130 camp (Welton Hall, near Brough) also took part in the service.

One of those killed in the accident was 25 year old Erich Schmidt. Erich was born on September 13th 1923 in Schwarzdorf (community Foritz) close to Sonneberg in the South of Thuringia. Erich was the son of Ernst and Emma Erna Olga Schmidt (nee Ruppert) and the brother of Lotte Helena Schmidt. Lotte got married but unfortunately died on the 17th December 1948 just three days after giving birth to her daughter Erika and just over a year after Erich had died in the Burton Agnes accident.

Erich Schmidt (from the archive of the family Schroder)

On Saturday 18th October 1947 it was announced that as a result of a recent appeal by the Bridlington Council of Churches Prisoner-of-War Social Centre Committee, 21 seven-pound parcels of food had been sent to the relatives of the victims of the Burton Agnes railway-crossing accident. Mr. J. H. Lambert-Smith told the Free Press that 53 people answered the appeal for gifts of rationed food. "It was a splendid gift from the people of Bridlington," he said, "and one that will do much to soften a most cruel blow and increase International understanding by the exercise of Christian love." A further collection of both food and clothing is to be organised for the middle of November to provide Christmas gifts for needy families in Europe.

*On the 22nd June 1962 the ten German Prisoners of War buried in Bridlington Cemetery were transferred to the Deutschen Soldatenfriedhof (German War Memorial) at Cannock Chase in Staffordshire.

On the 22nd December 2013, thanks mainly to the efforts of Richard Jones; a commemorative plaque was unveiled on the old signal box at Burton Agnes near to where the accident happened.

The Plaque (via Steve Adamson)

Bridlington Cemetery

During WW2 the cemetery was used for the burial of many of its citizens killed in the air raids on Bridlington together with various other casualties of war from German aircrew to allied servicemen. Bridlington Cemetery opened in 1886; The Chapel and Lodge were designed in 1879 by Hull architect Cuthbert Broderick who went on to design many famous buildings including the Grand Hotel in Scarborough and Leeds Town Hall.

The Chapel (F Bull)

The Bridlington Cemetery grave references quoted in this book consist of a letter/number combination, where the letter is the 'compartment' and the number is the grave number in that compartment. The diagram on the next page shows the layout of the compartments with the grave references taken from a plan drawing by Stonemason and Local Historian David Mooney.

The information on many of the headstones have been recorded and indexed (Bridlington Cemetery Memorial Inscriptions) by the East Yorkshire Family History Society (EYFHS). Copies are available from the EYFHS and reference copies can be viewed in Bridlington Local Studies Library.

Not all the Servicemen and civilians buried in Bridlington Cemetery in WW2 had their names recorded on wartime memorials. The following list gives the names of those burials which have no other memorial than the CWGC.

Bell Arthur Lawrell Commander Royal Navy, Service No, F8550. Bridlington Cemetery grave reference W42

Braithwaite Thomas Civilian Bridlington Cemetery grave ref X242

Ezard Henry Stancliffe Stoker 2nd Class Royal Navy Service No, D/KX 532410. Bridlington Cemetery grave reference Y 79

Finnerty Francis Joseph Warrant Officer Royal Air Force Service No. 330750. Bridlington Cemetery grave reference Z26

Garbutt Peter Denis Flying Officer (Nav.) Royal Air Force Service No.: 166299. Bridlington Cemetery grave reference W61

Martin Edward Francis Inkerfield Petty Officer Royal Navy, Service No. P/228794. Bridlington Cemetery grave reference X62

Pinkney George Olaf Private the West Yorkshire Regiment (The Prince of Wales's Own) Service No: 4395077
Bridlington Cemetery, grave reference Z9

Routledge George Elliott Fireman and Trimmer Merchant Navy. Bridlington Cemetery grave reference W 23

Stubbs Frank Private York and Lancaster Regiment, Service No. 1134437 Bridlington Cemetery grave reference J298

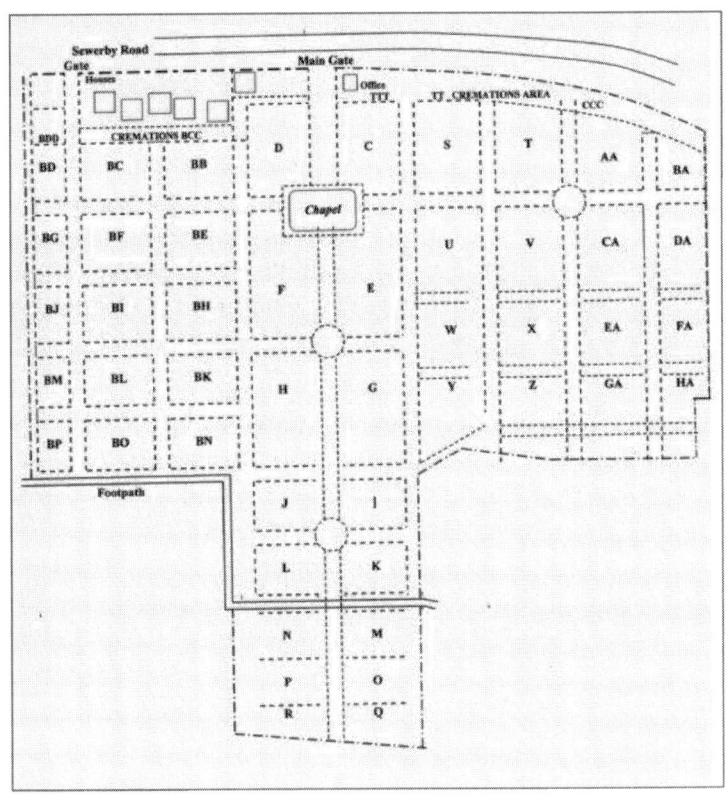

Bridlington Cemetery - layout of the compartments

5
The Bridlington Roll Of Honour for WW2

A to Z index of names from the Bridlington War Memorial, the Priory Parish Church, Bridlington School, Christ Church, Bridlington Trinity AFC, NALGO and Bridlington Cemetery.

They shall grow not old,
As we that are left grow old:
Age shall not weary them,
Nor the years condemn.
At the going down of the sun
And in the morning
We will remember them.

From `For the Fallen'
By Laurence Binyon

Flight Sergeant (Navigator) EDWIN RAYMOND ABELL

The Royal Air Force, Service No. 474271, Bridlington School Old Boy

Edwin Raymond Abell was born in the December quarter of 1911, the son of Edwin and Amy Helen Abell (nee Raymond) of 2 Marine Drive Bridlington. Edwin's father was a grocer and wine merchant. In 1922 Edwin attended Bridlington School and left in 1928. Edwin trained as a Chemist and before WW2 he was the manager of Taylors Drug Company Limited's shop at 20 Marine Drive, Bridlington. Before he enlisted he lived at 72 Queensgate, Bridlington.

Edwin Abell (Bridlington School)

During WW2 Edwin Abell joined The RAF and volunteered for air crew, serving as a Flight Sergeant (Navigator) RAFVR with 296 Squadron. 296 Sqd. was formed from the Glider Exercise Unit in 1942. In August 1944 it was stationed at Brize Norton, Oxfordshire and was part of Transport Command operating the Armstrong Whitworth Albemarle. The squadron's principal role was to tow glider borne troops into action, and, as such, took part in the invasions of Sicily and Normandy. The squadron also dropped agents into occupied Europe and supplies to the Resistance.

AW Albemarle (Wikipedia)

Edwin Raymond Abell was killed in action on the 9th August 1944 at the age of 32 when his aircraft Albemarle P1501 vanished without trace on a mission to drop supplies to agents of the Special Operations Executive (SOE) near Tours, France. Edwin was reported as 'missing' but was later confirmed as killed in action, he was unmarried. Edwin has no known grave and is commemorated on the Royal Air Force, Runnymede Memorial, Panel 215. He is also commemorated on the following memorials.

- Bridlington School Second World War Roll of Honour.
- The Bridlington War Memorial.
- St Mary (The Priory) Parish Church Roll of Honour.
- The Commonwealth War Graves Commission Website.

Note when names for the war memorial were requested in the Bridlington Free Press in 1950, Abell was misspelt as Abel.

Sergeant (Navigator/WOP) ALFRED HAROLD AKESTER

The Royal Air Force, Service No. 1129335, Bridlington School Old Boy

Alfred Harold Akester was born in the September quarter of 1914 the son of Alfred and Elizabeth Akester (nee Raylor) of Driffield. He came to Bridlington School in September 1925 with an East Riding County Minor Scholarship and won a bursary to Hull University College in October 1932. After leaving Hull University College he was employed in a Government office in Kingston upon Hull until he joined the RAF in 1940.

Alfred Akester (Bridlington School)

Alfred volunteered for air crew and was assigned to theRAFVR because RAF policy in WW2 was not to use conscripts as air crew, so conscripts who volunteered for air crew were assigned to the RAFVR. Alfred initially trained as an Observer with Fighter Command and in the September quarter of 1941 he married Cissie Eileen Wotton of Erdington, Birmingham. By 1942 Alfred was serving as a Navigator /Wireless Operator with 29 Squadron, a night fighter squadron equipped with Bristol Beaufighter aircraft and stationed at West Mailing in Kent.

Bristol Beaufighter (Wikipedia)

Sergeant Alfred Harold Akester RAFVR aged 28 died accidentally in a flying accident on the 21st October 1942 near Winchelsea, Sussex. His body was discovered on the ground and the cause of death was described as 'Due to War Operations'. Alfred was buried with full military honours in Driffield Cemetery, grave ref 1079, his coffin being conveyed from the railway station on a gun tender.

Alfred's grave in Driffield (C Bonnett)

As he was not a Bridlington resident Alfred Akester is not recorded on the Bridlington War Memorial or the Priory Roll of Honour but he is commemorated on the following memorials.
- Bridlington School Second World War Roll of Honour.
- The Commonwealth War Graves Commission Website.

WILLIAM STEWART ALLAN

Civilian, Bridlington School Old Boy

William was born in Sculcoates, Kingston upon Hull on the 13 February 1924 the son of Alfred George Allan and Elizabeth Louisa Allan (nee Tattersall). He came to Bridlington School in September 1939 from Hull where his father worked as a Pharmaceutical Chemist. His sister Peggy lived at 12 Third Avenue in Bridlington.

William Allan (Bridlington School)

17 year old William was a pupil of Bridlington School on the 18 June 1941 when he was caught up in an air raid. At 2.06 am an enemy aircraft dropped two 1,000 kg parachute mines which exploded in Lamplugh Road and St. Anne's Road. Several houses were completely destroyed and many others were badly damaged. William died at 4 Lamplugh Road, the only Bridlington School pupil to be killed as the result of enemy action; six other civilians were also killed in this air raid.

Lamplugh Road (Bridlington Local Studies Library)

William Stewart Allan was buried in Bridlington Cemetery on 21st June 1941, grave ref X94 and he is commemorated on the following memorials.

- Bridlington School Second World War Roll of Honour*.
- Bridlington War Memorial.
- St Mary (The Priory) Parish Church Roll of Honour.
- Christ Church Roll of Honour.
- The Commonwealth War Graves Commission Website (Civilian War Dead).

Note *William is the youngest person to be commemorated on the Bridlington School Roll of Honour and there was a Memorial Chair in the School dedicated to William. In 1944 his family endowed the Stewart Allan Bursary to assist boys who wanted to study medicine.

Lieutenant JOHN FREDERICK BROOKE ALLBUT

The Royal Engineers, Service No. 289136

John Frederick Brooke Allbut was born in Dudley Staffordshire in the June quarter of 1913. He married Hilda Richards in the June quarter of 1937 at Wednesbury, Staffordshire.

Prior to WW2 John Allbut was employed as a Town Planning and Engineering Assistant in the Bridlington Borough Engineering Department.

Lieutenant John Frederick Brooke Allbut served in the Royal Engineers during the Second World War and was 'killed by enemy action' on the 20th February 1944 in Paddington, London. He was 30 years old but the circumstances of his death are not recorded.

In a meeting of Bridlington Town Council on the 28th June 1944 the Mayor made a sympathetic reference to his death whilst in service with H.M. Forces.

John Frederick Brooke Allbut of 109 Dudley Road Tipton was buried in Tipton Cemetery, Staffordshire grave reference A/E 222.

The grave of John Allbut (public domain)

John Frederick Brooke Allbut is commemorated on the following memorials.

- Bridlington War Memorial.
- St Mary (The Priory) Parish Church Roll of Honour.
- Bridlington Trinity AFC Memorial.
- NALGO memorial in Bridlington Town Hall.
- The Commonwealth War Graves Commission Website

Warrant Officer *EDWIN JOHN THURSTON ALTHAM*

The Royal Air Force, Service No. 508800

Edwin John Thurston Altham was born in the June qtr. of 1910, the son of Harry and Dorothy Altham (nee Le Ray) of Stockwell Road, Lambeth, London.

Edwin was a regular officer in the RAF and first came to Bridlington with the 1st marine section in 1932. Edwin married Sarah Elizabeth Danby of Bridlington in the December quarter of 1932. When war broke out in 1939 Edwin was stationed in Bridlington and he and Sarah were living at 50 Wellington Road.

During WW2 Edwin was transferred to 205 Squadron. 205 was the RAF's first squadron to be permanently based at Singapore where it flew maritime reconnaissance patrols over the approaches to Singapore and the Indian Ocean, employing bases in Ceylon and the Nicobar Islands. The Squadron was re-equipped with PBY Catalina's in 1941 before being withdrawn from Singapore and relocated to Java, leaving three aircraft at Selatar Air Base. When Japanese forces invaded Java the squadron retired to the south of the island and then to Australia, where it disbanded on 31 March 1942. Reformed in Ceylon on 23 July 1942, the squadron's Catalina's flew anti-submarine and air-sea rescue patrols out of Koggala for the remainder of the war.

Warrant Officer Edwin John Thurston Altham was killed when his Catalina Flying Boat (probably FP 255) was forced to ditch during an air-sea rescue mission off Ceylon on the 11th June 1943. Edwin was 35 years old and is commemorated on Column 424 of the Singapore War Memorial and on the following memorials.

- Bridlington War Memorial.
- St Mary (The Priory) Parish Church Roll of Honour.
- The Commonwealth War Graves Commission Website.

ALFRED WILLIAM ANDERSON

Civilian

Alfred William was born in 1875 in Hoxton, Shoreditch, London the son of John and Anne Anderson. Alfred joined the Royal Navy and by 1891 was a Boy 2nd Class on the training ship HMS *Boscawen* at Portland. This was the second *Boscawen,* a sailing ship of the line converted into a training ship for boy seamen. By 1901 Alfred was at HMS *Vernon* the Torpedo School at Portsmouth. Alfred had married Alice Beatrice New, the daughter of James Thomas and Sarah New, in the December quarter of 1896 at Portsmouth Hampshire. By 1911 Alfred had joined the Coastguard Service and eventually became a Lieutenant in the Coastguard Service.

After 30 years' service Alfred retired to Bridlington about 1928. He was a member of the Bridlington Home Guard and lived with his wife at 'Cairn Ryan', 40 St. Wilfred Road Bridlington. They had one daughter whom they named Alice Louisa May Anderson. Alfred was employed as a telephone operator at the General Post Office (GPO) on Quay Road.

On the 20 August 1940 a lone Ju88 dropped a 250 kg HE bomb which hit the G.P.O, killed 65 year old Alfred and trapped eleven other people in the collapsed building. The people trapped were brought out alive thanks to the efforts of the ARP rescue party under its leader Tom Alderson.

The General Post Office after the raid
(Bridlington Local Studies Library)

Alfred William Anderson was buried in Bridlington Cemetery on the 23rd August 1940, grave ref V237 and is commemorated on the following memorials.
- Bridlington War Memorial.
- St Mary (the Priory) Parish Church Roll of Honour.
- The Commonwealth War Graves Commission Website (Civilian War Dead).

ANNIE MARIA ANDERSON

Civilian

Annie Maria was born in the March quarter of 1862, the daughter of Thomas and Elizabeth Anderson (nee Whitwell) of York.

Annie Maria never married and the 80 year old spinster was one of the seven civilians who were killed in the air raid on the 18 June 1941 that destroyed and damaged houses in Lamplugh Road and St. Anne's Road. Annie died at her home, 5 Lamplugh Road, Bridlington when her house was destroyed.

Lamplugh Road, 18 June 1941 (Bridlington Local Studies Library)

Annie Maria Anderson was buried in Bridlington Cemetery on the 21st June 1941, grave ref X24 and is commemorated on the following memorials.

- Bridlington War Memorial.
- St Mary (the Priory) Parish Church Roll of Honour.
- The Commonwealth War Graves Commission Website (Civilian War Dead).

Lieutenant JOHN NORMAN ANDREWS

The Royal Inniskilling Fusiliers, Service No. 140028
Bridlington. School Old Boy

John Norman Andrews was born in 1916 the son of Sydney and Jessie Andrews of Kettering, Northamptonshire. He came to Bridlington School in 1926 and while there he was awarded his Colours for Cricket and Rugby and was also a School Prefect. He left the School in 1932.

In WW2 John Andrews was serving with the 6th Battalion of the Royal Inniskilling Fusiliers. The Royal Inniskilling Fusiliers was an Irish infantry regiment of the British Army formed in 1881.

John Andrews (Bridlington School)

The 6th Battalion formed in 1939 and served with the 38th (Irish) Infantry Brigade in the Tunisian Campaign in North Africa as part of the 6th Armoured Division.

6th Armoured & 38 Brigade insignia

Lieutenant John Norman Andrews aged 27 of 107 Rockingham Road Kettering Northamptonshire was accidentally killed on the 10th January 1943 in Tunisia. His death is described in the Regimental War Diary as follows:

War Diary - 6th Battalion Royal Inniskilling Fusiliers.

10th January 1943 – IN THE FIELD. (Tunisia)
CO holds conference of O Group at 0900 hrs in Bttn. Admin HQ in farm. Bttn. at 2 hrs notice to move. It will be a difficult job. The hill is now a sea of mud after 5hrs of rain during the night. IO called to conference at Brigade HQ 1130hrs. 1000 An explosion is heard in C Coy area. A truck has blown up and it is found that Lieut Andrews has been killed. Also one fusilier, Cpl Christie, who was 60 yards away, receives an eye injury.

Lieutenant John Norman Andrews was buried in Medjez-el-Bob Cemetery in Tunisia, Grave I.F. 13, As he was not a Bridlington resident he is not recorded on the Bridlington War Memorial or the Priory Roll of Honour but he is commemorated on the following memorials.

- Bridlington School Second World War Roll of Honour.
- The Commonwealth War Graves Commission Website.

Aircraftman 1st Class *SIDNEY KENNETH ARKSEY*

The Royal Air Force, Service No. 1325764

Sydney Kenneth Arksey was born on the 23 January 1916 the only son of Sydney and Rose Annie Arksey (nee Everfield) of 59 Quay Road, Bridlington, East Yorkshire. His father, Private Sydney Arksey was killed in WW1 while serving with the East Yorkshire Regiment. Sydney Kenneth Arksey was a bell ringer at the Priory Church where in his boyhood days he was a chorister. He was also a member of the local Church Lads Brigade. Before the war he was employed by the Bridlington Relay Service and was also a member of the Bridlington Fire Brigade. He was engaged to Miss Lillian Sigsworth.

In August 1939 Sydney joined the Royal Air Force Volunteer Reserve (RAFVR) and in February 1941 he went out to the Middle East and then on to South Africa.

Sidney Arksey died in hospital in South Africa on the 19th December 1942 just two weeks after being admitted, he was 25 years old. Sydney was buried in Durban (Stellawood) Cemetery, Kwazulu Natal, South Africa, grave reference, block F. grave 299.

Stellawood Cemetery (CWGC)

Aircraftman 1st Class Sydney Kenneth Arksey was awarded the 1939/1945 medal and the Africa star medal.

Sidney Kenneth Arksey is commemorated on the following memorials.

- Bridlington War Memorial.
- St Mary (The Priory) Parish Church Roll of Honour.
- Christ Church Roll of Honour.
- The Commonwealth War Graves Commission Website.

Warrant Officer (Pilot) ERIC LEONARD ARMITAGE

The Royal Air Force, Service No. 1434790, Bridlington School Old Boy

Eric Leonard Armitage was born in 1923 the son of Leonard Shaw Armitage and Annie Amelia Armitage of Thorpe Egham, Surrey. He came to Bridlington School in 1933 and he joined the RAF in 1940 straight after leaving school.

Eric volunteered for air crew training with the Royal Air Force Volunteer Reserve (RAFVR) and in 1944 he was serving as a pilot with 357 Maintenance Unit in Malta where his duties included delivering new aircraft to operational stations.

Eric Armitage (Bridlington School)

On the 24th August 1944 Eric took off from Catania Sicily as part of a formation that was delivering North American Mustang fighters to mainland Italy. The formation ran into a heavy storm from which Eric did not emerge and he was presumed to have crashed into the sea.

Eric Leonard Armitage has no known grave and is commemorated on Panel 13, Column 2 of the Malta GC Memorial.

Malta GC Memorial (CWGC).

Warrant Officer (Pilot) Eric Leonard Armitage is also commemorated on the following memorials.

- Bridlington School Roll of Honour.
- Bridlington War Memorial.
- St Mary (the Priory) Parish Church Roll of Honour.
- The Commonwealth War Graves Commission Website.

Flying Officer (Pilot) DEREK WILSON ASTON

The Royal Air Force, Service No. 145048, Bridlington School Old Boy

Derek Wilson Aston was born in 1924 the son of Alexander Lake Aston and Beryl Kathleen Aston. He came to Bridlington School in 1935 and left in 1938

Derek married Margaret Lambert of Bridlington, East Yorkshire in July / August 1944. At that time Derek Aston was serving in the RAFVR as a Pilot Officer with 524 Squadron.

Derek Wilson Aston (Bridlington School)

No. 524 Squadron was formed as a Coastal Command Squadron at RAF Oban, Argyll and Bute in Scotland on 20 October 1943. Its initial role was to introduce the Martin Mariner flying boat into RAF service but by the end of 1943 when the aircraft was ready for operations the RAF decided not to operate the type and the squadron was disbanded. 524 squadron reformed at RAF Davidstow Moor, Cornwall on 7 April 1944 to operate the Vickers Wellington XIII on night operations off the French coast in preparation for D-Day, mainly attacking E-boats and submarines but also providing escort to Coastal Command Beaufighters carrying out night strikes. After the Normandy Invasion the squadron operated in a similar role along the Dutch coast from RAF Docking and Bircham Newton, Norfolk.

Wellington XIII (Wikipedia)

On the 30 August 1944 Derek W Aston, aged 20, was part of the crew of Wellington 7R-J of 524 Sqd. that took off at 10.59hrs on an anti-E Boat patrol off the Dutch coast. The aircraft vanished without trace. Pilot Officer Derek Wilson Aston has no known grave and is commemorated on the Royal Air Force Runnymede Memorial, Panel 204. He is also commemorated on the following memorials.

- Bridlington School Second World War Roll of Honour.
- Bridlington War Memorial.
- St Mary (The Priory) Parish Church Roll of Honour.
- The Commonwealth War Graves Commission Website.

Lieutenant-Colonel THOMAS SYDNEY ATHRON

The Royal Engineers, Service No. 40605, Bridlington School Old Boy

Thomas Sydney Athron's birth was registered at Doncaster in the March quarter of 1895. He was the son of Herbert and Louisa Athron (nee Braithwaite) of Doncaster. Thomas came to Bridlington School in 1909 and left in 1912.

In the First World War Thomas Sydney Athron joined the 21st (Service) Battalion, West Yorkshire Regiment (Wool Textile Pioneers) and was wounded in the first battle of the Somme.

Thomas Athron (Bridlington School)

He was promoted to Second Lieutenant and transferred to the Royal Fusiliers where he ended the war as a Captain. After WW1 ended Thomas served in the Army of Occupation in Germany. Thomas then practiced as an architect in Doncaster and in the March quarter of 1920 he married Florence Evelyn Burton of Doncaster and they lived at Westlands Avenue in Doncaster.

Between the wars Thomas was active as a territorial forces volunteer with the 5th Battalion (TF) KOYLI with the rank of Major. On the outbreak of the Second World War Thomas Athron joined the Royal Engineers. The Corps of Royal Engineers has a long heritage and can claim direct descent from the military engineers that William the Conqueror brought to England. Since then it has lived up to its Motto 'Ubique' ('Everywhere'), having had a significant presence at every large scale battle the British Army has ever fought.

Lieutenant-Colonel Thomas Sydney Athron died suddenly of illness on the13th March 1944 aged 49 in Sri Lanka (formerly Ceylon). He was buried in Livaramentu Cemetery Colombo, Grave reference I.M.3.

As he was not a Bridlington resident Thomas Sydney Athron is not recorded on the Bridlington War Memorial or the Priory Roll of Honour but he is commemorated on the following memorials.

- Bridlington School Second World War Roll of Honour.
- The Commonwealth War Graves Commission Website.

Sergeant (Flight Engineer) JOHN JOFFRE ATKINSON

The Royal Air Force, Service No. 1591782

John Joffre Atkinson was born on the 20th January 1916, the son of William and Mary Atkinson (nee Walker) of Bridlington, East Yorkshire. After leaving school John became a bricklayer and married Dorothy Newlove of Bridlington on the 3 Oct 1940. John and Dorothy lived at 40 St. Mary's Crescent and their daughter Jill was born on the 25 May 1944.

John joined the RAF on the 15 Mar 1943, volunteered for air crew training and was assigned to the Royal Air Force Volunteer Reserve (RAFVR). John Joffre Atkinson had been on operations since 1943 and by 1945 was serving as a Sergeant Flight Engineer with 51 Squadron. 51 Squadron had reformed in 1937 and by 1942 was equipped with Halifax bombers as part of No. 4 Group Bomber Command.

Handly Page Halifax (Wikipedia)

On the 16th January 1945 John Joffre Atkinson was the flight Engineer on Halifax III, LW461, (MH-Y), the other members of the 7 man crew being Ernest Malcolm Popplewell (Pilot), David Lewis Johns (Nav.), Andre Jean Julius Hisette (Air/Bmr.), Arthur Alfred Muddiman (WOP/AG), R.A Boydell (Air/Gnr.) and Leslie Annis (Air/Gnr.). Halifax LW461 (MH-Y) took off from R.A.F. Snaith as one of 371 aircraft tasked to bomb the city of Magdeburg in Germany. This raid was part of a force of 1238 aircraft dispatched to bomb Magdeburg and the synthetic oil plants at Brux, Zeitz and Wanne-Eickel. Halifax LW461 was one of the 17 aircraft lost on the Magdeburg raid and crashed near Meppen, Germany. 6 crew members including 29 year old John Joffre Atkinson were killed and Sgt. R.A Boydell was taken prisoner. John Joffre Atkinson was buried in collective grave 13. D. 9-14., Becklingen War Cemetery, Niedersachsen, Germany and is commemorated on the following memorials.

- Bridlington War Memorial.
- St Mary (The Priory) Parish Church Roll of Honour.
- The Commonwealth War Graves Commission Website.

Able Seaman EDWARD AYRE

The Royal Navy, Service No. P/JX 189626

Edward Ayre was born in 1914 the son of Alfred and Ellen Ayre of 13 Postill Square Bridlington. Before the war he was captain of Bridlington Central United AFC. Edward was the husband of Phyllis Ayre, of Leeds, Yorkshire whom he married in 1938, they had one child.

During WW2 Edward was serving in HMS *President III* a Royal Navy 'stone frigate' (shore establishment) at Dedworth Manor, Windsor, London, that was acquired by the Admiralty on the outbreak of World War II.

This establishment was responsible for the pay, accounts and administration of the D.E.M.S. (Defensively Equipped Merchant Ships) personnel, worldwide, and was directly responsible to D.N.A. (The Director of Navy Accounts) at the Admiralty. The staff consisted of regular and reserve naval officers, ratings and wrens. The male ratings were mainly those returning from sea service, including survivors.

26 year old Edward Ayre died on the 23 November 1940. Details of how and where he died have not been found.

Able Seaman Edward Ayre has no known grave and is commemorated on Panel 38, Column 1, of the Portsmouth Naval Memorial

Portsmouth Naval Memorial (CWGC)

Edward Ayre is also commemorated on the following memorials.

- Bridlington War Memorial.
- St Mary (The Priory) Parish Church Roll of Honour.
- The Commonwealth War Graves Commission Website.

Lieutenant VINCENT THOMAS BAILEY

The Durham Light Infantry, Service No. 259389
Bridlington School Old Boy

Vincent Thomas Bailey was born in the December quarter of 1916, the son of Fred and Louisa Mary Bailey (nee Fosberry), of 58 Eighth Avenue, Bridlington, East Yorkshire. He came to Bridlington School in 1925 and he left School in 1931 to go to Ratcliffe College. Before WW2 started he was on the staff of the Bridlington Borough Treasurer's Department and was Assistant Secretary of the Royal Yorkshire Yacht Club and a member of the Bridlington Amateur Operatic Society.

Vincent Bailey (Bridlington School)

Early in 1939 Vincent joined the newly-formed 7th Battalion, Green Howards and served in North Africa as a Sergeant. When he received his officer's commission in December 1942, Vincent was transferred to the 8th Battalion of the Durham Light Infantry. The 8th Battalion was a Territorial battalion that served in the 151st Brigade, 50th (Northumbrian) Division throughout the war. After the Allied success at El Alamein in 1943 the German and Italian forces withdrew to the Mareth Line in Tunisia. This was a system of concrete bunkers armed with anti-tank and AA guns protected by barbed wire, anti-tank mines and anti-personnel mines.

Lieutenant Vincent Thomas Bailey, age 26, was killed in action on the 22nd March 1943 by a shell during a night assault on the Mareth Line. Vincent has no known grave and is commemorated on Face 28 of the Medjez-el-Bab Memorial, Tunisia

Medjez-el-Bab Memorial (CWGC)

Vincent T. Bailey is also commemorated on the following memorials.
- Bridlington War Memorial.
- St Mary (The Priory) Parish Church Roll of Honour.
- NALGO memorial in Bridlington Town Hall.
- The Commonwealth War Graves Commission Website.

Lance Sergeant HARRY BAKER

The Royal Artillery, Service No. 1498637

Harry Baker was born in the September quarter of 1918 the son of Clara May Baker, and stepson of William Anthony Wolsey. They lived at 56 Belvedere Road, Bridlington, before the start of WW2.

In 1943 Harry was serving with the 78 Field Regiment, Royal Artillery in Italy. The 78 Field Regiment, Royal Artillery was formed in Edinburgh on 3rd September 1939 as the 78 (Lowland) Field Regiment RA (TA) of the 52 (Lowland) Infantry Division. By 1942 it was in North Africa as GHQ 8th Army Troops and participated in the battle for El Alamein as part of the 1st Armoured Division. In March 1943 it was part of 13 Corps, 5th Army Group Royal Artillery (AGRA) for the battles in Sicily & Italy.

Following the Allied invasion of Italy in September 1943 the Allied armies succeeded in conquering the southern part of Italy but by early October had come up against a series of fortified lines designed to block the Allied advance to Rome. On the 3rd October the Eighth Army breached the first line (Viktor) followed by the Barbara Line and the first of the Winter Line positions behind the Sangro River. On the night of 27/28 November, the Eighth Army attacked the Winter Line supported by heavy artillery fire.

It was during the initial stages of this battle on the 27th November 1943 that 25 year old Lance Sergeant Harry Baker RA was killed in action. He was buried in grave reference IX. C. 5. at the Sangro River War Cemetery in the Commune of Torino di Sangro in the Province of Chieti, Italy.

Sangro River War Cemetery (CWGC)

Harry Baker is also commemorated on the following memorials.

- Bridlington War Memorial.
- St Mary (The Priory) Parish Church Roll of Honour.
- The Commonwealth War Graves Commission Website.

Leading Airman RICHARD VIVIAN BARNBY

The Fleet Air Arm, Service No. FAA/FX89356
Bridlington School Old Boy

Richard Vivian Barnby was born in the September quarter of 1923, the youngest son of George Ernest and Annie Barnby (nee Stones) of 2 George Street Bridlington and later of Warlingham, Surrey.

Richard came to Bridlington School in 1932 and was an excellent gymnast, leaving the School in 1940. He was also well-known locally as a tennis, golf and badminton player.

Richard Barnby joined the Fleet Air Arm of the Royal Navy in September 1941 and was serving as a Leading Airman based at HMS *Daedalus*, Lee-on-Solent, Hampshire. HMS *Daedalus* was one of the primary shore airfields of the Fleet Air Arm and its main training establishment.

Richard Barnby (Bridlington School)

Richard Vivian Barnby RN died on the 15th April 1942 aged 18 and a few weeks short of his 19th birthday. The circumstances of his death are not recorded as the unit's records appear not to have survived, but it is probable that he was in an aircraft which crashed into the sea.

Richard Vivian Barnby has no known grave and is commemorated on Bay 3, Panel 2 of the Fleet Air Arm Memorial at Lee-on-Solent.

Lee-on-Solent Memorial (CWGC)

Richard Barnby is also commemorated on the following memorials.
- Bridlington War Memorial.
- St Mary (The Priory) Parish Church Roll of Honour.
- The Commonwealth War Graves Commission Website.

Fusilier WALTER FREDERICK BARRON

The Royal Scots Fusiliers, Service No. 14632556

Walter Frederick Barron was born in the September quarter of 1913, registered at Sculcoates, Hull. He was the eldest son of Walter and Mary Ellen Barron (nee Fenwick) of 'Askerne' 4 Fortyfoot Grove, Bridlington.

Walter Barron married Nora Elizabeth Cable, the marriage being registered in the June quarter of 1936 at Bridlington, East Yorkshire. By 1941 Walter was a builder and living with Norah at 'Askerne' 4 Forty Foot Grove, Bridlington, they had one son.

During WW2 Walter was serving as a Fusilier with the 6th Battalion Royal Scots Fusiliers (6RSF). The 6th Battalion was part of the 44th (Lowland) Infantry Brigade, which in turn was part of the 15th (Scottish) Division.

On the 13th June 1944 the Division landed in Normandy and took part in the breakout from the beachhead and the advance to the Rhine. In February 1945 the 44th (Lowland) Infantry Brigade, (15th (Scottish) Division) were ordered to take the Fortress town of Goch on the Rhine. On the night of 21st/22nd February the 6th Battalion Royal Scots Fusiliers made an attack on a wooded area around Schloss Kalbeck and suffered fairly heavy casualties in an enemy counter attack. One of the casualties was Fusilier Walter Frederick Barron who died from wounds received in action on the 22nd February 1945 Age: 31.

Walter Frederick Barron was buried in the Reichswald Forest War Cemetery, grave reference: 58. J. 2.

Reichswald Forest War Cemetery (CWGC)

Walter is also commemorated on the following memorials.

- Bridlington War Memorial.
- St Mary (The Priory) Parish Church Roll of Honour.
- The Commonwealth War Graves Commission Website.

Fusilier LOUIS ARTHUR BARRON

The Royal Fusiliers (City of London Regiment), Service No. 5577166

Louis Arthur Barron was born in the April quarter of 1922, registered at Sculcoates, Hull, the son of Walter and Mary Ellen Barron (nee Fenwick) of 'Askerne' 4 Fortyfoot Grove, Bridlington. Louis Arthur was the younger brother of Walter Frederick Barron who was killed in action on the 22nd February 1945. After leaving school Louis Arthur Barron worked with his father as a builder and then joined the Army in 1942 where he served with the 2nd Battalion of the Royal Fusiliers (City of London Regiment). This regiment had been formed in June 1685 out of two companies of Guards at the Tower of London and it was the first ever regiment with the 'Royal' title.

In WW2 the 2nd Battalion, Royal Fusiliers, was engaged throughout the withdrawal through Belgium and France until the remnants of the battalion were evacuated from Dunkirk. It remained in Great Britain from June, 1940 until March, 1943, when it formed part of the 12th Brigade of the 4th Infantry Division and took part in the Allied invasion of Tunisia where it fought at the Battle of Peter's Corner on 24 April, 1943. On 3 September 1943 the Allies invaded the Italian mainland, the invasion coinciding with an armistice made with the Italians who then re-entered the war on the Allied side. Progress through southern Italy was rapid despite stiff resistance, but the advance was checked for some months at Monte Cassino on the German Gustav Line. The line eventually fell in May 1944 and as the Germans fell back, Rome was taken by the Allies on 3 June. The Germans made their first stand after being driven north of Rome at Bolsena in June 1944.

22 year old Fusilier Louis Arthur Barron died of wounds on the 8th June1944 during the battle for Bolsena and was buried in the Bolsena War Cemetery Italy, grave reference: I, H, 21. He is also commemorated on the following memorials.

Bolsena War Cemetery (CWGC)

- Bridlington War Memorial.
- St Mary (The Priory) Parish Church Roll of Honour.
- The Commonwealth War Graves Commission Website.

Bombardier LESLIE BATTYE

The Royal Artillery, Service No. 915020

Leslie Battye was born in 1918 the son of John and Anne Battye, of 30 Elma Avenue, Bridlington. Leslie was brought up in the Foresters Orphanage in St, Johns Avenue Bridlington.

Leslie left Bridlington about 1935 and moved to Kentish Town, London, where he joined the local Territorial Army Unit, the 64th (London) Medium Regiment RA (TA), as a bombardier. In 1939/40 they were based in the London District on Aerodrome defence.

In 1941 they moved to Egypt as part of 13 Corps. The Regiment then transferred to Greece with 1 ANZAC Corps and when ordered to evacuate Greece, most of them were taken off the Marathon beaches by the AA Cruiser HMS *Carlisle* and landed at Suda Bay, Crete, others. were taken off by ships that went back to Alexandria. On Crete they were to defend Heraklion aerodrome while the remainder of the Regiment were at Perivolia near Canea as infantry. The gun party were evacuated on the night 29/30 May while the remainder marched over the mountains to Sphakia where most were evacuated on the night 30/31 May 1941, The Regiment then went back to Egypt where it joined the 8th Army and took part in its many battles. In Oct 1943 the Regiment handed in all heavy equipment and embarked for the UK, Arriving in Liverpool on 9 Dec 1943.

The Regiment landed in France in June 1944 and fought in the battles for Le Hamel, Vaux sur Seulles, Bayeux, Cahagnolles, Mont Pincon, Argentan, Laigle, Vernon, Antwerp and Escaut Canal before providing support for the 1st Airborne Division at Arnhem end of September1944.

However 26 year old Leslie Battye did not take part at Nijmegen, having been killed on the 15th September 1944 probably on the Escaut Canal. He was buried in Leopoldsburg War Cemetery Belgium grave/memorial reference VI. C. 15, and is also commemorated on the following memorials.

- Bridlington War Memorial.
- St Mary (The Priory) Parish Church Roll of Honour.
- Christ Church Roll of Honour.
- The Commonwealth War Graves Commission Website.

Corporal GEORGE BEECROFT

The Oxford and Bucks Light Infantry, Service No. 14620251

George Beecroft was born on the 2nd September 1923 at a farm near Kilnwick, he was the son of Mrs. Key (formerly Beecroft) and the stepson of Frederick Key of 115 St. Johns Avenue.

George was educated at Oxford Street School and then went to St. Georges School. After leaving school he worked for Mr. Jackson at North Dale Farm as a Farm Labourer. He joined the army in 1943 and served in the 1st. Battalion of the Oxford and Bucks Light Infantry.

The Battalion was part of the 6th Beach Group, landing on D-Day on 6 June 1944 to organise the units on the landing beaches and for Bridgehead defence. They took part in Operation Epsom, the Odon bridgehead, the battle for Caen and Falaise. They entered Belgium in early September and took part in the ground operation in support of the airborne corridor to Arnhem.

George Beecroft (family archive)

In February 1945 the battalion was involved in the Allied invasion of the German Rhineland, including taking part in the Battle of the Reichswald: the five-division assault on the Reichswald Forest, where the battalion was involved in heavy fighting against German paratroopers and armour at the village of Asperberg. The battalion crossed the Rhine in late March but George Beecroft was killed in action on the 30th March 1945.

23 year old George Beecroft was buried in Winterswijk Cemetery, Gelderland, the Netherlands, Grave Reference 42. He is also commemorated on the following memorials.

- Bridlington War Memorial.
- St Mary (The Priory) Parish Church Roll of Honour*.
- The Commonwealth War Graves Commission Website.

Note the Priory Roll of Honour has a George 'Beechcroft' and a George 'Beecroft'. George Beecroft is the correction for George Beechcroft.

Commander ARTHUR LAWRELL BELL

The Royal Navy, Service No. F8550

Arthur Lawrell Bell was born in 1884 the son of George and Georgina Bell of Bournemouth. Arthur had a lifelong association with the Senior Service As a young man he specialized in physical training. By 1903 Arthur was a Sub Lieutenant in the Royal Navy and by 1904 he was promoted to Lieutenant. In 1908 Arthur was transferred to the Emergency List

Arthur served as a Lieutenant Commander during WW1 with HMS Excellent. HMS Excellent was the Royal Navy shore based gunnery school at Portsmouth, Hampshire. He was awarded a Mentioned in Despatches (MID)

When he retired Arthur became a stock broker but when WW2 started he returned to Service and was in charge of a minesweeping flotilla and took part in the Dunkirk evacuation where he was severely wounded. He then served ashore under the Flag Officer(Humber). In 1944 Arthur, was based at HMS Beaver II at Immingham. HMS Beaver II was a shore establishment for Coastal Forces Motor Launches (ML's) based at Immingham.

Commander Arthur Lawrell Bell died suddenly at his home, 23 Pembroke Terrace, Bridlington; on the 31st January 1944 age 60 while he was being moved into hospital.

Arthur Lawrell Bell was buried with full military honours in Bridlington Cemetery, grave reference W42. Naval Ratings from Hull formed a guard of honour, the Royal Air Force fired three volleys over the grave and a R.A.F. bugler sounded the Last Post.

Grave W42 (C Bonnett)

Arthur Lawrell Bell is not recorded on any of the Bridlington War Memorials but he is commemorated on the following memorial.

- The Commonwealth War Graves Commission Website.

THOMAS HENRY BRAITHWAITE

Civilian

Thomas Henry Braithwaite was born in 1879, the son of Emma and William H. Braithwaite of Weston, North Yorkshire. Thomas married Elizabeth Pashley in the December quarter of 1902, registered at Bridlington. His wife Elizabeth was born in 1879, the daughter of William and Caroline Pashley of Swinton Bridge, South Yorkshire. In the 1911 census Thomas and Elizabeth and their family were living at 18 North Back Lane, Bridlington but by 1941 Thomas, a Coal Merchant, and Elizabeth were at 3 Elma Villas, Elma Avenue Bridlington. Thomas was an accomplished crown green bowls player and a member of the Dukes Park Bowling Club. The photograph of him was taken in 1933 when he won the Hospital Cup. Thomas also won the Challenge Trophy in 1928 and 1933, the Barker Cup in 1938 and the Moorhouse Trophy in 1940.

Thomas Braithwaite (family archive)

On the 11 July 1941 two 'C' type mines were dropped on a paddock at the rear of Elma Avenue and on Bessingby Road at its corner with St. Johns Avenue. Both mines caused extensive damage to property. 4 people were hospitalized and about 40 treated for their injuries. Although no one was fatally injured at the time Thomas was badly injured and was probably one of those hospitalized. Thomas eventually died of his injuries age 64 on the 25 July1943 and was buried in Bridlington Cemetery on 27 July 1943, grave ref X242.

Thomas Braithwaite's grave (C Bonnett)

Thomas is is not recorded on any of the Bridlington war memorials but he is commemorated on the following memorial.

- The Commonwealth War Graves Commission Website (Civilian War Dead).

Flight Lieutenant (Pilot) ALEXANDER (Alec) BREMNER

The Royal Air Force, Service No. 49772, Bridlington School Old Boy

Alexander (Alec) Bremner was born in 1919 the only son of Dr. Alexander Bremner and Mrs J. W. Bremner of 28 Ormonde Avenue in Hull. Alec came to Bridlington School in 1928 and left in 1933. Alec was employed as an architect by Messrs North and Andrew Architects of Hull and when WW2 began he received a commission in the Royal Artillery.

Alexandra Bremner (Bridlington School)

This he declined and volunteered for aircrew duties in the RAF and after training in Canada he became a qualified pilot in the Royal Air Force Volunteer Reserve (RAFVR). Alec married Eileen Mary Webb on the 4 November 1944 at St. John Newland Church in Hull when Alec was a serving pilot with No 2 (Army Co-operation) Squadron. No 2 (AC) Squadron was one of the four original RFC squadrons with a continuous existence since 1912. In the autumn of 1944 the squadron was equipped with Supermarine Spitfire Mark XIV aircraft based at Gilze-Rijen, Air Base in the Netherlands and specialising in tactical photo reconnaissance for the 21st Army Group.

Alec was shot down whilst on a reconnaissance flight over Belgium and after a period of home leave he returned to duty. He then collapsed when about to take off and it was discovered that he had suffered serious internal injuries as the result of being shot down. 25 year old Alec Bremner was flown back to the UK but died of his injuries on the 26 December 1944 in an RAF hospital, His death was registered in the Swindon, Wiltshire Registration District.

Alexander (Alec) Bremner was buried in Kingston-upon-Hull (Northern) Cemetery on the 29th December 1944, Compartment reference 23, Grave 40. He was the last war-related death of an Old Boy to be published in the Bridlingtonian magazine. As he was not a Bridlington resident Alec is not recorded on the Bridlington War Memorial or the Priory Roll of Honour but he is commemorated on the following memorials.
- Bridlington School Second World War Roll of Honour.
- The Commonwealth War Graves Commission Website.

Fusilier CHARLES ERNEST BROWN

The Royal Scots Fusiliers, Service No. 4464285

Charles was born in 1914 the son of Reginald and Elizabeth Alice Brown, of 15 Trinity Road Bridlington East Yorkshire.

In 1944 Charles was serving with the 11th Battalion of the Royal Scots Fusiliers.

In 1939 the 11th Battalion was part of the 147th Infantry Brigade and stayed with the same Brigade throughout the war. It became attached to 49th (West Riding) Infantry Division between 15–17 April 1940. It first saw action when it took part in the short and ill-fated landings in Norway that were intended to retake the ports of Trondheim and Narvik from the Germans. It withdrew from Norway in May 1940 and was sent to Iceland to relieve the Royal Marines. Here the Brigade adopted the polar bear on an ice floe as its insignia.

In April 1942 the Battalion along with 147th Brigade was transferred back to the UK and in June 1944, Shortly after D-Day, it moved to Normandy as part of XXX Corps and saw action along the river Odon and Operation 'Market Garden'.

Fusilier Charles Ernest Brown, age 30, died on the 29th October 1944 during the fierce battles for the liberation of Arnhem and was buried in Bergan-Op-Zoom War Cemetery in Noord-Brabant, Holland grave reference: 7. A. 16.

Bergan-Op-Zoom War Cemetery (CWGC)

Charles is also commemorated on the following memorials.

- Bridlington War Memorial.
- St Mary (The Priory) Parish Church Roll of Honour.
- The Commonwealth War Graves Commission Website.

Private FRANK BROWN

The Royal Army Service Corps, Service No. T/107621

Frank Brown was born in October quarter of 1901 the son of Mrs. C. Brown, and the grandson of Frank and Mary Jane Brown. In the 1911 census Frank, age 9, was living with his grandparents at 15 West Street Bridlington.

Frank was the husband of Elsie Brown, (nee Robinson), from Scarborough.

In 1942 Frank was serving with the Royal Army Service Corps. The Royal Army Service Corps (RASC) was a corps of the British Army and was responsible for land, coastal and lake transport, air despatch, barracks administration, the Army Fire Service, staffing headquarters' units, supply of food, water, fuel and domestic materials such as clothing, furniture and stationery and the supply of technical and military equipment.

Private Frank Brown (RASC) died in the Ministry of Pensions Hospital in Leeds on Saturday the 21st November 1942 aged 42 years and was buried in Bridlington Cemetery but details of how he died have not been found.

The grave of Frank Brown in Bridlington Cemetery (C Bonnett)

Frank Brown is not recorded on the Bridlington War Memorial but he is commemorated on the following memorials:

- St Mary (The Priory) Parish Church Roll of Honour.
- The Commonwealth War Graves Commission Website.

Ordinary Seaman *JOHN WILLIAM BURGESS*

The Royal Navy, Service No. D/JX 304613

John William Burgess was born in 1921, the son of John William Tom and Louise Burgess, of Flamborough, East Yorkshire.

In 1942 John Burgess was serving in the Royal Navy onboard H.M. Submarine *Unique*, a U class submarine built by Vickers Armstrong at Barrow-in-Furness. *Unique* joined the 10th Submarine Flotilla in Malta during early 1941 and spent most of her career operating in the Mediterranean. After a refit in the UK in 1941 she was deployed in Home waters. *Unique* left Holy loch on 7 October 1942 for a patrol in the Bay of Biscay while on passage from Britain to Gibraltar. She left her escort off the Scillies and no more was seen or heard from her after that. She was reported overdue on when she failed to arrive at Gibraltar. H.M. Submarine *Unique* is believed to have been sunk without survivors and the cause of her loss is unknown.

H.M. Submarine *Unique* (Luis Photos)

John William Burgess has no known grave and died about the 24 October 1942 Age 21. He is commemorated on the Plymouth Naval Memorial reference: Panel 67, Column 1. He is also commemorated on the following memorials.

- Bridlington War Memorial.
- St Mary (The Priory) Parish Church Roll of Honour.
- The Commonwealth War Graves Commission Website.

Warrant Officer Class II JAMES ARTHUR BUTCHER

The Royal Engineers, Service No. 1866444

James Arthur Butcher was born in 1908 and lived at 9 St John Street Bridlington. James worked as a bricklayer for local builder Messrs Sawdon and then joined the Army as a regular soldier before WW2 and was posted out to Singapore in 1936. He never returned to Bridlington and after his death his wife and two children went to live in Australia.

James rose to the rank of Warrant Officer Class II, Q.M.S. and was captured when Singapore surrendered in February 1942 and he became a POW. In October 1942 James was one of the POW's forced to work on the notorious Burma-Siam railway, a 424 kilometre long railway built to support the Japanese army in Burma.

Approximately 13,000 prisoners of war died, including 35 year old James Arthur Butcher on the 26th May 1943, and were buried along the railway. The graves of those who died during the construction of the Burma-Siam railway (except for the Americans, whose remains were repatriated) were transferred from camp burial grounds and isolated sites along the railway into three cemeteries at Chungkai and Kanchanaburi in Thailand and Thanbyuzayat in Myanmar.

James Arthur Butcher whose death was not made official until October 1945, was re-buried in Kanchanaburi War Cemetery, Thailand grave reference2. P. 2.

Kanchanaburi War Cemetery (CWGC)

James Arthur Butcher is also commemorated on the following memorials.

- Bridlington War Memorial.
- St Mary (The Priory) Parish Church Roll of Honour.
- The Commonwealth War Graves Commission Website.

Apprentice *MALCOLM ANDERSON CAMPBELL*

The Merchant Navy, No Service No., Bridlington School Old Boy

Malcolm Anderson Campbell was born in the December quarter of 1921 registered at Glossop, the son of Malcolm M. Campbell and Mary Llewellyn Campbell (nee Anderson). His mother Mary Campbell came to Spurn in 1930 as the village schoolteacher and lived in the school bungalow. Mary had been widowed twice and had 3 children, 2 daughters Gwen and Jackie with her first husband and Malcolm with her second husband. Malcolm came to Bridlington School from Spurn on a Boarder's Scholarship in 1933.

Malcolm Campbell (Bridlington School)

Malcolm went to sea soon after leaving school in 1938 and in 1940 he was a Merchant Navy Apprentice on *SS Orangemoor* a 5,775 ton steam merchantman built in 1923 by the Northumberland Shipbuilding Co Ltd, Howden-on-Tyne for her owners Walter Runciman & Co Ltd, Newcastle-upon-Tyne. She had a crew of 40 and her homeport was Newcastle. In May 1940 *SS Orangemoor* was bound from Bona (Annaba), Algeria to the River Tyne with a cargo of 8,150 tons of iron ore as part of Convoy HGF31. On the 31st May 1940 SS *Orangemoor* was torpedoed by *U-101* south-west of Roches Doures in the English Channel. Eighteen of the crew were lost including 18 year old Malcolm Campbell.

At Spurn school his Mother recorded in her logbook on the 7th June that *Orangemoor* had been torpedoed and her son was missing. His death was later confirmed and at the start of the new school term in late August Mrs Campbell was told her bungalow would be 'razed to the ground' to make way for a new concrete road to the Point.

Malcolm Anderson Campbell has no known grave and is commemorated on Panel 76 of the Merchant Navy Memorial at Tower Hill in London. As he was not a Bridlington resident he is not recorded on the Bridlington War Memorial or the Priory Roll of Honour but he is commemorated on the following memorials.

- Bridlington School Second World War Roll of Honour.
- The Commonwealth War Graves Commission Website.

Junior Ordinary Seaman DEREK CAPPLEMAN

The Merchant Navy, Service No. R.298973

Derek Cappleman was born in 1925 the youngest son of Rickman and Jane Elizabeth Cappleman of 7 Jubilee Avenue, Bridlington. Derek was educated at St. Georges School Bridlington and after leaving school he took up forestry work at Boynton.

Derek Cappleman joined the Merchant Navy in October 1943 as a Seaman Apprentice and by 1944 was one of the crew of the SS *Fort Maisonneuve*, a 'Fort' class merchant ship of 7,128 tons managed by the R.B. Chellew Steam Navigation Company on behalf of the Ministry of War Transport. The 'Fort' Ships were a class of 198 cargo ships built in Canada during World War II for use by the United Kingdom under the Lend-Lease scheme. They were built by ten different builders in eighteen different Canadian shipyards and their triple expansion steam engines were built by seven different manufacturers. Twenty-eight ships were lost due to enemy action and a further 25 due to accidents.

In December 1944 SS *Fort Maisonneuve* was on passage from New York to Antwerp. It had joined convoy TAM 18 consisting of 19 ships and two escorts. Passing off Flushing in the River Scheldt on the 15 December, the *Fort Maisonneuve* struck a mine and sank, three of her crew were killed, including 19 year old Derek Cappleman.

Derek Cappleman, who was awarded the 1939-1945 Star, has no known grave and is commemorated on Panel 50 of the Merchant Navy Memorial at Tower Hill, London.

Panel 50 of the memorial (benjidog.co.uk)

Derek Cappleman is also commemorated on the following memorials.

- Bridlington War Memorial.
- St Mary (The Priory) Parish Church Roll of Honour.
- The Commonwealth War Graves Commission Website.

Stoker (1st Class) GEORGE CARTER

The Royal Navy, Service No. C/KX 122509

George Carter was born in 1924 the son of George and Ethel Carter, of Bridlington, Yorkshire. His parents ran the fruit shop on the Promenade during WW2. George attended St George's School and then joined the Royal Navy when he was 18.

By 1945 George was serving as a Stoker on the frigate H.M.S. *Goodall*. HMS *Goodall* (K 479) was a Captain Class Frigate of 1,150 tons built in 1943 by the Boston Navy Yard, Boston MA, USA. for the Royal Navy.

HMS *Goodall* (Luis Photos)

On the 29 April 1945 HMS *Goodall* was part of the 19th Escort Group for Convoy RA-66 on route from Murmansk to the UK. About 22.00 hours U-286 hit HMS *Goodall* with a 'Gnat' homing torpedo in the entrance to the Kola Inlet 7 miles from Murmansk. The ships magazine exploded, blowing away the forepart of the vessel and killing the commander.. The next day, the abandoned ship was scuttled by gunfire from HMS *Anguilla* (K 500) and U-286 was sunk by other ships of the 19th Escort Group during the following night. This was the last confirmed U-boat success in the Northern Theatre.

HMS *Goodall* had a complement of 156 officers and men of which 44 survived and 112 died. One of those who died was 21 year old George Carter. It was initially reported that there were two George Carters on board and the 'Bridlington' one had survived, but this was incorrect.

Stoker (1st Class) George Carter has no known grave and is commemorated on Panel 81, 2. of the Chatham Naval Memorial and the following memorials.

- Bridlington War Memorial.
- St Mary (The Priory) Parish Church Roll of Honour.
- The Commonwealth War Graves Commission Website.

RAYMOND NOEL CARTER

The Air Training Corps, Service No. 46406.

Raymond was born in Jhansi, Bengal, India in 1926 the son of Sergeant Arthur Frederick Carter, Royal Field Artillery, and Sarah Alice Carter (nee White) of Sewerby Fields. Arthur was a regular soldier who had served overseas for nine years and was at Deepcut Barracks, Aldershot, when he married Sarah at Sewerby, St. John the Evangelist Church in the March quarter of 1921.

In 1926 when Raymond was born his father was stationed in India. By 1943 Arthur had retired from the Army and the family address was in Sedgley, Staffordshire. However it is believed that in WW2 Raymond was staying with his Grandfather Matthew White of 'Mount Pleasant', Mill Lane, Bridlington, where Raymond probably joined the Bridlington ATC. The ATC was an organisation to prepare young men for entry to the RAF and arranged visits to RAF stations with opportunities for air experience flights.

On the 2nd August 1943, 16 year old ATC Cadet Raymond Noel Carter was accidentally killed in an air crash at RAF Wyton, Cambridgeshire. Records show that at the time he was a member of 1066 (Hitchin) Squadron of Air Training Corps and was possibly a Cadet Corporal.

Raymond was buried in Sedgley (All Saints) Churchyard West Extension, grave reference plot B, new part, row 21, grave 1.

It is believed that Raymond's name was given to the Bridlington War Memorial Committee by his Grandfather Matthew White of Bridlington.

Raymond is commemorated on the following memorials.
- Bridlington War Memorial (as C H Carter – see page 310).
- St Mary (The Priory) Parish Church Roll of Honour.
- The Commonwealth War Graves Commission Website.

Gunner WILLIAM ROLAND CAWKILL

The Royal Artillery, Service No. 786338

William Roland Cawkill was born in the March quarter of 1908 and was the son of William Alfred and Sarah Ann Cawkill of 116 Durham Street Hull. In the 1911 census his father was a Journeyman Joiner and William age 3 is listed as Roland William. He has an 18 month old sister named Maria Hilda and the family surname is mis-transcribed as Cawkell.

In 1928 when he was 20 years old William joined the Army as a regular soldier and served for seven years, five of which were spent in India. He left the Army in 1935 and then worked in Bridlington. William married Ruth Broadbent in the June quarter of 1936 and they lived at 82 New Burlington Road, Bridlington. William and Ruth had three children, Michael, John and Catherine.

When reservists were called up in September 1939, William joined the Royal Artillery and served as a Driver/Gunner with 160 Battery, 54th Light A.A. Regiment, R.A. The 54th was part of III Corps in the BEF that was sent to France and was subsequentially part of the 9th Battalion, The Argyll and Sutherland Highlanders, when they converted to a light AA unit. The German Blitzkrieg in May 1940 smashed through the allied armies and the BEF began its retreat to Dunkirk. 32 year old William Roland Cawkill was killed in action on the 27th May1940 during this retreat and was buried in grave reference Row C. Grave 24.Cassel Communal Cemetery Extenstion, Nord, France,

William is commemorated on the following memorials.
- Bridlington War Memorial.
- St Mary (The Priory) Parish Church Roll of Honour.
- The Commonwealth War Graves Commission Website.

Note William Cawkill is incorrectly spelt as 'Cawkhill' on the War memorial and the Priory Roll of Honour.

ELSIE GERTRUDE CHATTERTON

Civilian

Elsie Gertrude Chatterton was born in the June quarter of 1891 in Hull, the daughter of Master Mariner Capt. Edward Newton, and Jane Newton (nee Stephenson). She married Walter F. S. Chatterton in the December quarter of 1915 at Sculcoates Hull. They had one son whom they named Reginald Walter Chatterton, he was born in Hull and became a farm stockman. Walter Chatterton died in 1933, and by 1941 Elsie Chatterton was living at 7 Lamplugh Road with her mother Jane, also a widow.

50 year old Elsie, together with her mother Jane Newton, were two more victims of the 18th June 1941 air raid on Bridlington and they were both killed at 7 Lamplugh Road.

Lamplugh Road after the Air raid (Bridlington Local Studies Library)

Elsie Chatterton and her mother Jane Newton were buried together in the Newton family grave, ref. J213, in Bridlington Cemetery on 22 June 1941.

The Newton family grave (C Bonnett)

Elsie Chatterton is commemorated on the following memorials.

- Bridlington War Memorial.
- St Mary (The Priory) Parish Church Roll of Honour.
- The Commonwealth War Graves Commission Website (Civilian War Dead).

Pilot Officer ARNOLD FOSTER CHEETHAM

The Royal Air Force, Service No. 103550, Bridlington School Old Boy

Arnold Foster Cheetham was born in 1915 the son of Eugene Wilberforce Cheetham and Amy Agnes Cheetham of 14 Blackburn Avenue Bridlington. He came to Bridlington School in 1925, became a School Prefect and was awarded his Colours for Cricket. He left the School in 1931 and was employed by the East Riding County Council in Beverley. He joined the RAF in WW2 and became a Pilot Officer with the RAFVR.

Arnold Cheetham (Bridlington School)

In May 1942 Arnold was a pilot with 149 (East India) Squadron in No. 3 Group, Bomber Command flying Short Stirling Bombers from RAF Lakenheath in Suffolk. On the 5th May 1942 his aircraft, Stirling N6124 (OJ-R), was part of a force of 77 aircraft on an operation to bomb Stuttgart Germany. The aircraft is believed to have crashed at Aguilcourt, Aisne, France, some 30 km south-east of Laon. There were no survivors and another three aircraft were lost.

Arnold Foster Cheetham aged 27 was buried in Len (St Just) Communal Cemetery, Aisne, France, grave reference 14. Arnold's death was not confirmed to his parents until September 1948 after his body was lifted from his grave and his name was found inside his tunic, the other members of his crew were not identified and were buried in a collective grave close to his. Arnold is also commemorated on the the following memorials.
- Bridlington School Second World War Roll of Honour.
- Bridlington War Memorial.
- St Mary (The Priory) Parish Church Roll of Honour.
- Bridlington Trinity AFC Memorial.
- The Commonwealth War Graves Commission Website.

Note Arnold Foster Cheetham was the older brother of Frank Alan Cheetham who was also a Bridlington School Old Boy and was also killed in action while serving with the RAF.

Sergeant (Navigator) FRANK ALAN CHEETHAM

The Royal Air Force, Service No. 1437917. Bridlington School Old Boy

Frank Alan Cheetham was born in 1921 the son of Eugene Wilberforce Cheetham and Amy Agnes Cheetham of 14 Blackburn, Avenue, Bridlington. He came to Bridlington School in 1933 and was awarded his Colours for Cricket. He left the School in 1938 and between leaving School and joining the RAF he worked in local government.

Frank Cheetham (Bridlington School)

After joining the RAF Frank became a Sergeant (Navigator) RAFVR and in 1943 was serving with 454 (Australian) Squadron in the Middle East. 454 (Australian) Squadron first formed in 1941 in Australia under the Empire Air Training Scheme. It was re-formed at Aqir in Palestine in 1942 and first saw action in Iraq.

In November 1943 it was the general reconnaissance unit of Middle East Command and conducted anti-submarine patrols and bombing raids on Crete and Greece using Martin Baltimore medium bombers.

The Martin Baltimore (Wikipedia)

On the 19th November 1943 a Baltimore of which Frank Cheetham, aged 22, was the Navigator took off from Berka III in Libya as part of a force of six aircraft on an antisubmarine patrol. His aircraft sent out an SOS message and was believed to be about 20 miles south of Crete, but searches were unsuccessful. Frank Alan Cheetham has no known grave and is commemorated on Column 270 of the El Alamein Memorial in Egypt. He is also commemorated on the following memorials.
- Bridlington School Second World War Roll of Honour.
- Bridlington War Memorial.
- St Mary (The Priory) Parish Church Roll of Honour.
- Bridlington Trinity AFC Memorial.
- Bridlington Town Hall Memorial (NALGO)
- The Commonwealth War Graves Commission Website.

Aircraftman 1st Class FRANK CHIVERS

The Royal Air Force, Service No. 985665

Frank Chivers was born in 1914 the only son of Reginald and Elsie Chivers of 20 Meadowfield Road, Bridlington.

Frank Chivers married Frances Rollitt of Bridlington at Christmas in 1939 and they lived at 3 St Mary's Crescent Bridlington. Frank worked for Modern Dairies of Bridlington and he volunteered for the RAF in April 1940 and was assigned to the Royal Air Force Volunteer Reserve (RAFVR). After training Frank was posted to 957 Balloon Squadron.

In 1939 there were about 42 Balloon Squadrons and the RAF was responsible for operating them. The Balloon Barrage system was part of the Air Defence of Great Britain and 1,455 balloons were established across the country with the higher densities covering the more strategically important areas.

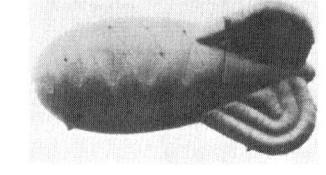

A Typical Anti-Aircraft Balloon

957 Balloon Squadron was part of No 32 Balloon Barrage Group, Romsey (No11 Balloon Centre Bristol) and operated 24 balloons at Yeovil.

Frank was returning to his unit from seven days leave at home in Bridlington on the 6th December 1940 when he was killed during an Air Raid on Bristol Temple Meads Railway Station.

Frank Chivers, who was 26 years old, was buried with full Military Honours in Bridlington Cemetery, grave reference X93.

Grave X93 (C Bonnett)

Frank Chivers is also commemorated on the following memorials.
- Bridlington War Memorial.
- St Mary (The Priory) Parish Church Roll of Honour.
- The Commonwealth War Graves Commission Website.

Sergeant (Air Gunner) GEORGE ELLIS CLARK

Royal Air Force, Service No. 628471, Bridlington School Old Boy

George Ellis Clark was born in 1919 the son of George and M. A. Clark of 'Nethergate', Marine Drive, Bridlington. He came to Bridlington School in 1931 and left the School in 1934. After leaving school George was employed by J. H. Licence & son, accountants and then moved to work for F. W. Woolworth at their Bridlington Branch. George joined the RAF as a Regular Airman in 1938 and by July 1943 was a Sergeant (Air Gunner) with 61 Squadron.

George Clark (Bridlington School)

61 Squadron was in No. 5 Group, RAF Bomber Command and based at Syerston in Nottinghamshire. The Squadron had re-formed as a bomber squadron in 1937 and by 1943 it was equipped with Avro Lancasters. On the 26th July 1943, George E. Clark aged 24 was a Sergeant (Air Gunner) on Lancaster ED613 (QR-?) which took off at 10.13 p.m. as part of a force of 705 aircraft on an operation to bomb Essen in Germany.

This was George's first flight over Germany and his aircraft crashed at Essen. There were no survivors and another 25 aircraft were also lost on this operation.

A Lancaster B1 (F Bull)

George Ellis Clark was buried in the Reichswald Forest Cemetery, Kleve, Nordrhein-Westfalen, Germany, grave reference 6.D.10, and he is also commemorated on the following memorials.

- Bridlington School Second World War Roll of Honour
- Bridlington War Memorial
- St Mary (The Priory) Parish Church Roll of Honour
- The Commonwealth War Graves Commission Website.

ROBERT ERNEST CLARK

Civilian (Civil Service), Bridlington School Old Boy

Robert Ernest Clark was born on the 12 December 1918 at 23 Elma Avenue the son of William and Gertrude Annie Clark (nee Bateman). The family moved to Cottingham in 1938 after living in Bridlington for over 16 years. During the war the family had no permanent address but Robert always considered himself to be a 'Brid Boy'. Robert came to Bridlington School in 1930 and left in 1935 to enter the Civil Service, having passed the Clerical Grade Examination.

Robert Clark (Bridlington School)

Robert was posted to the Royal Naval Victualing Service Yard at Deptford and was on the threshold of a promising career when war broke out. He was appointed Victualing Store Officer and saw service afloat on the RFA supply ship *Boniface* on the West Coast of Scotland and ashore at Scapa Flow for two years. Robert was involved in supplying naval craft supporting the North African operations and in February 1943 he was returning from Gibraltar on leave but failed to return home. His brother Captain M. Gordon Clark of the East Yorkshire Regiment submitted his name to the Bridlington War Memorial Committee and stated Robert's ship was torpedoed about the 8th February 1943. Bridlington School gives a possible date of 5 March 1943 as a passenger aboard SS *Trefusis* bound from Pepel Sierra Leone to London via Gibraltar as part of Convoy XK2 and sunk by *U130* off Cape Finisterre Spain. Three of those on board were lost and the rest were ultimately rescued but no names have been found for those lost so it cannot be confirmed that Robert was on board. Robert's death is not recorded by the CWGC or the GRO index. In a list of Old Boys on active service he is recorded as 'RN' but his name does not appear in the indices of the deaths of RN officers or ratings for WW2 so it seems probable that he remained a civil servant who worked for the Admiralty.

Robert Ernest Clark is commemorated on the following memorials.
- Bridlington School Second World War Roll of Honour
- Bridlington War Memorial
- St Mary (The Priory) Parish Church Roll of Honour.

Private *JOHN CLARK*

The Durham Light Infantry, Service No.4459771

John Clark was born in 1919 the only son of Henry and Elsie Clark of 9 Bridlington Road Flamborough.

In WW2 John Clark was serving with the 1st Battalion of the Durham Light Infantry (DLI). During the Second World War the DLI had Eighteen Active Battalions.

The 1st DLI Battalion (68th Light Infantry) arrived in Egypt in January 1940 as part of the 23 Infantry Brigade. After extensive training the Battalion moved into the front line and in July they moved into the 22 Infantry Brigade and over the following months lost several men due to enemy air attacks.

In December the 1st DLI formed Selby force to contain the enemy around Maktila while the main British forces attacked around Sidi Barrani.

Private John Clark age 21 died on the 3 December 1940 during the December battles and was buried in El Alamein War Cemetery, Egypt, grave reference: XXIX. H. 4.

El Alamein War Cemetery (CWGC)

John Clark is commemorated on the following memorials.

- Bridlington War Memorial
- St Mary (The Priory) Parish Church Roll of Honour.
- The Commonwealth War Graves Commission Website.

Private ARTHUR CLARKSON

The Green Howards, (Alexandra, Princess of Wales's Own Yorkshire Regiment), Service No.4394491

Arthur Clarkson was born in 1914 the son of Samuel and Martha A. Clarkson, of Bridlington, East Yorkshire.

He married Hilda May Jessop, of Bridlington in the September quarter of 1940 and they lived at 53 Nelson Street, Bridlington.

Arthur joined the Green Howards in WW2 and served with either the 6th or 7th Battalions. In 1944 both battalions were part of the D-Day landings, wading ashore on the morning of 6 June 1944. By the evening of the first day they had fought their way seven miles inland, further than any other British or American unit and 180 Green Howards had lost their lives.

On the 11 June 1944 the 6th Battalion of the Green Howards are North-West of Caen and capture the village of Ducy-Sainte-Marguerite.

The 7th Battalion of the Green Howards tries to attack in the South-west but does not manage to cross the line of fire set up by the SS Panzer Lehr Division who inflicts very heavy losses on the Battalion.

Private Arthur Clarkson, Age 30, of the Green Howards died in the Normandy battles on the 11th June 1944 and was buried in the Bayeux War Cemetery, Calvados, France, grave reference XV. C. 26.

Bayeux War Cemetery (CWGC)

Arthur is commemorated on his Mother's grave Z130 in Bridlington Cemetery and on the following memorials.

- Bridlington War Memorial.
- St Mary (The Priory) Parish Church Roll of Honour.
- The Commonwealth War Graves Commission Website.

Skipper-Lieutenant LEONARD CLAXTON

The Royal Navy, Service Number not known

Leonard Claxton was born in September quarter of 1909 the son of Henry (Harry) Claxton and Ada Foots of Hull. His father was lost at sea during WW1.

The family lived in Somerset Street, Hull and Leonard attended Somerset and Wawne Street Schools. After leaving school Leonard went to sea on Trawlers. He married Alice Kemp in the June quarter of 1929 in Hull and they had three daughters and one son. Prior to WW2 Leonard was working for Messrs. Pickering & Haldane's Steam Fishing Co., Ltd. of Hull.

During WW2 Leonard was a Skipper Lieutenant in the Royal Naval Reserve and was at the Dunkirk evacuation.

On the 26th October 1944 Leonard Claxton was lost overboard from H.M.B.Y. Minesweeper 2006 during minesweeping operations in India. At the time of his death Leonard Claxton's grandmother, Mrs. H. Edmond, was living in Grundall Yard, Bridlington and two aunts, Mrs. Langton and Mrs. Loughton, were also living in Bridlington. Leonard's three brothers, Harold, John and Ernest were serving at sea.

Leonard Claxton (Hull Daily Mail)

Leonard Claxton, age 35.was buried in Calcutta (Bhowanipore) Cemetery Kolkata India, grave reference, Plot L. Grave 191.

Calcutta Cemetery (CWGC)

Skipper Lieutenant Leonard Claxton is commemorated on the following memorials.

- Bridlington War Memorial.
- St Mary (The Priory) Parish Church Roll of Honour.
- The Commonwealth War Graves Commission Website.

Gunner WILLIAM NOEL COATES

The Royal Artillery, Service No. 942178

William Noel Coates was born in India in 1919 the son of William Joseph and Mabel Victoria Coates who later resided at 'The Limes' 28 Cardigan Road Bridlington. William and his wife lived at 10 Portland Place in Bridlington. His Mother submitted his name for the War Memorial because 'his wife had gone away'.

In WW2 William was serving as a Gunner with the 74th Field Regiment, RA, (TA). The 74th Regiment mobilized as divisional Artillery within the 50th (Northumbrian) Infantry Division, supporting the 151st Durham Light Infantry Brigade, with whom it served from 1939 to 1944. The Regiment deployed to France in 1940 as part of the (BEF) and returned to the UK in the Dunkirk evacuation.

In 1941 the Regiment embarked with the 8th Army for the Mediterrancan and Middle East Theatre where it took part in the Battle of Gazala, and the Second Battle of El Alamein, followed by the assault on the Mareth Line.

On 10 July 1943 the 74th took part in the Allied invasion of Sicily as part of the 50th Infantry Division where it was engaged in the battle of Primosole Bridge (Operation Fustian) from the 13 to the 16th of July 1944. Gunner William Noel Coates died on the 17th July 1943 age: 24, just after the battle ended.

William Noel Coates was buried in Catania War Cemetery Sicily, grave reference: II. D. 1.

Catania War Cemetery (CWGC)

William is also commemorated on the following memorials.

- Bridlington War Memorial
- St Mary (The Priory) Parish Church Roll of Honour.
- The Commonwealth War Graves Commission Website.

Leading Seaman KENNETH GORDON COLE

The Royal Navy, Service No. C/SSX 33510

Kenneth Gordon Cole was born on the 15th November 1918 the eldest son of Albert William and Doris Cole of 21 St. Hilda Street, Bridlington. As a boy he attended Hilderthorpe and Oxford Street Schools and after leaving school he became a bricklayer with Spink builders. Kenneth joined the Royal Navy at Christmas, 1939 and had seen active service in many waters.

By 1944 Kenneth was on HMS *Verulam* (R28) a V class destroyer completed by Fairfield Govan in December 1943. She was part of the Home fleet force that attacked the German battleship Tirpitz in Altenfjord and also took part in the D Day Landings on the 6th June 1944.

HMS *Verulam* (Wikipedia)

On the 12/13 November 1944 *Verulam* together with *Kent, Bellona, Myngs, Zambesi,* and *Algonquin* took part in Operation Counterblast. Operation Counterblast was an attack on an escorted convoy off the south-west coast of Norway. There were seven enemy freighters in the convoy and six were sunk as well as three of the four escorts. This highly successful attack was fought entirely within range of enemy shore batteries which had opened fire on our ships during the action. The only Allied ships damaged were *Zambesi* and *Verulam*, six 20mm rounds hit *Zambesi* and 32 rounds of 37mm and 20mm gunfire struck *Verulam,* killing two men and wounding five others.

One of the two men killed in action on the 13th November 1944 was 26 year old Leading Seaman Kenneth Gordon Cole who was buried at sea and is commemorated on the Chatham Naval Memorial, panel reference: 74, 3. and on the following memorials.

- Bridlington War Memorial.
- St Mary (The Priory) Parish Church Roll of Honour.
- The Commonwealth War Graves Commission Website.

Note HMS *Verulam* survived WW2 and was reconstructed as a Type 15 A/S frigate (F29) in1954. She was decommissioned c1970.

Driver ROBERT WILLIAM COLMAN

The Royal Signals, Service No. 2335355

Robert William 'Bob' Colman was born in Bridlington on the 16th December 1916, Robert and his twin brother Alfred were the sons of Charles George and Eliza Colman (nee Pinder) of 'Danes Lea' 73 South Back Lane, Bridlington. Robert was educated at Burlington School and was a Butcher before the war. He married Dorothy Dunning of West Hartlepool County Durham in the September quarter of 1939. Robert's Bridlington address before he enlisted was 78 Brookland Road but at his death it was in West Hartlepool, County Durham where their daughter June Cynthia Colman was born in 1940.

Bob Colman (P Wiles)

Robert volunteered for the Army Corps of Signals and served in six campaigns in the Middle East during the two years he was out there. Robert William Colman died of multiple wounds on the 6th November 1942 during the final stage of the allied victory at the battle of El Alamein. He is believed to have driven over a landline in a jeep, He was 25 years old. Robert was buried in El Alamein War Cemetery, Egypt, grave reference plot IX, grave J18.

El Alamein War Cemetery (G Colman)   Robert's grave (P Wiles)

Robert William Colman is commemorated on the following memorials.
- Bridlington War Memorial.
- St Mary (The Priory) Parish Church Roll of Honour.
- The Commonwealth War Graves Commission Website.

Note Robert's surname is incorrectly spelt as 'Coleman' on the Bridlington War memorial and on the Priory Roll of Honour.

Trooper ARTHUR ROBERT CONSTABLE

The 24th Lancers, Royal Armoured Corps, Service No. 320758

Arthur Robert Constable was born in the April quarter 1921 in Hull, the son of Thomas Wilfred and Ellen Constable (nee Binks) of Beverley. Arthur was educated at Osbourne Street School in Hull and was the husband of Martha Elizabeth Constable (nee Clarkson) whom he married in the December quarter of 1943. Arthur and Martha lived at 33 Little Beck Road Bridlington, East Yorkshire.

Arthur first enlisted in the Horse Guards in 1938 and was transferred to the 24th Lancers at the beginning of the war. The 24th Lancers was raised in December 1940 from the 9th Queen's Royal Lancers and the 17th/21st Lancers, originally assigned to 29th Armoured Brigade; it was later reassigned to 8th Armoured Brigade. The regiment landed on Gold Beach in the second wave of the Operation Overlord landings, supporting the 50th (Northumbrian) Infantry Division. Shortly after landing, it was involved in the fighting around Putot-en-Bessin and Villers Bocage.

Sherman VC Firefly of 24th Lancers (Wikipedia)

Arthur received serious burns in the Normandy Landings and was brought back to England but died of pneumonia caused by his injuries on the 1st July 1944 age 23 in Queen Elizabeth Hospital Birmingham.

Trooper Arthur Robert Constable was buried with full military honours in Bridlington Cemetery, grave reference W191.

Arthur's grave (C Bonnett)

Arthur is also commemorated on the following memorials.

- Bridlington War Memorial.
- St Mary (The Priory) Parish Church Roll of Honour.
- The Commonwealth War Graves Commission Website.

Note the CWGC incorrectly names his parents as John & Helen.

Sergeant JOHN DAWSON COOPER

The Royal Electrical and Mechanical Engineers, Service No.4539520
Bridlington School Old Boy

John Dawson Cooper was born in the December quarter of 1918, the eldest son of John and Marjorie Cooper (nee Dawson) of Westwood Road, Beverley. John Dawson Cooper attended Beverley Grammar School and then came to Bridlington School in 1932, leaving in 1935. John's father had been at Bridlington School between 1902 and 1904 and all three of his sons eventually attended the School as well.

John Cooper (Bridlington School)

After leaving school John was articled as a solicitor to Mr. R. F. Paterson who was a partner in the family firm of Cooper and Paterson Solicitors of Butcher Row, Beverley.

John joined the Kings Own Yorkshire Light Infantry in 1939 but transferred to the REME later. He married Brenda Houlton, formerly of Beverley but who was living in Long Eaton, Nottinghamshire in 1945 when John died.

Sergeant John Dawson Cooper, aged 26, died suddenly in India on the 15 March 1945 having suffered from ill health for virtually all of the two years that he was abroad.

John was buried in Delhi Cemetery in India grave reference 5.K.5.

Delhi Cemetery (CWGC)

As he was not a Bridlington resident John Dawson Cooper is not recorded on the Bridlington War Memorial or the Priory Roll of Honour but he is commemorated on the following memorials.

- Bridlington School Roll of Honour.
- Commonwealth War Graves Commission Website.

Lieutenant KENNETH GEORGE COOPER

The Royal Artillery, Service No. P/194424, Bridlington School Old Boy

Kenneth George Cooper was born in 1918 the son of Mr. and Mrs. Charles Cooper of 22 St. Aidan Road, Bridlington. His father was a Colliery Agent. Kenneth, together with his twin brother Geoffrey, came to Bridlington School in 1926 and left in 1930.

In WW2 Kenneth saw service in North Africa with the 81st Battery of the 25th Light Anti-Aircraft Regiment RA (TA). This LAA Regiment was formed in Liverpool in 1939 and was deployed around the Mersey defences. In February 1941 the Regiment sailed to Egypt. In December 1942 it joined 50th Division and fought through North Africa, Tunisia and the invasion of Sicily before it returned to Britain.

Kenneth Cooper (Bridlington School)

While serving in Egypt Kenneth was captured by the Italians, escaped from a German prisoner of war camp in Italy and managed to reach Allied lines. However his war experiences undermined his health and he met his death after the war under a railway locomotive and died of his injuries on the 16th March 1946 aged 28 in Northfield Military Hospital in Birmingham. At the inquest the Coroner concluded that he had taken his own life.

Kenneth George Cooper was buried in Bridlington Cemetery, grave reference W52. His requiem mass and funeral service were conducted by his twin brother, Father Geoffrey Cooper at the Church of Our Lady and St. Peter, Bridlington.

The grave of Kenneth George Cooper (C Bonnett)

Kenneth George Cooper is also commemorated on the following memorials.

- Bridlington School Second World War Roll of Honour.
- Bridlington War Memorial.
- St Mary (The Priory) Parish Church Roll of Honour.
- The Commonwealth War Graves Commission Website.

Sapper FREDERICK COPSEY

The Royal Engineers, Service No. 1918032

Frederick Copsey was born in Bridlington in 1913 the son of George William Thomas and Isabella Annie Copsey of 67 Brookland Road. His father, George, was killed in WW1 while serving with the Royal Engineers. Frederick Copsey married Ethel Brigham and they lived at 64 Gypsey Road Bridlington and had three children.

Before the war Frederick was a member of the local TA (Green Howards) and also a member of their band. He joined 666 Artisan Works Company Royal Engineers in January 1940 and went to France as part of the B.E.F. in June 1940 the Company had retreated to the port of St. Nazaire where they were to be evacuated from France. On the 17th June 1940 they were told to board the *Lancastria*, a Cunard liner that had been requisitioned as a troop ship. However *Lancastria* received three direct hits from German bombers. 20 minutes later the 16,243-ton luxury liner sank, taking with her more than 4,000 people including units from the Army and RAF as well as civilians, men, women and young children. The news of the loss of the *Lancastria* was not made public in Britain until 26th July, 1940.

Lancastria War Memorial in St. Nazaire (Wikipedia)

Among the dead was Sapper Frederick Copsey age 27 of the Royal Engineers. Frederick Copsey was buried in Pornic War Cemetery, Loire-Atlantique, France, special memorial 'C' 2. E. 10. He is also commemorated on the following memorials.

- Bridlington War Memorial.
- St Mary (The Priory) Parish Church Roll of Honour.
- The Commonwealth War Graves Commission Website.

Note by a tragic co-incidence both father and son enlisted in the Royal Engineers on the same Day and Month of the year and both died in the month of June.

Private GEORGE S. CORNELL

The East Yorkshire Regiment (The Duke of York's Own)
Service No. 4342258

George S. Cornell was born in the June quarter of 1914, the son of Ernest and Annie Elizabeth Cornell (nee Robinson) of No 1 Paul's Yard Bridlington.

George married Bella Cornell in the March quarter of 1943 registered in York. Bella was the widow of his brother Sydney Cornell and they lived at 78 Gypsey Road Bridlington.

During WW2 George served with the 7th Battalion East Yorkshire Regiment as a private. The East Yorkshire Regiment raised six 'hostilities-only' battalions in the Second World War, and took part in the Invasion of Normandy and the liberation of Western Europe. It was during the battles for The Netherlands that George Cornell was wounded and died of wounds on the 18th October 1944 age 30.

George Cornell was buried in Mierlo War Cemetery, (12km East of Eindoven), Noord-Brabant, The Netherlands, grave reference: I. D. 3.

The cemetery was started in the spring of 1945 when graves were brought in from the surrounding district, most of them being casualties from the main fighting to clear the region south and west of the Maas and with opening up the Scheldt estuary further west.

Mierlo War Cemetery (CWGC)

George Cornell is also commemorated on the following memorials.

- Bridlington War Memorial.
- St Mary (The Priory) Parish Church Roll of Honour.
- The Commonwealth War Graves Commission Website.

Driver SYDNEY CORNELL

The Royal Engineers, Service No. 1894765

Sydney Cornell was born in the September quarter of 1912 the son of Ernest and Annie Elizabeth Cornell (nee Robinson) of No 1 Paul's Yard, Bridlington and the older brother of George Cornell. His father Ernest was a farm labourer from Cambridge and his mother was from Bridlington, they married in the Sept qtr. 1904 in Bridlington.

Sydney Cornell married Bella Cape in the December quarter of 1938 registered in Buckrose district which covers Bridlington. After their marriage they lived at 22 Watsons Avenue in Bridlington.

Sydney was a driver (Sapper) with the Royal Engineers when he was killed on active service on the 28th October 1940 age: 28. He had been in the Army for just over six months and died in Princess Alice Hospital Carew Road Eastbourne though details of what caused his death have not been recorded by the CWGC.

Sydney Cornell was buried in Bridlington Cemetery, grave reference: S161.

The grave of Sydney Cornell
(C Bonnett)

Sydney Cornell is also commemorated on the following memorials.
- Bridlington War Memorial.
- St Mary (The Priory) Parish Church Roll of Honour.
- The Commonwealth War Graves Commission Website.

Sergeant ARTHUR KENNETH DACRE

The Royal Air Force, Service No. 997219, Bridlington School Old Boy

Arthur Kenneth Dacre was born in 1922 the son of Harold and Clarice Dacre of 'Rose Lea' Bankfield Drive, Nab Wood, Shipley in Yorkshire.

He came to Bridlington School in 1936 and left in 1938. On leaving School he started training as an accountant and then joined the RAF on his 18th birthday and was assigned to the Royal Air Force Volunteer Reserve (RAFVR). He was sent to No. 20 Service Flying Training School that had been formed on 10 July 1940 at Cranboume, near Salisbury in Southern Rhodesia.

Arthur Dacre (Bridlington School)

On the 24 December 1940 Sergeant Arthur Kenneth Dacre aged 18 was involved in a motor-cycle crash while on leave and was admitted to Gatooma Hospital, Southern Rhodesia. He died of his injuries on the 28 December 1940.

Sergeant Arthur Kenneth Dacre was buried in Harare (Pioneer) Cemetery in Southern Rhodesia (now Zimbabwe) European War Graves Plot, Grave 17.

Harare (Pioneer) Cemetery (CWGC)

As he was not a Bridlington resident Arthur Dacre is not recorded on the Bridlington War Memorial or the Priory Roll of Honour but he is commemorated on the following memorials.

- Bridlington School Second World War Roll of Honour.
- The Commonwealth War Graves Commission Website.

Sergeant GEOFFREY GEORGE DARWEN

The Royal Air Force, Service No. 539874

Geoffrey George Darwen was born in April 1917 the son of William James and Floss Darwen. Geoffrey married Marjorie Elizabeth Gray in the September quarter (i.e. July-August-September) of 1939. The marriage was registered in Buckrose district which covers Bridlington

Geoffrey and Marjorie lived at 58 Marshall Avenue Bridlington, East Yorkshire and Geoffrey was a member of the Bridlington Musical Comedy Society.

Geoffrey Darwen joined the RAF and in 1943 was serving as a Sergeant with 84 Squadron RAF. No.84 Squadron had a relatively short active career during the Second World War, handicapped by a lack of aircraft or by the choice of aircraft for much of the time. After fighting in Greece between November 1940 and April 1941 No.84 Squadron was one of a number of squadrons that moved from the Middle East to the Far East, reaching Sumatra in late January 1942 where it joined up with survivors of the defeat in Malaya. This combined force was soon threatened by the Japanese invasion of Sumatra and Java. 84 Squadron was overrun by Japanese forces in Java and all were taken prisoner except a small party including the CO and 11 aircrew.

Geoffrey George Darwen died age 26 on the 29th November 1943 while a prisoner in the hands of the Japanese, He had been held captive for two years. The information supplied to The Bridlington War Memorial Committee states 'Torpedoed, drowned whilst a POW in Japanese hands' which indicates that he was probably being transferred by ship to another POW camp when it was sunk by allied forces.

Geoffrey George Darwen has no known grave and is commemorated on Column 425 of the Singapore Memorial and also on the following memorials.

The Singapore Memorial (CWGC)

- Bridlington War Memorial.
- St Mary (The Priory) Parish Church Roll of Honour.
- The Commonwealth War Graves Commission Websitee

Third Radio Officer GEOFFREY DOBSON

The Merchant Navy, No Service No., Bridlington School Old Boy

Geoffrey Dobson was born in the December quarter of 1927, the only son of Edwin and Winifred Muriel Dobson (nee Tottle) of 'Dalewood' 94 Queensgate Bridlington. His father Edwin was a Railway Clerk and Geoffrey came to Bridlington School in 1935 and left in 1943. After leaving school he joined the Merchant Navy and trained in Hull. Geoffrey commenced his first voyage on Good Friday (7 April) 1944.

Geoffrey Dobson (Bridlington School)
On the 18 April 1945, Geoffrey was the Third Radio Officer on-board the London registered *SS Empire Gold*, a tanker that displaced 8,028 tons and had a crew of 42 seamen and five gunners. *SS Empire Gold* was part of Convoy HX348 bound from Philadelphia, to Antwerp Belgium via New York, with a cargo of 10,278 tons of motor spirit.

At 10.15 hours on the 18th April, 1945, U-1107 fired a spread of three torpedoes at two overlapping ships in the convoy about 70 miles west of Brest and reported two hits. Both ships, the *Cyrus H. McCormick* and the *Empire Gold* were hit and sunk. The master (Henry Cecil Cansdale), 37 crew members and five gunners from the *Empire Gold* were lost. Four crew members were picked up by the British rescue ship *Gothland*.

Geoffrey Dobson aged 17 was one of the 37 crew who were killed in Action, he was the youngest Old Boy to lose his life through enemy action during the war, and was also the last Old Boy to be killed in action in the Second World War.

Geoffrey Dobson has no known grave and is commemorated on Panel 41 of the Merchant Navy Memorial, Tower Hill in London. He is also commemorated on the family grave, ref. Z46, in Bridlington Cemetery and on the following memorials.

- Bridlington School Second World War Roll of Honour.
- Bridlington War Memorial.
- St Mary (The Priory) Parish Church Roll of Honour.
- The Commonwealth War Graves Commission Website.

Sergeant (WOP/AG) LEONARD DOWSE

The Royal Air Force, Service No. 1484106

Leonard Dowse was born in 1922, the son of John Albert and Lucy Annie Dowse, of 3 Midway Terrace Bridlington.

Leonard was the younger brother of Wilfred Lawrence Dowse who was killed in action on the 31st May 1942 in Libya. Both brothers were members of the Christ Church Company of the Church Lads Brigade.

Before WW2 Leonard was an employee of Messrs. W.H. Smith and worked in their bookstalls at Bridlington, Darlington and Harrogate before he joined the RAF in 1941. Leonard volunteered for air crew training and was assigned to the Royal Air Force Volunteer Reserve (RAFVR) where he became a Sergeant (Wireless Operator/Air Gunner).

22 year old Sergeant Leonard (Len) Dowse RAFVR was 'killed on duty with the RAF, somewhere in England' on the 4th January 1944. Neither the CWGC nor reports in the newspapers give any indication of his unit or specific details of how he was killed.

Leonard Dowse was buried with full military honours in Bridlington Cemetery grave reference, X152. The coffin was draped with the Union Jack and borne by six sergeants, the RAF provided an escort and a firing party fired a salute at the graveside. A bugler sounded the 'Last Post' as the coffin was lowered into the grave.

Leonard Dowse's grave (C Bonnett)

Leonard is also commemorated on the following memorials.

- Bridlington War Memorial.
- St Mary (The Priory) Parish Church Roll of Honour.
- Christ Church Roll of Honour.
- The Commonwealth War Graves Commission Website.

Lance Corporal WILFRED LAWRENCE DOWSE

The Green Howards (Alexandra, Princess of Wales's Own Yorkshire Regiment), Service No. 4388920

Wilfred Lawrence Dowse was born in 1920 the son of John Albert and Lucy Annie Dowse, of 3 Midway Terrace Bridlington, Yorkshire. He was educated at Oxford Street School and was the elder brother of Leonard Dowse. Wilfred and Leonard were members of the Christ Church Company of the Church Lads Brigade in which Wilfred was a drummer. Wilfred worked for the Bridlington Corporation Gardens Department and in 1941 he married Rose Marion Cope, the marriage was registered in Weston-Super-Mare district. At the time of his marriage Wilfred was serving in the 5th battalion Green Howards and had been to France with the BEF and evacuated from Dunkirk, the 5th Green Howards being among the last British units off the beaches.

Reorganised and retrained the 5th (and 6th) battalions were then sent to the Middle East as part of the 150th Infantry Brigade, 50th (Northumbrian) Division. In May 1942 they were part of the defensive positions known as The 'Gazala Line', a series of occupied 'boxes' set out across the desert with minefields and wire. In late May 1942 the Afrika Corps attacked the Gazala Line, overran some boxes and isolated the 150th Infantry Brigade Box. The enemy committed parts of German 15th Panzer Division, 101 Motorised Division Trieste and German 90th Light Infantry Divisions, supported by heavy bombing attacks against the isolated 150th brigade. After 72 hours of very heavy fighting in this area, which become known as 'The Cauldron', the position was overrun and forced to surrender. It was during this battle that 22 year old Lance Corporal Wilfred Lawrence Dowse was killed in action on the 31st May 1942 and was buried in Knightsbridge War Cemetery Acroma in Libya Special Memorial 16 G 12.

Knightsbridge War Cemetery (CWGC)

Wilfred Dowse is also commemorated on the following memorials.
- Bridlington War Memorial.
- St Mary (The Priory) Parish Church Roll of Honour.
- Christ Church Roll of Honour.
- The Commonwealth War Graves Commission Website.

Leading Writer *JOHN FEATHERSTONE DRISCOLL*

The Royal Navy, Service No. D/MX67653

John Featherstone Driscoll was born in 1921, the eldest son of William and Georgina Driscoll, of 19 Albion Terrace Bridlington. His Father was a joiner and after leaving school John worked in the auditing department at Bridlington Town Hall and played cricket for Bridlington Cricket Club second eleven.

John joined the Royal Navy in 1939 and by 1942 he was serving on H.M.S. *Exeter* a heavy cruiser of the Royal Navy that fought against the German pocket battleship *Graf Spee* at the 1939 Battle of the River Plate.

HMS *Exeter* (Luis Photos)

In 1941 HMS *Exeter* was engaged on escort duty for Atlantic convoys and then went to the Far East as part of a naval force intended to defend the Dutch East Indies (now Indonesia) from Japanese invasion.

On 27 February 1942, *Exeter* was damaged in the Battle of the Java Sea and two days later she was intercepted by Japanese heavy cruisers and destroyers. The Second Battle of the Java Sea ensued, and *Exeter* was badly damaged by gunfire and torpedoes and finally sank about noon. Her escorting destroyers, HMS *Encounter* and USS *Pope* were also lost. About 800 Allied seamen were picked up by the Japanese and became prisoners of war. 153 of *Exeter's* crew died while in captivity and three more died after being liberated at war's end due to their treatment by the Japanese.

Leading Writer John Featherstone Driscoll was one of HMS *Exeter's* crew who died in captivity on the 8th April 1945 age 24. He was buried in Ambon War Cemetery Indonesia, Grave Reference: 29. A. 9. John Featherstone Driscoll is commemorated on the following memorials.

- Bridlington War Memorial.
- St Mary (The Priory) Parish Church Roll of Honour.
- Bridlington Town Hall Memorial (NALGO).
- The Commonwealth War Graves Commission Website.

Lieutenant ERIC DUNKERLEY

The Royal Navy, Service No. not known, Bridlington School Old Boy

Eric Dunkerley was born in 1909, the son of Herbert and Alice Dunkerley of 29 Harland Road, Bridlington. He came to Bridlington School in 1918 and left in 1924. Eric became a Merchant Navy officer with wide seagoing experience as an engineer and in the June quarter of 1935 he married Ethel Mona Kathleen Ritherdon and they lived at 32 Alton Gardens Twickenham. Eric then worked for Middlesex County Council before receiving a commission in the Royal Naval Reserve in 1941.

Eric Dunkerley (Bridlington School)

By 1942 Lieutenant Eric Dunkerley RNR was serving on the escort carrier HMS *Avenger* that was the first aircraft carrier to escort an Arctic convoy. *Avenger* had a ship's company of 555 officers and men and could carry up to 15 aircraft. After taking part in the North African landings in November 1942 *Avenger* departed Gibraltar for the Clyde with convoy MKF 1 on the 14 November. At 0305 on 15 November *Avenger* was torpedoed by U155 off Gibraltar. She was hit on the port side amidships, which in turn ignited her bomb room, blowing out the centre section of the ship. Her bow and stern sections rose in the air and sank within 2 minutes leaving only 12 survivors.

HMS Avenger (Luis Photos)

34 year old Lieutenant Eric Dunkerley RNR was among those killed in action on the 15 November 1942. Eric has no known grave and is commemorated on Column 1, Panel 2, of the Royal Naval Reserve Memorial in Liverpool Lancashire. He is also commemorated on the following memorials.
- Bridlington School Second World War Roll of Honour.
- Bridlington War Memorial.
- St Mary (The Priory) Parish Church Roll of Honour.
- The Commonwealth War Graves Commission Website.

Sergeant (Navigator) GEORGE CHARLES DYNES

The Royal Air Force, Service No. 1501437, Bridlington School Old Boy

George Charles Dynes was born in 1922, the son of Muriel Dynes of 5 Eastmoor Drive, Roundhay Leeds. He came to Bridlington School in 1936 and left in 1939. George joined the RAF, volunteered for air crew training, and was assigned to the Royal Air Force Volunteer Reserve (RAFVR) where he became a Sergeant (Navigator) with 35 Squadron. No. 35 Squadron (also known as No. XXXV (Madras Presidency) Squadron first formed in 1916 and disbanded in 1919.

George Dynes (Bridlington School)

35 Squadron reformed at Bircham Newton on 1 March 1929 and in 1939 on the outbreak of WW2 the Squadron was designated a training unit, with Battles, Ansons and Blenheims. The Squadron disbanded again after being absorbed into No. 17 OTU along with No. 90 Squadron at Upwood. It reformed on 5 November 1940 at RAF Linton-on-Ouse in Yorkshire as the first Handley Page Halifax squadron. In August 1942 it became a pathfinder unit in No. 8 Group at Graveley.

George Charles Dynes was killed in action on the 27 March 1943 aged 21 when his aircraft Halifax II W7907 (TL-M) was shot down over Germany. His Halifax took off at 7.50 p.m. as part of a force of 396 aircraft on an operation to bomb Berlin. The aircraft was hit by anti-aircraft fire and crashed at 9.35 p.m. to the north of Habichhorst, about 3 km east of Stadthagen. There were no survivors and eight other aircraft were lost on this raid.

George Charles Dynes was buried in Collective Grave reference 11.G.1-6.a in Becklingen War Cemetery Niedersachsen in Germany.

Becklingen War Cemetery (CWGC)

As he was not a Bridlington resident George is not recorded on the Bridlington War Memorial or the Priory Roll of Honour but he is commemorated on the following memorials.
- Bridlington School Second World War Roll of Honour.
- The Commonwealth War Graves Commission Website.

Aircraftman 1st Class *DENIS EARNSHAW*

The Royal Air Force, Service No. 631813, Bridlington School Old Boy

Denis Earnshaw was born in 1922, the son of Alfred and Edith Annie Earnshaw (nee Vary) of North Street, Bridlington. He came to Bridlington School in 1932 and left in 1937. His father Alfred was a stonemason who died in 1933 a year after Denis came to the School and Denis's Grandfather was the well-known architect Joseph Earnshaw. On leaving School Denis worked at Bridlington Town Hall as an assistant in the Valuation Department, he enlisted in the RAF shortly before the war started.

Denis Earnshaw (Bridlington School)

In 1941 Denis Earnshaw was serving with No. 214 (Federated Malay States) Squadron, part of No. 3 Group, Bomber Command and stationed at Stradishall, Suffolk equipped with Vickers Wellingtons.

Denis Earnshaw aged 19 took his own life at Stradishall airfield by shooting himself with a service rifle. He died of his injuries on the 18th April 1941 and was buried in grave reference U136, in Haverhill Cemetery, Withersfield Road, Haverhill in Suffolk.

Haverhill Cemetery has 44 burials from the 1939-45 war, the majority having served with the air forces of the Commonwealth. Most are buried in a service plot in Section U.

Haverhill Cemetery (CWGC)

Denis Earnshaw is also commemorated on the following memorials.

- Bridlington School Second World War Roll of Honour.
- Bridlington War Memorial.
- St Mary (The Priory) Parish Church Roll of Honour.
- The Commonwealth War Graves Commission.

Note Bridlington School Roll of Honour Booklet has his Christian name misspelt as Dennis.

Aircraftman 1st Class GEORGE EDWARDS

The Royal Air force, Service No. 997740

George Edwards was born in 1913 the son of Joseph Appleby Edwards and Jane Elizabeth Edwards of South Shields.

George was serving in the RAFVR in WW2 and in 1941 he was billeted in the Promenade, Bridlington.

At 24 minutes past midnight on Thursday morning the 17th July 1941 a German aircraft dropped four HE's bombs which exploded along the Promenade in Bridlington completely destroying the properties at 101, 103, 105 and 107 the Promenade. The houses hit were occupied by the RAF and at Numbers 103 and 105 twenty two airmen had a miraculous escape. George Edwards was not so lucky and he and fellow airman Edward Redding were killed in this air raid together with civilian George Ireland who lived at 105 the Promenade.

Air Raid damage at the Promenade   (Bridlington local Studies Library)

George Edwards was buried in section F, grave reference 4873 of South Shields (Harton) Cemetery.

George is not recorded on the Bridlington War Memorial but he is commemorated on the following memorials.

- St Mary (The Priory) Parish Church Roll of Honour.
- The Commonwealth War Graves Commission Website.

Note the CWGC does not reveal the RAF unit to which George Edwards was attached when he died.

Sergeant (Air Gunner) FRANCIS GORDON ELLIS

The Royal Air Force, Service No. 1108093, Bridlington School Old Boy

Francis Gordon Ellis was born in 1920, the son of George Henry and Doris Ellis of the Brentwood Hotel in Bridlington and then of Harrogate. He came to Bridlington School in 1934 and left in 1940. Francis joined the RAF, volunteered for air crew training and was assigned to the Royal Air Force Volunteer Reserve (RAFVR). Francis served with 28 (Army Co-operation) Squadron which had formed in 1915 and served in India continuously from 1920.

Francis Ellis (Bridlington School)

By July 1942 28 (AC) Squadron was equipped with Westland Lysander aircraft and was based at Kohat North West Frontier Province in India.

22 year old Francis Gordon Ellis was killed in action on the 27 July 1942 when three aircraft took off on a mission to bomb `rebellious tribesmen' at Narakai. The aircraft in which Francis Ellis was flying as Air Gunner was seen to force-land and turn over onto its back about a mile from Dargai. The aircraft and the bodies of the crew were then looted by local natives. Later the bodies of Francis Ellis and another crew member were retrieved by Khasadars (Indian police officers) and were buried with full military honours at Kohat Cemetery.

Their remains were later moved to Karachi Cemetery and Francis Gordon Ellis was reburied in Grave 4A1 at Karachi Cemetery in Pakistan.

Karachi Cemetery (CWGC)

In 1943 his parents presented the Ellis Cup to Bridlington School in his memory which was competed for in Junior House Cross Country. Francis Gordon Ellis is commemorated on the following memorials.

- Bridlington School Second World War Roll of Honour.
- Bridlington War Memorial.
- St Mary (The Priory) Parish Church Roll of Honour.
- The Commonwealth War Graves Commission Website.

Chief Engineer FRED ELLIS

The Merchant Navy, Service No. not known, Bridlington School Old Boy

Fred Ellis was born in 1901, the son of Fred and Catherine Alice Ellis of 8 Kingsgate, Bridlington. He came to Bridlington School in 1913 and left in 1916. He was the eldest of nine brothers who all attended Bridlington School. Fred joined the Merchant Navy on leaving School and was the husband of Minnie B. Ellis of Hull, they had one daughter whom they named Patricia (Pat).

Fred Ellis (Bridlington School)

Fred Ellis was awarded the King's Commendation for Brave Conduct (published in the London Gazette on 12 May 1942). The collective citation stated that the awards to Merchant Navy personnel were for *"brave conduct when their ships encountered enemy ships, submarines, aircraft or mines"*. The award consisted of a stylised bronze oak leaf which was affixed to the ribbon of the 1939-1945 War Medal.

On the 3rd February 1943 Fred Ellis was a Chief Engineer on MV *Inverilen* a 9,456 ton motor tanker, registered in Glasgow with a crew of 39 seamen and six gunners. She was bound from New York to Stanlow, Cheshire with about 13,000 tons of clean petroleum products as part of Convoy HX224. At 02.57 hours the *Inverilen* (Master Joseph Mann) was torpedoed by U-456 south of Iceland. She was abandoned and sank later. The master, 24 crew members and six gunners were lost. 14 crew members and two passengers were picked up by HMS *Asphodel*, unfortunately Chief Engineer Fred Ellis, age 42, was not among the survivors.

Fred Ellis has no known grave and is commemorated on Panel 58 of the Merchant Navy Memorial, Tower Hill, London. There was a Memorial Chair to him in Bridlington School and he is commemorated on the following memorials.

- Bridlington School Second World War Roll of Honour.
- Bridlington War Memorial.
- St Mary (The Priory) Parish Church Roll of Honour.
- The Commonwealth War Graves Commission Website

Second Lieutenant JOHN ELLIS (MM)

The Royal Army Pay Corps, Service No. 195695, Bridlington School Old Boy

John Ellis was born in Beeston about 1895, the son of Joe and Alice Jane Ellis. He came to Bridlington School in 1911. John was awarded his Colours for Cricket and Football and left the School in 1912. During the First World War John served in ranks of the 10th (Service) Battalion, East Yorkshire Regiment (Hull Commercials) and was awarded the Military Medal for gallant conduct in 1917. He was discharged as unfit for further service in 1918.

John Ellis (Bridlington School)

On the 22nd February 1922 John Ellis married Dorothy May Martin, daughter of George Elliott Martin, in the parish of Potternewton, St Martin in West Yorkshire. After their marriage they lived at 12 Hartley Crescent Birkdale Southport in Lancashire.

47 year old John Ellis joined the Royal Army Pay Corps in 1940, but his health broke down and he died of Illness on the 29th September 1941 aged 48, his death being registered in the Southport Lancashire Registration District.

John Ellis was buried in grave H717 of the Southport (Birkdale) Cemetery in Lancashire.

As he was not a Bridlington resident Second Lieutenant John Ellis (MM) is not recorded on the Bridlington War Memorial or the Priory Roll of Honour but he is commemorated on the following memorials:

- Bridlington School Second World War Roll of Honour.
- The Commonwealth War Graves Commission Website.

Captain JOHN ELLISON

The Green Howards (Alexandra, Princess of Wales's Own Yorkshire Regiment), Service No. 164551, Bridlington School Old Boy

John Ellison was born in 1913, the son of William Ernest and Beatrice Ellison of Hull. He came to Bridlington School in 1923 and left in 1928. On leaving School he entered the electrical industry and was employed by Edison Swan Electricians Ltd in Hull. John was the husband of Beatrice Ellen Ellison and they lived at 46 Parkstone Road off Beverley Road in Hull. John joined the Territorial Army (TA) in 1939 serving with the 7th Battalion the Green Howards.

John Ellison (Bridlington School)

John Ellison was one of the early members of the 7th battalion serving in the ranks in France before being evacuated from Dunkirk and subsequently receiving an officer's commission. The 7th Battalion (T A) had a particular link with Bridlington and the School. It was formed in Bridlington in April 1939 as a duplicate of the 5th Battalion (TA). The appointed second-in-command of the battalion was Major J. B. Lister, a member of the School staff who also commanded the School contingent of the OTC. Following a meeting in the lecture room at the School on 2nd May, 1939 between Major J. B. Lister, a senior officer and a number of Old Boys resident in the district. 38 Old Boys enlisted at the Drill Hall three days later and this number was quickly increased to 46.

Captain John Ellison was seconded to the 2nd Battalion of the East Yorkshire Regiment and crossed to France shortly after D-Day. On the 12th August 1944 31 year old Captain John Ellison was killed in action by a land mine near Villers Bocage in Normandy France. He was buried in grave XVI.C.15. of the Bayeux Cemetery in Calvados France.

As he was not a Bridlington resident John Ellison is not recorded on the Bridlington War Memorial or the Priory Roll of Honour but he is commemorated on the following memorials.

- Bridlington School Second World War Roll of Honour.
- The Commonwealth War Graves Commission Website.

Private WILLIAM EMMERSON

The Border Regiment, Service No. 3602810

William Emmerson was born on the 28 December 1915 the son of George R. and Annie Emmerson (nee Creaser) of Bridlington. In 1936 William Emmerson married Mary E. Wiles at Bridlington and they lived at 19 South Back Lane.

During WW2 William joined the 1st Battalion of the Border Regiment. The Battalion was amongst the first troops to cross the Channel with the B.E.F. They were heavily engaged in the German Blitzkrieg of May 1940, which ended in their successful evacuation from Dunkirk. The 1st Battalion subsequently converted into airborne (glider) troops and were retitled the Border Regiment 1st (Airborne) Battalion and joined the 1st Airlanding Brigade of the 1st Airborne Division. In 1943 the division was deployed to Tunisia for operations in the Mediterranean theatre. The 1st Airlanding Brigade then took part in 'Operation Ladbroke' as part of the invasion of Sicily.

'Operation Ladbroke' was a glider assault by the 1st Airlanding Brigade near Syracuse that began on 9 July 1943. The brigade was equipped with 144 Waco and six Horsa gliders. Their objective was to land near the town of Syracuse, secure the Ponte Grande Bridge, and ultimately take control of the city itself. On the way to Sicily, 65 gliders were released too early by the towing aircraft and crashed into the sea, drowning around 252 men. Only 87 men arrived at the Pont Grande Bridge, which they successfully captured and held beyond the time they were to be relieved. With their ammunition expended and only 15 soldiers remaining unwounded, they surrendered to the Italian forces.

William Emmerson, age 27, was one of the soldiers who died on the 9 July 1943 and has no known grave. He is commemorated on Panel 7 of the Cassino War Memorial in Italy and also on the following memorials.

Cassino War Memorial (CWGC)

- Bridlington War Memorial.
- St Mary (The Priory) Parish Church Roll of Honour
- The Commonwealth War Graves Commission Website.

Stoker 2nd Class HENRY STANCLIFFE EZARD

The Royal Navy, Service No. D/KX 532410

Henry Stancliffe Ezard was born on the 15th September 1909 at The Grange in Market Weighton East Yorkshire. In the 1911 census Henry was living with his Grandparents Henry and Mary Ezard near Market Weighton.

In the December quarter of 1936, Henry married Nora Mary Boddy of Bridlington. They lived at 27 Horsforth Avenue where Henry was a bricklayer. His wife Nora was a taxi driver for her father who was a Taxi Proprietor with his business premises at 43 West Street.

Henry Ezard (family archive)

Henry joined the Royal Navy on the 27th April 1943 and served aboard HMS *Excalibur* until the 3rd June 1943 when he transferred to HMS *Victory* at Portsmouth. He then went to HMS *Daedalus* on the 7th October 1943 until he was taken sick on the 22nd October 1943 and moved to the Royal Naval Hospital at Chatham. Henry was in hospital from the 23rd October 1943 until the 21st January 1944.

Henry Ezard was discharged from the Royal Navy on the 18th February 1944 and died at 43 West Street, age 36, on the 28th April 1946. Henry was buried in Bridlington Cemetery grave reference Y 79.

The grave of Henry Stancliffe Ezard (C Bonnett)

Henry Stancliffe Ezard is not recorded on the Bridlington War Memorial or the Priory Roll of Honour but he is commemorated on the following memorial.

- The Commonwealth War Graves Commission Website.

Gunner FRANK FEATHERSTON

The Royal Artillery, Service No. 1541678

Frank Featherston was born in 1919, the son of Elizabeth Featherston, (nee Jimmison) of Wetwang. His last address before enlistment was given as 32 Horsforth Avenue Bridlington.

Frank was a Gunner with the Royal Artillery and in 1940 was stationed with 411 Coast Battery, St. Margarets Bay, Dover, Kent. The Royal Artillery manned various coastal batteries, particularly on the South Coast of England where three new heavy gun batteries were built near Dover. The beach at St Margaret's Bay was seen as a possible landing place for an invasion fleet, so it was well defended during the war and old photographs show barbed wire entanglements and a pillbox and an underground tunnel system. It was also a crucial point as powerful gun batteries were located close by, and would have been a target for sabotage. The overall coastal command for Dover was from an operations room in one of the casemates below Dover Castle.

Gunner Frank Featherston died on the 25 November 1940 age 21 at Dover Castle through enemy action, but details of exactly how he died have not been found.

Frank Featherston was buried in Bridlington Cemetery grave reference X81.

The grave of Frank Featherston
(C Bonnett)

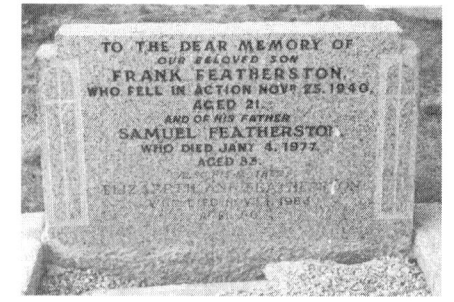

Frank Featherston is commemorated on the following memorials

- Bridlington War Memorial.
- St Mary (The Priory) Parish Church Roll of Honour.
- The Commonwealth War Graves Commission Website.

Note: The Bridlington War Memorial and the Priory have his surname incorrectly spelt as Featherstone.

Warrant Officer FRANCIS JOSEPH B. FINNERTY

The Royal Air Force, Service No. 330750

Francis Joseph Finnerty was born in 1902 the son of Joseph Michael and Mary Finnerty. Frances married Nellie Braithwate of Bridlington in 1932 and they lived at 93 Sewerby Road.

In WW2 Francis was a Warrant Officer in the Royal Air Force and died 'on war service' on the 11th January1945 age 43 at the King Edward VII Sanatorium, Midhurst, Sussex.

Details of the unit or squadron to which he was attached are not recorded on the Commonwealth War Graves Commission Website but it was reported in the Hull Daily Mail of the 1st March 1946 that he died from cancer.

Francis Joseph Finnerty was buried in Bridlington Cemetery, grave reference Z26.

Bridlington Cemetery (F Bull)   Francis's grave (C Bonnett)

Francis Joseph Finnerty is not recorded on the Bridlington War Memorial or the Priory Roll of Honour but he is commemorated on the following memorial.

- The Commonwealth War Graves Commission Website.

Note: In 1946 his wife Nellie Finnerty applied for a pension in respect of her husband's death, the outcome of this application is unknown.

Chief Engineer *JAMES GOLIGHTLY FIRMAN*

The Merchant Navy, Service No. not known

James Golightly Firman was born in the July quarter of 1890, the son of James Lowry and Sarah Elizabeth Firman of Stranton, West Hartlepool. His father was a Railway Signalman who died at Lloyds Cottage Hospital in 1955 when their address was 37 Trinity Road Bridlington.

James G. Firman married Minnie Crowe in the March quarter of 1919, the marriage being registered in Goole. After their marriage they lived at 36 Park Spring Gardens, Bramley, Leeds but James gave his address before enlistment as 19 St. Stephen Road, Bridlington.

During WW2 James Firman served in the Merchant Navy. On the 23 Feb 1941 he was Chief Engineer on the S.S. *Marslew* of London, a steam merchantman of 4,542 tons with a complement of 36 and carrying 6000 tons of general cargo on route Glasgow - Liverpool - Montevideo - Villa Constitucion, Argentina, as part of Convoy OB-288.

At 23.39 hours on 23 Feb, 1941, the unescorted *Marslew* which had dispersed from the convoy, was hit on the starboard side amidships in the boiler room by one G7e torpedo from U-69 about 265 miles west-northwest of Rockall. The explosion immediately broke the ship in two, its bow and stern rising slowly with the forepart sinking first after approximately 30 minutes and the stern sinking after floating vertically for a while. The master (Hubert Roland Watkins) and twelve crew members were lost. 21 crew members and two gunners were picked up by the British steam merchantman *Empire Cheetah* from the same dispersed convoy

James G Firman age 51 was among those lost; he has no known grave and is commemorated on Panel 69 of the Merchant Navy Memorial, Tower Hill, London. He is also commemorated on the following memorials:

- Bridlington War Memorial.
- St Mary (The Priory) Parish Church Roll of Honour.
- The Commonwealth War Graves Commission Website.

Warrant Officer (Pilot) CHARLES HENRY FLETCHER

The Royal Air Force, Service No. 1375522

Charles Henry Fletcher was born in 1915 the youngest son of Thomas and Emma Harriet Fletcher, of 26 Springfield Avenue, Bridlington.

Prior to WW2 Charles was a musician touring the country with his own dance band. He was 'discovered' by Hermon Darewski who introduced his professional career.

In 1940 Charles joined the RAF, volunteered for air crew training and was assigned to the Royal Air Force Volunteer Reserve (RAFVR). He served in the Middle East and in Malta during the siege. He also served in South Africa as an Instructor. Charles became engaged to Miss Pauline Guy and they were due to marry at Christ Church in May 1945 but Charles was killed in a flying accident on the 22 March1945 while serving as a pilot with 526 Squadron RAF. 526 Squadron was formed on 15 June 1943 at RAF Longmans Airport, Inverness, Scotland from the calibration flights of Nos. 70, 71 and 72 Wing RAF to carry out calibration duties in northern Scotland. It had a mixture of mainly twin-engined aircraft, including the Bristol Blenheim, Airspeed Oxford, the de Havilland Dominie and Hornet Moth, which apart from calibration were also used for communications duties. 526 Squadron also had detachments at RAF Tealing, Angus, Scotland and in Northern Ireland.

Charles was 30 years old when he accidentally died on the 22 March1945 but no details of this flying accident have been found to date. Charles was buried in March1945 at Moor Allerton (St. John) Churchyard Yorkshire.

Charles Henry Fletcher is commemorated on the following memorials:

- Bridlington War Memorial.
- St Mary (The Priory) Parish Church Roll of Honour.
- Christ Church Roll of Honour.
- The Commonwealth War Graves Commission Website

Gunner CHARLES FREDERICK (FRED) FLOWER

The Royal Artillery, Service No. 1782198

Charles Frederick (Fred) Flower was born on the 15th October 1910, the son of Herbert and Jane Ellen Flower (nee Cooper) of Arthur Street, Anlaby Road in Hull.

Fred married Dorothy Simpson and they lived at 29 Westbourne Avenue, Bridlington and had one son, David, and three daughters, Jean, Dorothy & Diana.

Fred worked as a Farm Worker and Milk Roundsman before joining the Army in 1941 where he served in the R.H.Q., 141 Light A.A. Regiment. The 141 was formed from batteries of 47, 62, 73 & 75 LAA Regiments.

Fred Flower saw war service in England, North Africa, Gibraltar, Sicily and Italy.

Charles Frederick (Fred) Flower
(via David Flower}

34 year old Charles Frederick (Fred) Flower had an accident and died on the 7th April 1945 following an operation in a Military Hospital in Italy. Fred was buried in Salerno War Cemetery, Grave Reference VI. F. 30.

Salerno War Cemetery (CWGC)

Charles Frederick (Fred) Flower is also commemorated on the following memorials:

- Bridlington War Memorial.
- St Mary (The Priory) Parish Church Roll of Honour.
- The Commonwealth War Graves Commission Website

Ordinary Seaman ALEC EDWARD FORBES

The Merchant Navy, Service No. not known

Alec Edward Forbes was born on the 1st April 1913 the son of Edward and Rhoda Forbes (nee Harrison) of 2 Prickett Road in Bridlington.

Alec was educated at Burlington School and before he joined the Merchant Navy he was a well-known local comedian who was popular with visitors and he used to entertain passengers on the pleasure boats sailing from Bridlington Harbour. Alec was the husband of Marion Emma Forbes (nee Fulcher) and after their marriage they lived at 21 Medforth Road, Bridlington where they had three children, Ralph, Betty and Brenda.

Alec Forbes (family archive)

In WW2 Alec Forbes was serving in the Merchant Navy and on the 7 June 1940 he was a member of the crew of the S.S. *Frances Massey*, a steam merchantman of 4,212 tons owned by W.A. Massey & Sons Ltd, of Kingston upon Hull. At 00.07 hours on 7th June 1940, the unescorted *Frances Massey* on route from Wabana, Conception Bay to Glasgow with a cargo of 7500 tons of iron ore, had been missed by a first torpedo which passed underneath her. At 02.13 hours when the ship was 14miles northwest of Tory Island, Ireland, she was hit in the foreship by one G7a torpedo from U-48. The vessel sank within 30 seconds, taking 33 crew members and one gunner with her. The sole survivor, the master, Walter Whitehead, was picked up by HMS *Volunteer*.

27 year old Alec Edward Forbes was among the crew members who died; he has no known grave and is commemorated on Panel 51 of the Merchant Navy Memorial, Tower Hill London. He is also commemorated on the following memorials:

- Bridlington War Memorial.
- St Mary (The Priory) Parish Church Roll of Honour.
- The Commonwealth War Graves Commission Website

Note U-48 was scuttled on the 3rd May 1945 off Neustadt, Germany.

THOMAS ATKIN FORSTER

Civilian

Thomas (Tom) Atkin Forster was born in 1881, the son of Charles (Chas) Forster and Isabel Matilda Forster (nee Atkin) of 6 the Promenade Bridlington. His father Chas was born in 1851 and was the founder of Messrs C Forster & Company, Printers. The Company printed the Bridlington and Quay Gazette. Chas Forster died in 1891 at the young age of 40 and his widow Isabel married John William Watson in the December quarter of 1894 at Bridlington. John and Isabel Watson (nee Forster) continued running the company and lived at 6 the Promenade. In the 1901 census John W Watson is described as born inYork c1853, Librarian (books), Printer, Newspaper Proprietor. By 1941 Isabel Matilda Watson (formerly Forster) was living at 9 Fort Terrace in Bridlington.

Tom Forster was employed by Messrs C Forster & Company, Printers as a compositor/printer and he married Annie Jane Simpson in the December quarter of 1912, registered at Bridlington. Tom was a member of the Bridlington Miniature Rifle Club. During WW2 Tom became a Bridlington Firewatcher.

60 year old Tom Forster of 5 Lamplugh Road was killed in the air raid of the 18th June 1941 that destroyed and damaged houses in Lamplugh Road and St. Anne's Road in Bridlington.

Thomas (Tom) Atkin Forster was buried in Bridlington Cemetery on the 21st June 1941 grave ref V195.

The grave of Tom Forster (C Bonnett)

Tom Forster is also commemorated on the following memorials:
- Bridlington War Memorial.
- St Mary (The Priory) Parish Church Roll of Honour.
- The Commonwealth War Graves Commision Website(Civilian War Dead)

Private HARRY FOSTER

The Green Howards, (Alexandra, Princess of Wales's Own Yorkshire Regiment), Service No. 4396332

Harry Foster was born on the 26th April 1911, the son of William Henry and Gertrude Maud Foster of 41 Quay Road, Bridlington.

Harry joined up on his 29th birthday, the 26 April 1940, from Butlins Camp buildings. He left work about 17 July 1940 to go to Richmond Camp where he joined the 7th Battalion of the Green Howards. The 7th Battalion served in France and Flanders and was evacuated from Dunkirk. In April 1941 the 7th Green Howards were part of the 69th Brigade, 50th (Northumbrian) Infantry Division, and went to the Middle East via Cyprus, Iraq, Syria, Egypt and then into Libya as part of XIII Corps in the Eighth Army. In May 1942 they took part in the Battle of Gazala and later in the battles for El Alamein They landed in Sicily on the 9th July 1943, the first day of the Allied forces invasion.

After Sicily they were one of the units recalled from the 8th Army in Italy to prepare for the invasion of North-West Europe. The 7th Battalion, Green Howards were part of the D-Day landings, wading ashore on the morning of 6 June 1944. By the evening of the first day they had fought their way seven miles inland, further than any other British or American unit. Then followed the exhaustive battles for Normandy in which Private Harry Foster was killed while with S Coy Mortar Platoon.

Harry died of wounds on the 10th August 1944 age 33 and was buried in grave III. F. 8, Tilly-Sur-Seulles War Cemetery, Calvados, France.

Tilly-Sur-Seulles War Cemetery (CWGC)

Harry Foster is also commemorated on the following memorials:

- Bridlington War Memorial.
- St Mary (The Priory) Parish Church Roll of Honour.
- The Commonwealth War Graves Commission Website

Seaman NORMAN CHARLES FOWLER

The Merchant Navy, Service No. not known

Norman Charles Fowler was born in 1924 the son of William Henry and Margaret Ann Fowler of Bridlington East Yorkshire. He lived at 31 Fairfield Road Bridlington and was a Merchant Seaman.

In 1940 Norman was a crew member of the S.S. *Lulworth Hill*, a London registered cargo ship of 7,628 GRT with a complement of 39 and owned by Dorset Steamships Co Ltd. SS *Lulworth Hill* had sailed from Alexandria to Mauritius to load 10,000 tons of sugar, fibre and 400 tons of rum. She then refueled at the Cape before sailing to Walvis Bay to rendezvous with other ships for the convoy home. However for some unknown reason *Lulworth Hill* was instructed to make her way home alone.

On the 19th March 1943 *Lulworth Hill* was in the South Atlantic, off the western coast of Africa, when she was torpedoed and sunk by the Italian navy submarine *Leonardo da Vinci* based at Bordeaux, France. The *Leonardo da Vinci* captured and took on board one survivor and 14 survivors made it onto a life raft. On the 7th May after 50 days adrift, the Royal Navy destroyer HMS *Rapid* picked up the life raft but only two seamen remained alive from the 14 men that had survived the sinking.

According to the CWGC 19 year old Norman Charles Fowler died on the 9th April and was therefore among the 14 crew members on the life raft. He has no known grave and is commemorated on Panel 66 of the Merchant Navy Memorial, Tower Hill, London and on the following memorials:
- Bridlington War Memorial.
- St Mary (The Priory) Parish Church Roll of Honour.
- The Commonwealth War Graves Commission Website.

Note:
On 23 May 1943 the Italian navy submarine *Leonardo da Vinci* was sunk in the North Atlantic, west of Vigo Spain, by the Royal Navy destroyer HMS *Active*. There were no survivors.

Lance Corporal DAVID NORMAN FREEMAN

The Coldstream Guards, Service No. 2659120

David Freeman was born the 8th September 1924 the eldest son of Henry Freeman and Margaret Ellen Freeman (nee Nicholson) of 37 North Street Bridlington. David was educated at Kilham School and joined the Army as a boy soldier / drummer when he left school at the age of 14.

David was evacuated from Dunkirk between May 26 and June 4 1940 where he was a stretcher bearer, probably with the 1st or 2nd battalions of The Coldstream Guards who were part of the British Expeditionary Force in France. David then served as a lance Corporal with the 5th Battalion of the Coldstream Guards. The 5th battalion was formed for the duration of the war and fought as part of the Guards Armoured Division.

David Freeman was the husband of Isabel May Freeman (nee Honey), of Luton, Bedfordshire. They married in August 1944.

In 1944 the 5th Coldstream Guards were part of the 32 Guards Infantry Brigade, Guards Armoured Division. The Division landed in Normandy on 26 June 1944 as part of VIII Corp, British Second Army, 21st Army Group and took part in Operations Goodwood and Bluecoat. After their action in Normandy, the Guards went on to liberate Brussels and take part in operation Market Garden (Arnhem). In early 1945 the Guards Armoured Division advanced into Germany and crossed the Rhine.

21 year old David Freeman was killed in action on the 5th March 1945 at Enpaleen (Kafaleen) in Germany during the Rhine battles. And was buried in the Reichwald Forest War Cemetery, grave ref: 43. B. 18.

David is also commemorated on the following memorials:

- Bridlington War Memorial.
- St Mary (The Priory) Parish Church Roll of Honour.
- The Commonwealth War Graves Commission Website.

Private WARD FREEMAN

The Durham Light Infantry, Service No. 4466445

Ward Freeman was born in the June quarter of 1910, the son of Henry and Selina Freeman (nee Walkington) of Nightingale Cottages, North Back Lane, Bridlington. Ward became a plumber before WW2 and married Isabel M. Mathews in 1934. They lived at Horseforth Avenue and Marshall Avenue in Bridlington.

Private Ward Freeman joined the 8th Battalion, Durham Light Infantry in WW2. The 8th battalion DLI formed part of the 151st Infantry Brigade, 50th (Northumbrian) Infantry Division and was part of the BEF. It arrived in France in late January 1940, and took part in the Arras counter-attack and defended the Dunkirk perimeter. It transferred to the Middle East in April 1941 the battalion garrisoned Cyprus and later Kirkuk and Mosul in Iraq. Returning to North Africa as part of the 8th Army it was placed into the line at Gazala and fought in the Gazala, Mersa Matruh and El Alamein battles.

At the Battle of Gazala in May 1942, Rommel attacked the Allied position at Gazala. During the battle, 151st Brigade remained facing east and repulsed a feinting attack by Italian troops. By 14 June, Rommel had won a decisive victory, and Eighth Army ordered the evacuation of the Gazala line.

32 year old Private Ward Freeman was killed in action on the 12 June 1942 during the battle of Gazala. He is commemorated on Column 68 of the Alamein Memorial.

His Mother Selina Freeman of 13 St Oswalds Road submitted his name to the Bridlington War Memorial Committee and he is commemorated on the following memorials:

- Bridlington War Memorial.
- St Mary (The Priory) Parish Church Roll of Honour.
- Christ Church Roll of Honour
- Commonwealth War Graves Commission Website.

Telegraphist HARRY LANCELOT FRIEND

The Royal Navy, Service No. C/JX236947

Harry Lancelot Friend was the son of Harry Lancelot Harston Friend and Florence May Friend of 48 North Parade Grantham. Before enlistment Harry gave his address as 21 Westgate, Bridlington.

Harry was serving as a Telegraphist on the destroyer HMS. *Electra* (H27). On 27th February 1942, the British destroyers *Electra*, *Jupiter*, and *Encounter*; the cruiser *Exeter*, the Dutch cruiser *De Ruyter*, USS *Houston*, HMAS *Perth*, and HNLMS *Java* plus two Dutch and four American destroyers left Surabaya for the Battle of the Java Sea.

H.M.S. *Electra (Luis Photos)*

That afternoon, they made contact with the enemy. *Exeter* was hit which caused her to lose speed and *Electra*, *Jupiter*, and *Encounter* headed toward the enemy ships to cover the *Exeter*'s escape. *Electra* scored several hits on the Japanese light cruiser *Jintsu* and the destroyer *Asagumo* but sustained several hits herself, came to a stop and started to list to port. 'Abandon ship' was ordered and *Electra* sank shortly afterwards, bow first with the White Ensign still flying. The next day 54 survivors of the 173 men on board were picked up by the United States submarine S-38 and taken to hospital in Australia. Many of the survivors were later put on the liner *Nankin*, bound for Ceylon and home to Britain, but the *Nankin* was sunk by the German raider *Thor* and after seven weeks on the raider's supply ship *Regensburg* they were handed over to the Japanese.

29 year old Harry Lancelot Friend died of dysentery and malaria in a Japanese POW camp on the 31st May 1943. He is buried in grave reference 10. B. 12 in Ambon War Cemetery, Indonesia and is also commemorated on the following memorials:
- Bridlington War Memorial.
- St Mary (The Priory) Parish Church Roll of Honour.
- The Commonwealth War Graves Commission Website.

Shipwright 4th Class GILBERT FUSSEY

The Royal Navy, Service No. P/MX 637473

Gilbert (Gillie) Fussey was born in 1923 the only son of Gilbert and Olive Fussey of 1 Rhodena Avenue in Bridlington and the grandson of Mr. & Mrs. Richard Fussey of Long Lane Bridlington. Gilbert's father died in 1938 just before the start of WW2.

As a boy Gillie attended Burlington and St George's Schools and was a member of Burlington Sunday School and Scout Troop. Before joining the Royal Navy Gillie worked for the Yorkshire Yacht Building and Engineering Co. In 1944 Gillie was serving as a shipwright (Joiner) on the old battleship H.M.S. *Iron Duke,* a depot ship based at Scapa Flow. *Iron Duke* was built by the Royal Portsmouth Dockyard and launched on the 12th October 1912. She was completed in 1914 and was the flagship of Admiral Sir John Jellicoe at the Battle of Jutland. In 1919 the outdated ship was sent to the Mediterranean and joined in the operation in the Black Sea to help the White Russians. She joined the Atlantic fleet between 1920 and 1929 when she was disarmed and reduced in engine power for use as a gunnery training ship. In 1939 she was turned into a depot ship based at Scapa Flow. Post war she was sold for scrap and broken up at Faslane in 1946.

21 year old Gilbert (Gillie) Fussey died in the Royal Naval Hospital at Shotton Bridge, Co. Durham on the 24th September 1944 following an operation.

Gillie Fussey was buried in the family grave (ref. V105) in Bridlington Cemetery.

The Fussey family grave (C Bonnett)

Gilbert (Gillie) Fussey is commemorated on the following memorials:

- Bridlington War Memorial.
- St Mary (The Priory) Parish Church Roll of Honour.
- The Commonwealth War Graves Commission Website

Master *JOHN LAWRENCE GANT*

The Merchant Navy, Service No. not known

John Lawrence Gant was born in the December Qtr. of 1900, the son of Charles and Emily Gant of 22 Holyrood Avenue Bridlington. His father was a builder and by the 1911 census the family was living at 3 Flamborough Road Bridlington and before John enlisted they were at 36 Forty-foot Bridlington. John joined the Merchant Navy and gained his 2nd Mates certificate (1921), 1st mate's certificate (1923), Extra Master and Masters certificates in 1926. In 1941 John L, Gant was master of the M.V. *Arthur F. Corwin*.

The Motor tanker *Arthur F. Corwin* (uboat.net)

The *Arthur F. Corwin* was a British Motor tanker of 10,516 tons completed in 1938 by Blohm & Voss, Hamburg for Oriental Tankers Ltd (Standard Transp. Co Ltd), Hong Kong. She had a Complement of 46 and her homeport was London.

On the 13 February 1941 the *Arthur F. Corwin,* with a cargo of 14.500 tons of motor spirit, was a straggler from Convoy HX-106 sailing Aruba - Halifax - Avonmouth when she was damaged by two torpedoes from U-103 which left the burning tanker in a sinking condition southeast of Iceland. At 19.50 hours the same day, U-96 came across the wreck of *Arthur F. Corwin*, which was still afloat and sank her. The master, John Lawrence Gant, 43 crew members and two gunners were lost.

40 year old John Lawrence Gant is commemorated on Panel 10 of the Tower Hill Memorial in London. The Memorial commemorates men and women of the Merchant Navy and Fishing Fleets who died in both World Wars and who have no known grave. John Lawrence Gant is also commemorated on the following memorials:
- Bridlington War Memorial.
- St Mary (The Priory) Parish Church Roll of Honour.
- The Commonwealth War Graves Commission Website.

Flying Officer LESLIE PERCIVAL GARBETT

The Royal Air Force, Service No. 91055, Bridlington School Old Boy

Leslie Percival Garbett was born in the December quarter of 1897 the son of Richard Percival and Winifred Constance Garbett of York. He came to Bridlington School in 1912 and was awarded his First XI Colours for Cricket and Football. He left the School in 1915.

Leslie served in the First World War and received his Auxiliary Air Force (AAF) commission in 1939. The Auxiliary Air Force was the voluntary reserve element of the Royal Air Force providing a primary reinforcement capability for the regular service. its motto is Comitamur Ad Astra - "We go with them to the stars".

Leslie married Kitty Webber of Boscastle, Cornwall in June 1935 at Exeter and after their marriage they lived at Pencombe Stoney Hill, Newton Abbot in Devonshire.

Leslie Percival Garbett (Bridlington School)

In WW2 Flying Officer Leslie Percival Garbett served with No. 934 (County of Devon) Balloon Barrage Squadron, part of, No. 32 (Balloon Barrage) Group, Romsey, No. 13 Balloon Centre, Plymouth. 934 was based at Collaton Cross, Yealmpton, Devon with 24 balloons. The first balloon squadrons were part of the Auxiliary Air Force and operated hydrogen-filled balloons attached to metal cables about 5,000 feet long. The balloons were situated at vulnerable points in order to deter attacks by dive bombers and low flying aircraft.

Leslie Percival Garbett died on the 8th August 1941 aged 43 in the St. German's, Cornwall Registration District. He was buried in Plymouth (Efford) Cemetery, Devon, grave reference C8849. As he was not a Bridlington resident he is not recorded on the Bridlington War Memorial or the Priory Roll of Honour but he is commemorated on the following memorials.

- The Bridlington School Second World War Roll of Honour.
- The Commonwealth War Graves Commission Website.

Flying Officer (Nav.) PETER DENIS GARBUTT

The Royal Air Force, Service No.: 166299

Peter Denis Garbutt was born on the 20th December 1924, the only son of Denis George and Florence Marjorie Garbutt (nee Spink) of Bradford. His father was born in Hull and was employed as an Indian Traveller.

Peter joined the RAF, volunteered for air crew training and was assigned to the Royal Air Force Volunteer Reserve (RAFVR). During WW2 Peter served as a Flying Officer Navigator but the name of his unit or squadron is not recorded on the Commonwealth War Graves Commission Website.

Peter Denis Garbutt died on the 20th June 1946 age 21 and was buried in Bridlington Cemetery, grave reference W61. His death was registered in East Elloe registration district in Lincolnshire and several major RAF stations were in this area. The Yorkshire Post of the 24th June 1946 reported his death as follows:

Bradford Flying Officer killed in Accident.
Notification has been received by Mr. and Mrs. D. G. Garbutt of Highfield Crescent, Heaton, Bradford that their only son Peter Denis Garbutt (21) RAF has died as the result of a flying accident.

As he was not a Bridlington resident Peter Denis Garbutt is not recorded on the Bridlington War Memorial or the Priory Roll of Honour. His connection to Bridlington other than his burial is that his father and mother probably had a holiday home here with the intention of moving permantly to Bridlington. This they did and they lived at 4 Nightingale Drive Bridlington and when they died in 1971 and 1981 respectively they were also buried in Bridlington Cemetery, family grave W61.

The Garbutt's grave W61 (C Bonnett)

Flying Officer Peter Denis Garbutt is also commemorated on the following memorial:

- The Commonwealth War Graves Commission Website.

Driver RAYMOND GARRETT

The Royal Army Service Corps, Service No. T/14508562

Raymond Garrett was born in 1920 the son of Roy and Annie Garrett of 4 Edge Cliff Villas, Bridlington, East Yorkshire.

After leaving school Raymond worked at Boynton for Mr. Wells, timber merchant of Beverley. He joined the Army in 1942 and married his wife Sylvia in February 1944.

In WW2 Raymond was serving with 106 Bridge Company of the Royal Army Service Corps. The Bridge Companies carried bridging and water assault equipment for engineers or infantry to use. Pontoons and folding boats needed special vehicles but increasingly bridging equipment was carried in 3 ton General Service Lorries.

The first Bailey Bridge to be built in France was completed 2 days after D Day and was a pontoon Bailey over the Caen Canal, about 700m away from the famous Pegasus Bridge. Many others soon followed over the River Orne and Caen Canal in the build-up to Operation Goodwood, many were built under constant enemy fire and one of the casualties was Raymond Garrett.

A WW2 Bailey bridge   (thinkdefense)

20 year old Raymond Garrett died from wounds on the 14 June 1944 and was buried in Hermanville War Cemetery, Calvados, France. Grave reference 1. Q. 16.

Raymond Garrett is also commemorated on the following memorials

- Bridlington War Memorial.
- St Mary (The Priory) Parish Church Roll of Honour.
- The Commonwealth War Graves Commission Website.

Private ARTHUR GEE

The Durham Light Infantry, Service No. 4469893

Arthur Gee was born in the September quarter of 1917 the son of Arthur and Harriet Gee (nee Williams) of 10 Savage Road, Bridlington East Yorkshire. Arthur was educated at Hilderthorpe School, and afterwards took up employment under the late Walter Barron as a bricklayer.

He was the husband of Florence 'Terry' Gee and they lived at 20 Olinda Road Bridlington.

Arthur joined the Army in 1941 and was later posted overseas as a driver with the 16th Battalion, Durham Light Infantry (DLI). In the Second World War the 16th Battalion reformed in 1940 and joined the 139th Infantry Brigade, 46th Division of the British First Army. Landing in Algiers in North Africa in January 1943 it fought in Northern Tunisia and North Africa. It then took part in the Salerno landing on 9 September where the battalion fought toward Naples. In October it made a silent crossing of the River Volturno, holding the bridgehead it established for 8 days until relieved. The battalion took part in the forcing of the Winter Line. In February 1944 the 46th Division was withdrawn for rest and retraining to Egypt and Palestine, where the battalion aided the civil authorities during a riot in Tel-Aviv. It returned to Italy in July and fought hard on the Gothic Line at Gemmano and Cosina Canal.

Driver Arthur Gee was killed in action on the 31st August 1944 age: 27, during the fighting on the Gothic Line and was buried in Gradara War Cemetery, situated in the Commune of Gradara in the Province of Pesaro. Italy, grave reference II B 8. Arthur Gee is also commemorated on the following memorials:

- Bridlington War Memorial.
- St Mary (The Priory) Parish Church Roll of Honour.
- The Commonwealth War Graves Commission Website

Corporal FREDERICK HENRY GEE

The Gloucestershire Regiment, Service No. 4394830

Frederick (Fred) Henry Gee was born on the 12th May 1914, the son of Arthur and Harriet Gee of 10 Savage Road, Bridlington. He was the elder brother of Arthur Gee who was killed in action in August 1944 in Italy while serving with the Durham Light Infantry.

After leaving Hilderthorpe School, Fred was employed as a painter and decorator by Garland's. Frederick Henry Gee married Doris Wiles and they lived at 162 Hilderthorpe Road, Bridlington. Fred and Doris had one son Keith born in 1936.

In WW2 Fred was serving with the 43rd (2/5th Bn. Gloucestershire Regt.) Reconnaissance Corps, R.A.C. The 43rd Recce was formed on 14 October 1941 and on the 1 January 1944 the Reconnaissance Corps became part of the Royal Armoured Corps.

43rd Recce went overseas a month after the D Day landings and saw action in the battles for Normandy and the pursuit towards the River Orne and Falaise. They crossed the River Seine at Vernon and then drove on across Belgium. 43 Recce took part in Operation Market Garden and afterwards was stationed on 'the Island' (between the Rivers Waal and Nederrijn), guarding the western end of the Island, co-operating with the Dutch Resistance and facilitating the escape across the river of British paratroops who had evaded capture.

30 year old Corporal Frederick (Fred) Henry Gee was killed in action by a mortar bomb on the 27th November 1944, He was buried in Brunssum War Cemetery, Limburg, The Netherlands, grave reference III. 113. After the war his wife Doris went to see his grave and collapsed and died there.

The graves of Fred and Doris Gee (Roud Scholten, Brunssum War Cemetery)

Frederick Henry Gee is commemorated on the following memorials:
- Bridlington War Memorial.
- St Mary (The Priory) Parish Church Roll of Honour.
- The Commonwealth War Graves Commission Website

Lieutenant GEOFFREY ROBSON GIBB

The Royal Navy, Service No. not known, Bridlington School Old Boy

Geoffrey Robson Gibb was born in Hull in 1909 the only son of Thomas & Lillian Gibb (nee Stephenson). His father Thomas was a commercial traveller in paints and varnish and in the 1911 census the family was at 30 Ella Street in Hull. Later they lived at 7 Trafalgar Crescent in Bridlington, In 1921 Geoffrey came to Bridlington School which he left in 1925. On leaving School Geoffrey worked in the paint industry and in advertising.

Geoffrey Gibb (Bridlington School)

He lived at 'Sungates' Belvedere Parade in Bridlington and was an amateur golfer and member of Bridlington Golf Club as well as a singer and actor with Bridlington Amateur Operatic Society. With other local yachtsmen he joined the Royal Naval Volunteer Reserve before the war. In 1940 Geoffrey now a Lieutenant was serving on the aircraft carrier HMS *Glorious* an aircraft carrier that could carry up to 48 aircraft. Her ship's company consisted of about 1,200 officers and men. On the 6th June 1940, HMS *Glorious* was returning to the UK after operating in support of the Norwegian Campaign when she was intercepted and engaged by the German battle cruisers *Scharnhorst* and *Gneisnau* about 200 miles off the Norwegian coast near Narvik. HMS Glorious and her two destroyer escorts were sunk by shell fire, with the loss of about 1,500 lives. One of the 1500 killed in action on the 6th June 1940

HMS *Glorious* (Luis Photos)

was Lieutenant Geoffrey Robson Gibb. 31 year old Lieutenant Geoffrey Robson Gibb has no known grave and is commemorated on Panel 44, Column 1 of the Royal Navy Memorial in Plymouth Devon. He is also commemorated on the following memorials:

- Bridlington School Second World War Roll of Honour.
- Bridlington War Memorial.
- St Mary (The Priory) Parish Church Roll of Honour.
- The Commonwealth War Graves Commission Website

Leading Seaman RONALD ERNEST GIBSON

The Royal Navy, Service No. C/JX 238783

Ronald Ernest Gibson was born in 1920 the son of William and Ethel Gibson (nee Mirfield) of Wharfdale, Leeds. Before he enlisted Ronald lived at 'Firth Holme', South Back Lane, Bridlington.

During WW2 Ronald was serving on H.M.S. *Boadicea* (H65), a B-class destroyer built c 1930. During World War II *Boadicea* spent the bulk of the war on convoy escort duty in British waters and participated in the Battle of the Atlantic, Operation Torch, the Russian Convoys, and in the Normandy landings.

H.M.S. Boadicea   (Luis Photos)

In preparation for Operation Overlord, *Boadicea* was transferred to Portsmouth where she escorted convoys arriving in England as well as the convoys across the Channel. On the 13 June 1944 *Boadicea* was sunk off Portland Bill by two torpedoes dropped by Junkers Ju 88 medium bombers while escorting a convoy of merchant ships to France. Only 12 of her crew of 182 survived.

One of those killed was 24 year old leading seaman Ronald Ernest Gibson, he has no known grave and is commemorated on Panel 74, 3. of the Chatham Naval Memorial, Kent.

Ronald's name was submitted to the Bridlington War Committee by Mary Jane Gibson of 46 Hermitage Road, Bridlington. Ronald Ernest Gibson is commemorated on the following memorials:

- Bridlington War Memorial.
- St Mary (The Priory) Parish Church Roll of Honour.
- The Commonwealth War Graves Commission Website

Private FREDERICK GILBERT

The King's Own Scottish Borderers, Service No.: 3185291

Frederick Gilbert was born in 1910 the son of William and Alice Gilbert, of Lincoln.

Frederick Gilbert married Maud Helen Holmes of Bridlington in the September quarter of 1937, registered in Lincoln.

In WW2 Frederick served with the 1st Battalion of the King's Own Scottish Borderers (KOSB).

The 1st KOSB embarked for France in 1939 with the BEF (3rd Infantry Division). They crossed the Belgian frontier in May 1940, from where, facing an enemy of overwhelming numerical superiority, they were at length ordered to withdraw. On the night of 31st May/1st June they were evacuated from the beaches at Dunkirk.

KOSB Cap Badge

Private Frederick Gilbert, 30 years old, was killed during the evacuation from the Dunkirk beaches. He has no known grave and is commemorated on Column 54 of the Dunkirk Memorial in France. The Memorial stands at the entrance to the British War Graves Section of Dunkirk Town Cemetery.

The Dunkirk Memorial

Frederick Gilbert is not commemorated on the Bridlington War Memorial or the Priory Church Roll of Honour. His wife remarried in 1949 to John W Bowman, the marriage being registered in the Buckrose registration district which covers Bridlington.

Private Frederick Gilbert is commemorated on the following memorials:

- Christ Church Roll of Honour.
- The Commonwealth War Graves Commission Website

Seaman WILLIAM ARTHUR GILMOUR

The Royal Navy, Service No. LT/X 19248A

William Arthur Gilmour was born in 1913 the eldest son of Mr. and Mrs. John Gilmour of 3 Pump Slipway, Bridlington.

After leaving school William worked as a fisherman along with his father on the coble *Rose*. In 1934 he became a naval reservist (RNR). The RNR was originally a reserve of seamen whose experience and professionalism could be called upon on by the RN in time of war.

Royal Naval Reserves were mobilised in August 1939 and most of them joined the Royal Naval Patrol Service which used small ships for minesweeping and other duties. In 1939 while on leave William married Miss M. E. Mercer at the Holy Trinity Church in Bridlington. His wife was the youngest daughter of Mr. and Mrs. J. T. Mercer of Patrington.

Seaman William Arthur Gilmour RNR was assigned to H.M.T. *James Ludford*, a Mersey Class, Admiralty designed trawler stationed at North Shields. The *James Ludford* was built by Cochranes of Selby in 1919. Her Pennant number was T16 and she displaced 438 tons. The Mersey Class trawlers could make 11 knots on their 600 IHP engines and nominal armament was 2 x 3inch guns. Crew Complement was around 20 and they were equipped for minesweeping.

26 year old William Gilmour died on the 3rd December 1939 at North Shields. It is believed that he fell into the sea while boarding his vessel. His body was later recovered and was brought back to Bridlington for burial in Bridlington Cemetery, grave reference S213A.

William Arthur Gilmour is commemorated on the following memorials:

- Bridlington War Memorial.
- St Mary (The Priory) Parish Church Roll of Honour.
- Christ Church Roll of Honour.
- The Commonwealth War Graves Commission Website

Note: The *James Ludford* was sunk by a mine off the Tyne on the 14 December 1939. There was only one survivor.

Marine *JOHN WILLIAM GILSON*

The Royal Marines, Service No. CH/X 109252

John William Gilson was born on the 4th March 1923 the eldest son of John William and Edith Gilson of 21 Jameson Road Bridlington. Before the war John was employed as an assistant butcher at Mr. L. S. Fletcher's on Quay Road.

John Gilson (family archive)

John joined the Royal Marines in 1942 and in early 1944 he married Marjorie Elsie Sawden of 15 Hermitage Road Bridlington. They were married for only seven months when Marine John Gilson Age: 21, was killed on the 1st November 1944.

John and Marjorie Gilson (family archive)

John Gilson was a RM gunner serving on H.M.L.C.F. No 37, (His Majesties Landing Craft Flak No 37.). The LCF was intended to give anti-aircraft support to the landings and were equipped with several light anti-aircraft guns, a typical 'fit' being eight 20 mm Oerlikons and four QF 2 pdr "pom-poms". They had a crew of 60, the operation of the craft was the responsibility of RN crew and the guns were manned by Royal Marines.

A typical LCF (Wikipedia)

On the 1st November 1944, H.M.L.C.F.37 was the leading ship giving support for Operation Infatuate, the assault on Westkappel, Walcheren in the Netherlands. The ship suffered badly from gunfire from the shore batteries and John, who was manning a gun next to the magazine, was killed instantly when the magazine received a direct hit and the ship blew up. John Gilson and at least 40 other crew members died on LCF. 37. Marine John William Gilson has no known grave and is commemorated on Chatham Naval Memorial, Panel Reference: 79, 2. He is also commemorated on the following memorials:

- Bridlington War Memorial.
- St Mary (The Priory) Parish Church Roll of Honour.
- The Commonwealth War Graves Commission Website.

Sergeant (W. Op.) PIETRO ALFREDO GIOVETTI

The Royal Air Force, Service No. 997911

Peitro Alfredo Giovetti was born in Portugal in 1914.

He was educated at Pocklington Grammar School and was in business in Bradford. From the age of seven, Pietro lived with his aunt Miss Byass at 4 Station Avenue Bridlington. Peitro was well known in amateur Rugby circles having played for Bridlington, Scarborough, Bradford and Yorkshire.

Peitro joined the RAF at the outbreak of the war, volunteered for air crew training and was assigned to the Royal Air Force Volunteer Reserve (RAFVR). Peitro served in No 144 Squadron as a wireless Operator / Air Gunner on numerous operations including the daylight raid on German warships in Brest Harbour.

144 Squadron was equipped with Handley Page Hampdens on the outbreak of the Second World War, flying its first mission on 26 September to search for, and attack, German naval forces in the North Sea. The squadron started to fly night-time leaflet dropping raids over Germany from February 1940, and on 6 March it flew its first bombing raid against the seaplane base at Hörnum on the island of Sylt. The squadron continued to operate in the night bomber role through the rest of 1940 and 1941.

On the 21st September 1941, 26 year old Sergeant Peitro Alfredo Giovetti was part of the crew of Hampden AD872 coded PM-? on a raid from North Luffenham to Frankfurt, His aircraft flew into fog and came down near Conningsby in Lincolnshire. All of the crew were killed in the crash.

Peitro Alfredo Giovetti was buried with full military honours in South Kyme (St Mary and all Saints) Churchyard Lincolnshire. He is also commemorated on the following memorials:

- Bridlington War Memorial.
- St Mary (The Priory) Parish Church Roll of Honour.
- Christ Church Roll of Honour.
- The Commonwealth War Graves Commission Website.

Stoker 2nd Class FRANCIS BRIAN GLAZIER

The Royal Navy, Service No. D/KX 99647

Francis Brian Glazier was born in 1922, the son of Robert Arthur and Ada Marie Glazier, of Bridlington, Yorkshire. His address before enlistment was 79 South Back Lane, Bridlington. During WW2 Brian was serving in the Royal Navy as a Stoker 2nd Class on HMS *Fame*.

HMS *Fame*   (Luis Photos)

HMS *Fame* (H78) was an F class destroyer of the Royal Navy. In 1939 *Fame* was assigned to the 8th Destroyer flotilla and attached to the Home Fleet, acting as anti-submarine escort. In 1940 she served in the Norwegian Campaign, and was involved in the Bodø evacuation.

18 year old Stoker 2nd Class Francis Brian Glazier died of wounds sustained at action station and was buried at sea on the 6th July 1940. The circumstances of his death are not recorded but it is known that on the 6th July 1940 HMS *Fame* deployed for screening major units of the Home Fleet during a search for H.M. Submarine *Shark*. *Fame* came under air attack and sustained splinter damage which required her to take passage to Robb's shipyard, Leith, for repairs.

Francis Brian Glazier has no known grave and is commemorated on Panel 41, Column 3 of the Plymouth Naval Memorial. He is also commemorated on the following memorials:
- Bridlington War Memorial. (as Glazier B.F[1]).
- St Mary (The Priory) Parish Church Roll of Honour. (as Brian F. Glazier[2]).
- The Commonwealth War Graves Commission Website.

Note[1] & [2]: for reasons unknown his initials have transposed as Glazier B. F. and Brian F. Glazier.

Sergeant SYDNEY GLEDHILL

The King's Own Yorkshire Light Infantry, Service No. 4687851

Sydney was born in 1912 the son of Mr. and Mrs. John Gledhill who lived at 3 Medford Road Bridlington. After his mother's death his father remarried and Sydney became the stepson of Sarah Gledhill.

After leaving school Sydney worked for Messrs Rowntree and Taylor at the Promenade Café in Bridlington. Sydney soon joined the Army as a regular soldier and with the exception of one leave had spent 9 years in India and Burma.

In WW2 Sydney was serving in Burma as a machine gun instructor with the 2nd Battalion of the King's Own Yorkshire Light Infantry.

When Japan attacked Burma on January 15th 1942, only two British battalions, 2nd Battalion King's Own Yorkshire Light Infantry and 1st Battalion Gloucestershire Regiment were stationed in Burma. Completely outnumbered, the army lost the battle for Rangoon and control of the Burma Road to China. It was during these battles that Sergeant Sydney Gledhill was killed in action on the 23rd February 1942 age 30 years.

Sydney Gledhill was buried in Taukkyan War Cemetery, Mingaladon, Burma (now Myanamar), Grave Reference 23A. B. 17.

Taukkyan War Cemetery (CWGC)

Sydney Gledhill is also commemorated on the following memorials:

- Bridlington War Memorial.
- St Mary (The Priory) Parish Church Roll of Honour.
- The Commonwealth War Graves Commission Website.

Pilot Officer PATRICK GLENVILLE

The Royal Air Force, Service No. 15830, Bridlington School Old Boy

Patrick Glenville was born in 1922 the son of William Cornelius and Mary Violet Glenville of 'Merry Friars', 6 Midway Avenue Bridlington. His father William was a commercial traveller. Patrick came to Bridlington School in 1929 and left in 1937.

On leaving School Patrick worked in local government. During the war he joined the RAF, volunteered for air crew training and was assigned to the Royal Air Force Volunteer Reserve (RAFVR).

In 1945 Patrick was serving with 189 Squadron which had been formed in 1944. By February 1945 it was operating Avro Lancaster heavy bombers in 5 Group, Bomber Command and stationed at Fulbeck in Nottinghamshire.

Patrick Glenville (Bridlington School)

Patrick had almost completed 2 operational tours when he was killed with only 2 more ops to go. His last trips were all over the Rhine and strongly defended places such as Munich, Dusseldorf, Cologne and the V2 sites.

On the 21st February 1945 Lancaster NG321(CA-V) with Patrick Glenville as pilot, took off at 5.27 p.m. as part of a force of 177 aircraft on an operation to bomb the Dortmund Ems Canal in preparation for an advance by allied troops in Osnabruck region. The aircraft was seen to explode in mid-air when hit by enemy gunfire. Six of the crew were killed and one was taken prisoner. Another eight aircraft were lost on this raid.

Patrick Glenville aged 23 was buried in the Reichswald Forest Cemetery, Kleve, Nordrhein-Westfalen, Germany, Grave reference 231.11. Patrick is also commemorated on the following memorials:

- Bridlington School Second World War Roll of Honour.
- Bridlington War Memorial.
- St Mary (The Priory) Parish Church Roll of Honour.
- The Commonwealth War Graves Commission Website

Flight Sergeant (Nav) CHARLES HENRY GOW

The Royal Air Force, Service No. 1320000

Charles Henry Gow was born in the March quarter of 1917 the birth being registered in the Oldham Lancashire district, Charles was the son of Thomas Henry and Evelyn Gow (nee Birch) of Broughton Lancashire. By 1939 his Mother Evelyn, sister Evaline and younger brother Ian were living at 7 Sewerby Crescent, Bridlington which was probably the family home in WW2. His brother Ian Malcolm Gow died when HMS Broadwater was sunk in 1941.

In WW2 Charles served in the Royal Air Force Volunteer Reserve as a Flight Sergeant (Navigator) with 44 Squadron. In December 1941 No.44 became the first squadron to receive the Avro Lancaster and carried out the first Lancaster mission on 3 March 1942. The squadron was renamed 44 (Rhodesia) Squadron in honour of the Rhodesian contribution to Britain's war effort and spent the rest of the war as part of Bomber Command's main bombing force. The squadron suffered the third highest overall casualties of RAF Bomber Command.

On the 30th January 1944 Charles Henry Gow was the navigator on the seven man crew of Avro Lancaster Mk.III serial number JA843, coded KM-O that was airborne at 16:56 from Dunholme Lodge to bomb a target in Berlin. Approaching the aiming point at 19,500 feet the aircraft was hit by flak and fell out of control. At 13,000 feet the Lancaster exploded, throwing the pilot, P/O A. Johnston clear (he survived and became a POW in camp L3). The other six members of the crew including 27 year old Charles Henry Gow were killed when the Lancaster exploded.

Charles Henry Gow was buried in Berlin 1939-1945 War Cemetery grave reference 7 F 9 and he is also commemorated on the following memorials.

- Bridlington War Memorial.
- St Mary (The Priory) Parish Church Roll of Honour.
- The Commonwealth War Graves Commission Website.

Engine Room Artificer 3rd Class IAN MALCOLM GOW

The Royal Navy, Service No. D/MX 52839

Ian Malcolm Gow was born in 1910 the birth being registered in the Salford district of Manchester. Ian was the son of Thomas Henry and Evelyn Gow (nee Birch) and the older brother of Charles Henry Gow.

In WW2 Ian was living at 7 Sewerby Crescent Bridlington and was serving in the Royal Navy as an Engine Room Artificer 3rd Class on H.M.S. *Broadwater*. HMS. *Broadwater* was a US Belmont Class destroyer built in 1919 as USS *Mason*. In WW2 she was one of 50 over age ships of this class turned over to the UK in exchange for 99-year leases on strategic bases in the Western Hemisphere.

USS Mason (Wikipedia)

On 15 October 1940 HMS *Broadwater* departed Halifax for the British Isles, via St. John's, Newfoundland, arriving in the Clyde River, Scotland, on the 26th for service with the 11th Escort Group, Western Approaches Command. During the early part of 1941 HMS *Broadwater* escorted convoys, carrying troops and military supplies, around the Cape of Good Hope to the Middle East and spent May and June at Southampton, England. Assigned to the Newfoundland Escort Force in July, HMS *Broadwater* patrolled the North Atlantic and guarded convoys against the German submarine wolfpacks. Early in the morning of 18th October 1941 HMS *Broadwater* was torpedoed by U-101 and sank at 1340 hours the same day. Four officers and forty crew lost their lives including Engine Room Artificer 3rd Class Ian Malcolm Gow, age 22.

Ian has no known grave and is commemorated on Panel 51, Column 1 of the Plymouth Naval Memorial. He is also commemorated on the following memorials:

- Bridlington War Memorial.
- St Mary (The Priory) Parish Church Roll of Honour.
- The Commonwealth War Graves Commission Website.

Flight Sergeant GEORGE KENNETH GRAINGER

The Royal Air Force, Service No. 936229

George Kenneth Grainger was born in the September quarter of 1919, the son of James William and Betsy Grainger (nee Bourne) of Beverley. The family moved to Bridlington and George played football for Bridlington Trinity AFC. Before George enlisted the family were living at 'The Minries' 65 St Columba Road in Bridlington.

In WW2 George served in the Royal Air Force Volunteer Reserve as a Flight Sergeant (Wireless Operator / Air Gunner) with 45 Squadron.

No.45 Squadron was part of the Desert Air Force and received its Bristol Blenheims in June 1939, only a few weeks before the outbreak of the Second World War. With the Italian declaration of war on 10 June 1940 No.45 Squadron began bombing operations, initially against Italian positions in Libya. The area of operations expanded in July when a detachment was sent south to the Sudan to take part in attacks against Italian East Africa, and the entire squadron moved south in September 1940, remaining in the Sudan for three months. After returning from the Sudan the squadron returned to operations over the Western Desert.

George Kenneth Grainger died on the 26th May 1941 when his aircraft was reported missing flying over Crete. The exact circumstances of his death have not been found.

He was buried in Suda Bay War Cemetery, Greece, joint grave reference 14. B. 16-17.

Suda Bay War Cemetery (CWGC)

George Kenneth Grainger is also commemorated on the following memorials:

- Bridlington War Memorial.
- St Mary (The Priory) Parish Church Roll of Honour.
- The Commonwealth War Graves Commission Website.

Craftsman CYRIL GRAY

The Royal Electrical and Mechanical Engineers, Service No. 10569862

Cyril Gray was born in the December quarter of 1902 registered in Wharfedale, the son of Mr. and Mrs. William Gray. Cyril married Kathleen Ward in the September quarter of 1927 registered in Huddersfield. In 1928 they had one son whom they named Lionel G Gray, the birth being registered in Huddersfield.

Before he enlisted Cyril worked for the G.P.O. in Bridlington and in WW2 he joined the Royal Electrical and Mechanical Engineers. By 1942 Cyril was serving in the Middle East and on 8 November 1942 Commonwealth and American troops made a series of landings in Algeria and Morocco. The Germans responded immediately by sending a force from Sicily to northern Tunisia, which checked the Allied advance in early December.

40 year old Cyril Gray was killed in action on the 16 December 1942 and was buried in Tabarka Ras Rajel War Cemetery, Tunisia, Grave Reference 2. B. 8. Tabarka was just behind the limit of the advance that winter. His son Lionel was serving in the Royal Navy at the time of his father's death.

Tabarka Ras Rajel War Cemetery contains 500 Commonwealth burials of the Second World War, 60 of them unidentified.

Tabarka Ras Rajel War Cemetery

Cyril Gray is also commemorated on the following memorials:

- Bridlington War Memorial.
- St Mary (The Priory) Parish Church Roll of Honour.
- The Commonwealth War Graves Commission Website.

DAVID ANTHONY GRAY

Civilian (Infant)

David Anthony Gray was born on January 25th 1939, the son of Corporal Albert William and Margaret Gray (nee Beeforth).
His father, Albert William Gray was the son of Albert E and Jane Ann Gray and his Mother was Margaret Beeforth the daughter of Frederick and Margaret Beeforth. His parents were married in the September quarter of 1936, registered at Bridlington.

Bridlington was attacked on the 10th April when 75 incendiary and 20 high explosive bombs were dropped on the town. Many houses and commercial properties were damaged in the central area and as far out as Sewerby. 12 people were seriously injured and 16 made homeless by this raid which killed two year old baby, David Anthoney Gray.

David was killed when house numbers 54 and 56 New Burlington Road were completely destroyed. The Bridlington Cemetery book gives his death as being at Hamilton Road which we believe is incorrect.

New Burlington Road
(Bridlington local Studies Library)

David Anthony Gray was buried in the Gray family grave ref. J318 in Bridlington Cemetery on 14 April 1941. His Mother was so distraught that she was unable to attend the funeral.

Davids grave (C Bonnett)

David is commemorated on the following memorials:

- Bridlington War Memorial.
- St Mary (the Priory) Parish Church Roll of Honour.
- Christ Church Roll of Honour.
- Commonwealth War Graves Commission Website (Civilian War Dead).

Private ALAN SWANN GREENSIDES

The Hertfordshire Regiment, Service No. 14272865
Bridlington School Old Boy

Alan Swann Greensides was born in 1924 the son of of Albert Edward and Carry Greensides of 9 St James Road, Bridlington. His father Albert was a builder. Alan came to Bridlington School in 1932 and left in 1939.

On leaving School he went into farming and then worked for the Inland Revenue.

Alan joined the Army in 1942 and served with the 1st Battalion of the Hertfordshire Regiment.

On the outbreak of war the battalion joined the 54th Division on coastal defence until March 1943, when it was sent overseas. It arrived in Gibraltar on 22 April, and remained there in training for over a year, before being deployed to Italy in July 1944 where it joined 66th Brigade of the 1st Infantry Division.

Alan Greensides (Bridlington School)

The Battalion moved into the frontline on 19 August, northeast of Florence. On the 31 August the battalion advanced on Fiesole, clearing the village of the enemy by midnight. On 2 September it moved up the main axis of the advance north of the city, codenamed 'Arrow Route'.

It was during this advance on the 2nd September 1944 against an enemy withdrawing to the Gothic Line positions that 20 year old Alan Swann Greensides of the 1st Battalion, The Hertfordshire Regiment, was killed in action.

Alan Swann Greensides was buried in Florence War Cemetery, grave reference IV. K. 14.and is commemorated on the following memorials:

- Bridlington School Second World War Roll of Honour.
- Bridlington War Memorial.
- St Mary (The Priory) Parish Church Roll of Honour.
- The Commonwealth War Graves Commission Website.

F. W. GREGORY

Not Identified

An F W Gregory is commemorated on the following Bridlington memorials:

- Bridlington War Memorial.
- St Mary (The Priory) Parish Church Roll of Honour.

We know that an F. W. Gregory attended Holy Trinity Church in Bridlington but have no other important details such as his arm of service or date of death. There are four people with the name Gregory F W recorded on the CWGC Website.

The authors have looked at these four possibilities but none of them seem to have any connection with Bridlington.

1) Frederick William Gregory Bombardier Service No:827092 Date of Death:12/09/1944 Age:27 Royal Artillery 3 H.A.A. Regt. Panel Reference: Column 7. Singapore Memorial Son of William and Florence Gregory; husband of Beatrice Lilian Gregory, of Crabbs Cross, Worcestershire.

2) Frederick William Gregory Petty Officer Stoker Service No:C/KX 80267 Date of Death:18/04/1942 Age:30 Royal Navy H.M. Submarine Upholder Awards:D S M Panel Reference: 60, 3. Chatham Naval Memorial. Son of Frederick William and Louisa May Gregory; husband of Nora Gregory, of Runcorn, Cheshire.

3) Francis Wynell Gregory Sergeant Service No:580512 Date of Death:12/05/1940 Age:23 Royal Air Force 139 Sqdn. Grave Reference: Coll. grave 6. F. 17-19. Heverlee War Cemetery Belgium. Son of Lt.-Col. Edward Denys Wynell Gregory and Julia Wadsworth Gregory of Halberton, Devon.

4) Frederick William Gregory Civilian Date of Death:10/10/1940 Age:50 Reporting Authority: Wimbledon Municipal Borough A.R.P. Repair Service; of 38 Russell Road husband of M. A. E. Gregory Died at 38 Russell Road Wimbledon.

Bombardier ERNEST VICTOR GUTHERLESS

The Royal Artillery, Service No. 856653

Ernest Victor Gutherless was born at 48 St. Johns Walk, Bridlington on the 7th November 1918 the son of John William and Hannah Gutherless (nee Doyle) of 20 Littlebeck Road Bridlington. He was named Ernest after his uncle who was killed in WW1 and he had a sister Doreen M.

Ernest was educated at the Catholic School and Burlington School. After leaving school he worked at the High Street branch of the Hull Co-operative Society. In 1936 he was living in Hull where he enlisted in the Royal Artillery.

He married Florence (Flo) in Mauritius in 1942 and they had one daughter whom they named Doreen. Doreen never met her father as she was born while Ernest was serving overseas.

Ernest Victor Gutherless died accidentally on the 19 May 1944 Age 26 while serving in No 3 Coastal Battery of the Royal Artillery. Ernest had been swimming in the sea and was resting on a ledge when a large wave swept him off and carried him towards shark infested waters. Swimming strongly he made for a small bay where the water was calmer. A naval launch was sent to his aid but before he could be reached he was attacked by a shark. He was picked up but later died on the launch due to loss of blood.

Ernest Gutherless (family archive)

Ernest's grave (family archive)

Ernest Victor Gutherless was buried with full military honours in Nairobi War Cemetery, Grave Reference 3. D. 8.
He is also commemorated on the following memorials.

- Bridlington War Memorial.
- St Mary (The Priory) Parish Church Roll of Honour.
- The Commonwealth War Graves Commission Website.

Corporal LUCAS SAMUEL HANTON

The Royal Air Force, Service No. 340278

Lucas Samuel Hanton was born in 1899 in Yarmouth, the son of William and Mary Hanton. He served for three years in France in WW1 with the 16th Battalion of the Manchester Regiment, service number 252873. He married Francis A. Carr in 1916 and they had twin boys named Lucas and Herbert, registered in Glanford Brigg district of Lincolnshire. Unfortunately baby Lucas died and Lucas and Mary came to Bridlington shortly afterwards. Their marriage ended in divorce in 1935 when they lived at 4 Blenheim Road, Bridlington, In 1938 Lucas Samuel Hanton married Ella M. Tose and they lived at 13 Rosberry Avenue Bridlington.

Lucas was called up as a reservist in September 1939 and went to France as a Physical Training Instructor with 12 Squadron RAF. He remained in France until June 1940 when he came back to England and became a PT instructor stationed at Wirral, Cheshire.

RAF PTI Badge

Corporal Instructor Lucas Samuel Hanton RAF, age 41, died on the 9th December 1940 in West Kirby Hospital, The Wirral, Cheshire, due to the effects of an operation on his nose.

Lucas Samuel Hanton was buried in Bridlington Cemetery, grave reference X46, with full Military Honours. Members of the RAF acted as bearers and formed a guard of honour. A firing party fired three rounds over his open grave and a bugler sounded the 'Last Post'.

Lucas Samuel Hanton's grave (C Bonnett)

Lucas Samuel Hanton is also commemorated on the following memorials.
- Bridlington War Memorial.
- St Mary (The Priory) Parish Church Roll of Honour.
- The Commonwealth War Graves Commission Website.

Flying Officer (Nav / Air Bomber) GEORGE JAMES HARDEN DFC.

The Royal Air Force, Service No. 61077

George James Harden was the eldest son of James Alfred and Lily Maud Harden, of 3 'Greensides', St Oswald's Road Bridlington, Yorkshire and formerly of Keyingham. George was educated at Hymers College Hull and then Cambridge where he read History and gained his B.A., Hons. (Cantab). He then spent two years in Germany as a teacher of English. Later he worked for the Anglo Iranian Oil Company in Iran. George then joined the RAF in 1940, volunteered for air crew training and was assigned to the Royal Air Force Volunteer Reserve (RAFVR). He went to No. 7 OTU in South Africa for training as a navigator and air bomber.

George Harden saw war service with 106 Squadron (Lancaster Heavy Bombers) and was awarded the DFC. His citation quoted from the Hull Daily Mail of the 10th September 1943 reads. *"Flying Officer Harden is an outstanding navigator and air bomber who has consistently achieved good results often supported by photographs of the target area. His many sorties have had as objectives such places as Berlin, Hamburg and Spezia while he has attacked the Ruhr Centers on 15 occasions. His intelligent and accurate map reading has given his captain invaluable assistance. This officer has always displayed courage, zeal and determination".*

George then joined 617 Squadron, the famous 'Dam Busters'. On the 24 April 1944 George Harden was one of the eight man crew of Lancaster DV394 coded KC-M. The aircraft took off from Woodhall Spa at 20.51 hrs. on a mission to bomb Munich. After hitting the target the Lancaster was shot down at 02.43 hrs. on the 25 April 1944 by a German Night Fighter. George was killed and the other members of the crew became POW's. This was George's 42nd operational flight.

George James Harden was buried in Durnbach War Cemetery Bayern, Germany, grave reference: 4. E. 16. He is also commemorated on the following memorials:

- Bridlington War Memorial.
- St Mary (The Priory) Parish Church Roll of Honour.
- The Commonwealth War Graves Commission Website.

Flight Lieutenant (*Pilot*) ALAN BRUCE HARRISON DSO

The Royal Air Force, Service No. 39732, Bridlington School Old Boy

Alan Bruce Harrison was born in 1918 the eldest son of Captain and Mrs. S. A. Harrison who lived at 'Avalon' on Eight Avenue in Bridlington. They later moved to 'Welldone' 2a Waterden Road in Guilford, Surrey. Alan Bruce Harrison attended a preparatory school in Pickering and came to Bridlington School in 1931 and left in 1935. At School he was remembered as a fearless boxer.

Alan Bruce Harrison was a pre-war Regular, having joined the RAF in 1937, and had been on many missions over enemy territory for which he was awarded the Distinguished Service Order. 1n 1941 Alan was serving with 61 Squadron, unofficial name 'Hull's Own ', stationed at North Luffenham in Rutland. 61 Squadron had re-formed in 1937and in 1941 it was serving in 5 Group Bomber Command and operating the Avro Manchester heavy bomber.

Alan Harrison (Bridlington School)

The Manchester was difficult to fly owing to the tendency for its engines to overheat. On the 3rd September 1941, Flight Lieutenant (Pilot) Alan Bruce Harrison was one of the crew of Avro Manchester L7388 (QR-?) that took off at 8.30 p.m. as part of a force of 49 aircraft on an operation to bomb Berlin. Avro Manchester L7388 and four other aircraft were shot down by anti-aircraft fire over Berlin, there were no survivors from L7388 and in addition to its normal crew the aircraft was carrying, as supernumeraries, Wing Commander G. E. Valentine DSO, Commanding Officer of 61 Squadron and Group Captain J. F. Barrett DSO and Bar, DFC, Station Commander of RAF North Luffenham.

23 year old Flight Lieutenant (Pilot) Alan Bruce Harrison D.S.O. was killed in action on the 3rd September 1941 when his aircraft was shot down over Berlin. Alan was buried in Brandenburg Cemetery: Berlin, grave reference 52.6. As he was not a Bridlington resident he is not recorded on the Bridlington War Memorial or the Priory Roll of Honour but he is commemorated on the following memorials.

- Bridlington School Second World War Roll of Honour.
- The Commonwealth War Graves Commission Website.

Leading Aircraftman HAROLD EDWARD HARTLEY

The Royal Air Force, Service No. 944034, Bridlington School Old Boy

Harold Edward Hartley was born in 1912 the son of Chris and Nellie Hartley of Eastgate Cottage, Rudston. He came to Bridlington School in 1924 and left in 1928.

Harold was a chemist before the war and was employed by Messrs. Taylors of Bridlington. He married Alice Mary Simpson of Norton, near Malton in 1940. Harold was a member of the Civil Air Guard and the Junior Branch of the League of Frontiersmen. He had also been the Secretary of the local Miniature Rifle Association. His elder brother, C. E. Hartley, went to Bridlington School between 1924 and 1926 and was a Regular RAF Wing Commander.

Harold Hartley (Bridlington School)

Harold Edward Hartley joined the RAF and was assigned to the Royal Air Force Volunteer Reserve (RAFVR) and was sent for flying training with No. 4 British Flying Training School at Mesa in Arizona USA.

30 year old Leading Aircraftman Harold Edward Hartley was killed in a flying accident on the 15th April 1942 at Mesa, Arizona, USA.

Harold Edward Hartley was buried in Mesa City Cemetery, Arizona, USA, grave reference Lot 1, Block 528, Grave 3.

Mesa City Cemetery (CWGC)

As he was not a Bridlington resident Harold Edward Hartley is not recorded on the Bridlington War Memorial or the Priory Roll of Honour but he is commemorated on the following memorials.

- Bridlington School Second World War Roll of Honour.
- The Commonwealth War Graves Commission Website.

Note; the index to the Bridlington School WW2 Roll of Honour has his Christian name as Howard instead of Harold.

Lieutenant ROBERT KEMPLAY HAWKINS

The Green Howards (Alexandra, Princess of Wales's
Own Yorkshire Regiment), Service No. 91888,
Bridlington School Old Boy

Robert Kemplay Hawkins was born in the December quarter of 1913 the son of Philip and Fanny Hawkins (nee Barr) of Bridlington. His father was a chemist, with a shop at 200 Quay Road. He came to Bridlington School in 1921 and was the youngest of five brothers who all attended the School and was a School Prefect and Captain of Cricket & Football. After leaving School in 1931 he trained as a teacher at the college of St. Mark & St.John Chelsea and gained his qualified teacher's certificate from the Universitity of London. Robert held teaching posts at schools in Kilham and Sherburn followed by being Assistant Master at Oxford Street School in Bridlington. In the December quarter of 1938 Robert married Ailsa Mary Rickaby, the marriage was registered in Ryedale. After their marriage they lived at 15 Borough Road in Bridlington. Robert was one of the first recruits to the 7th battalion Green Howards in 1939 and during the Battle of Alamein in 1942 his truck ran over a land mine and the explosion caused him to suffer multiple injuries and the loss of use of his right arm. He spent a long time in hospital and was invalided out of the Army and returned to teaching in Bridlington using his left arm only.

Robert Hawkins (BridlingtonSchool)

33 year old Robert Kemplay Hawkins eventually died of wounds on the 26th December 1946 in Lloyd Hospital in Bridlington and was buried in Bridlington Cemetery, grave reference W70 on the 30th December 1946 after a memorial service at Christ Church in Bridlington. Robert is commemorated on the following memorials.

The Hawkins family grave (C Bonnett)

- Bridlington School Second World War Roll of Honour.
- Bridlington War Memorial.
- St Mary (The Priory) Parish Church Roll of Honour.
- Christ Church Roll of Honour.
- The Commonwealth War Graves Commission Website.

Flight Sergeant RICHARD WILLIAM ALBERT HAWKSWORTH

The Royal Air Force, Service No. 551586

Richard William Albert Hawksworth was born in Cologne Germany in 1920 the only son of William John and Barbara Helena Hawksworth (nee Fuchs). His father was serving with the RASC in Germany at the time and after the family returned to England they lived at 4 Seventh Avenue Bridlington. Richard was well known locally as a good swimmer. Richard joined the RAF as an apprentice at the age of 16 and after training he served with 76 Squadron Royal Air Force as a Flight Sergeant, Wireless Operator / Air Gunner.

76 Squadron reformed on 30 April 1940 at RAF West Raynham as a Hampden unit before being disbanded on 2 May 1940. On 1 May 1941, the squadron reformed properly at RAF Linton-on-Ouse as the second Handley Page Halifax bomber squadron, part of the newly created No. 4 Group, RAF Bomber Command.

The Squadron moved to RAF Middleton St. George in June 1941, returning to Linton-on-Ouse in July 1942. The squadron bombed targets of the widest variety and also participated in a series of three attacks on the Tirpitz in the Trondheim area in March and April 1942 On the night of 10/11th April 1942, it dropped the first 8,000lb High Capacity bomb in a raid on Essen.

76 Squadron Halifax (Wikipedia)

Richard Hawksworth RAFVR received a 'Mentioned in Despatches' in WW2. Richard Hawksworth was killed in action over Germany on the 13 April 1942 he was 22 years old and was buried in the Reichwald Forest War Cemetery Germany, grave reference 19. B. 3-8. He is also commemorated on the following memorials:

- Bridlington War Memorial.
- St Mary (The Priory) Parish Church Roll of Honour.
- The Commonwealth War Graves Commission Website.

Private WILLIAM HENRY 'DON or DONOVAN' HEBDON

The Green Howards (Alexandra, Princess of Wales's Own Yorkshire Regiment), Service No. 4392084

William Henry Hebdon was born in the December quarter of 1918, the son of George Henry and Fanny Hebdon (nee Phillips) of Low Hall Scotton near Richmond Yorkshire. William Henry's address before enlistment was the Fish Shop, 2 Queen Street Bridlington the proprietor of which was a Thomas William Hebdon. For reasons unknown William Henry was known locally as 'Don' or 'Donovan'.

In WW2 'Don' Hebdon served with the 7th Battalion (TA) of the Green Howards. The 7th Battalion had a particular link with Bridlington and was formed here in April 1939. 'Don' was seconded to the HQ of the 69th Infantry Brigade that in the Battle of France was in the 23rd (Northumbrian) Division. The 23rd suffered such heavy losses that it was disbanded and the 69th brigade became part of the 50th (Northumbrian) Infantry Division. In April 1941 the 50th Infantry Division was dispatched to the Middle East via Cyprus, Iraq, Syria, Egypt and then into Libya as part of XIII Corps in the British Eighth Army where it took part in the Battle of Gazala in May 1942. The battle was a defeat for the 8th Army and the 69th Brigade and the remaining units of 50th Northumbrian Division had to escape by attacking west through the enemy lines then sweeping back east to the south of the enemy forces, eventually they reached the El Alamein line by 1 July.

23 year old 'Don' Hebdon died on the 22nd July 1942 while his unit and the HQ. 69th Inf. Brigade was in the El Alamein line. 'Don' Hebdon has no known grave and his name is recorded on Column 60 of the El Alamein Memorial in Egypt which commemorates more than 8,500 soldiers who have no known grave. 'Donovan' Hebdon is also commemorated on the following memorials.

- Bridlington War Memorial.
- St Mary (The Priory) Parish Church Roll of Honour.
- The Commonwealth War Graves Commission Website*.
- The Cleveland Memorial *

Note* The CWGC states Private Hebdon but the Cleveland Memorial states Lance Corporal Hebdon.

Leading Aircraftman HERBERT CECIL HERMON

The Royal Air Force, Service No. 614311, Bridlington School Old Boy

Herbert Cecil Hermon was born in the March quarter of 1906 the eldest son of Thomas and Nellie Hermon (nee Gatenby) of 2 Cambridge Street, Bridlington. By the 1911 census the family were at 47 Market Place Bridlington. Herbert came to Bridlington School in 1918 and left in 1921 to join his father in business as an estate agent. Herbert was a prominent Snooker player and a member of the Old Town Working Men's Club Team.

Herbert Hermon (Bridlington School)
In the June quarter of 1925 at Nafferton Herbert married Miss Lillian Dorothy Hall, the daughter of Mr. and Mrs. P. Hall of the Kings Head Nafferton. Herbert and Dorothy Hermon had two children whom they named Harold and Audrey. The family lived at 14 Lamplough Road and 53 St. John Street Bridlington and in 1939 Herbert was an unsuccessful candidate in the Borough of Bridlington council elections.

Herbert joined the RAF and in 1941 was serving as a Leading Aircraftman on the Island of Malta where its naval base and airfields, suffered heavy aerial bombardment by both the Italians and the Germans from autumn 1940 until late 1942.

35 year old Herbert Cecil Hermon was killed at Valetta Malta on the 29th April 1941. This was probably in an Air Raid but no details have been found and his RAF unit at that time is not given by the CWGC. Herbert Cecil Hermon was buried in Capuccini Naval Cemetery, Malta GC, grave reference, Protestant Section, Plot F Collective Grave 28.

Capuccini Naval Cemetery (CWGC)

Herbert is also commemorated on the following memorials.

- Bridlington School Second World War Roll of Honour.
- Bridlington War Memorial.
- St Mary (The Priory) Parish Church Roll of Honour.
- The Commonwealth War Graves Commission Website.

CLARA EDITH HILDREW

Civilian

Clara was born in 1917 the daughter of Mr. and Mrs. F. Waines, of 19 High Street, Flamborough. She married William Hildrew in the June quarter of 1939, registered at Buckrose, which covers Flamborough.

23 year old Clara of Peace Cottage, Stylefield road, Flamborough worked at the Ship Inn, Flamborough. On the 11th July 1940 she was at an hairdresser's salon in Hilderthorpe Road, Bridlington having obtained a cancelled appointment. Suddenly an enemy aircraft appeared and dropped a stick of high explosive bombs between Bridlington Railway Station and Hilderthorpe Road. Clara was fatally injured when the salon was destroyed and died 3 days later on the 14th July at Lloyd Hospital Bridlington as a result of her injuries.

Hilderthorpe Road (Bridlington local Studies Library)

Clara Edith Hildrew was buried in Flamborough Cemetery on the 17th July 1940 grave ref 1161, she is also commemorated in Flamborough Church.

Clara did not live in Bridlington so she is not recorded on the Bridlington War Memorial or the Priory Roll of Honour but she is commemorated on the following memorial.

- The Commonwealth War Graves Commission Website (Civilian War Dead).

Sergeant *CYRIL HILLS*

The Royal Air Force, Service No. 411621

Cyril Hills was born on the 15th December 1914 in Derbyshire, the son of William and Elizabeth Hills. When Cyril was eleven he was the Schoolboy Boxing Champion of Derbyshire. He continued boxing and his experience was won the hard way in fairground boxing booths in Hull and many other parts of the country. Cyril was better known under his boxing name of 'Darkie Ellis'. He had over 400 fights and was only defeated in twelve of them. In his professional career he boxed in this country and on the Continent and never lost a fight.

Cyril Hills as Darkie Ellis in 1939 (Hull Daily Mail)

Cyril moved to Bridlington from Manchester in 1935 and in the June quarter of 1936 he married a Bridlington girl Joyce Durham. The marriage was registered in South Manchester and after their marriage they lived at 9 Westmorland Avenue where they had two daughters.

When the outbreak of WW2 interrupted his boxing career Cyril was the Northern Counties Middleweight Champion. In 1939 Cyril joined the Green Howards and served in France, he was evacuated from Dunkirk and he later transferred to the Royal Air Force where he served as a Sergeant Physical Training Instructor. Cyril organised boxing shows for charity as well as participating in them himself. After being demobed at the end of 1945 Cyril began a vocational training course in Architecture which he was unable to finish because of illness. Cyril died of Bronchial Pneumonia in Beverley Base Hospital on Saturday the 14th December 1946. He was 32 and died the day before his 33rd Birthday. Cyril Hills was buried in Bridlington Cemetery grave reference W15.

Cyril Hills grave (C Bonnett)

Cyril Hills is also commemorated on the following memorials.
- Bridlington War Memorial.
- St Mary (The Priory) Parish Church Roll of Honour.
- The Commonwealth War Graves Commission Website.

Sergeant (Pilot) DENIS AUBREY HINCHLIFFE

The Royal Air Force, Service No. 1622911, Bridlington School Old Boy

Denis Aubrey Hinchliffe was born in the June quarter of 1924, the eldest son of Joseph and Sarah Annie Hinchliffe (nee Atkin) of 44 Fortyfoot in Bridlington. He came to Bridlington School in 1934 and left in 1940. On leaving School he worked in banking and was one of the earliest members of 252 (Bridlington) Squadron, Air Training Corps where he attained the rank of Flight Sergeant. Dennis joined the RAF, volunteered for air crew training and was assigned to the Royal Air Force Volunteer Reserve (RAFVR).

Denis Hinchliffe (Bridlington School)

Denis became a Sergeant Pilot with 114 (Hong Kong) Squadron. 114 Squadron took its Blenheim IV light bombers to France and lost most of its aircraft during the German invasion. By November 1942 the squadron had moved to Algeria to take part in the invasion of North Africa. While in North Africa the Blenheim's were finally replaced by Douglas Boston twin-engine bombers. In 1943 the squadron moved to Sicily and mainland Italy and by October 1944 it was stationed at Cecina on the coast of Tuscany. On the 2nd October 1944, Sergeant Pilot Denis Hinchliffe and his crew, in a Douglas Boston IV, BZ559 were part of a force of twelve aircraft on an armed reconnaissance of the River Sangro area in order to harass the retreating enemy, unfortunately Denis and his crew failed to return from this, his 30th operational flight. His death was not confirmed until September 1945. Denis Aubrey Hinchliffe, age 20, was buried in Argenta Gap War Cemetery, Italy, collective grave H.A. 19-21 and he is commemorated on the following memorials.

- Bridlington School Second World War Roll of Honour.
- Bridlington War Memorial.
- St Mary (The Priory) Parish Church Roll of Honour.
- Christ Church Roll of Honour.
- The Commonwealth War Graves Commission Website.

The Hinchliffe Cup for a Sabre Competition was presented to Bridlington School by his father in memory of his son and there was also a Memorial Chair.

Leading Aircraftman *JOHN DERRICK HOBSON*

The Royal Air Force, Service No. 1044216

John Derrick Hobson was the foster son of Robert and Clara Taylor, of Pauls Yard Bridlington.

In WW2 John Hobson joined the RAF and was assigned to the Royal Air Force Volunteer Reserve (RAFVR) and by 1943 John was serving as a Leading Aircraftman (LAC).

John Derrick Hobson died on the 4th April 1946. Age 23. His death occurred at RAF Debden Essex which at that time housed the Empire Radio School, a unit of the Technical Training Commission. The circumstances of his death have not been found and his unit or squadron is not recorded by the Commonwealth War Graves Commission.

John Derrick Hobson was buried in Bridlington Cemetery, Grave Reference W60.

Grave W60 (C Bonnett)

John Derrick Hobson is also commemorated on the following memorials.

- Bridlington War Memorial.
- St Mary (The Priory) Parish Church Roll of Honour.
- The Commonwealth War Graves Commission Website.

Sergeant (WOP/AG) ALBERT WILLIAM HODGSON

The Royal Air Force, Service No. 636770

Albert William Hodgson was born on the 15 July 1920 the son of Albert and Lavinia Ellen Hodgson (nee Jackson) of 55 Scarborough Road Bridlington.

Albert was a member of the Priory Church Scout Troop for six years and in the Priory Choir for four years. He joined the RAF in 1939 and became a Wireless Operator/Air Gunner with 214 (Federated Malay States) Squadron.

Albert Hodgson (L Ellis)

On the 19th December 1940 Albert married Marjorie Anne Leggott in Hatfield Church Doncaster. Marjorie was the only daughter of Mr. & Mrs. Leggott of Hatfield Moors in Doncaster.
Albert and Marjorie had one child, a boy, whom they named Anthony.

214 (Federated Malay States) Squadron was in No 3 group Bomber Command and equipped with Vickers Wellingtons. On the 28 Dec 1940 Albert was part of the 6 man crew of Wellington Mark IC L7849 that had taken off from its base at Stradishall in Suffolk for a night bombing raid on Le Havre. On its return the aircraft came down in the North Sea off the Norfolk Coast. Three crew members died including 20 year old Albert and three were rescued by a Coast Guard vessel. Albert William Hodgson had been killed just nine days after his marriage.

On the 3rd January 1941 Albert was buried with full military honours in Bridlington Cemetery. His coffin was borne to the cemetery on a gun carriage and a salute was fired over the grave by an RAF party. Albert was buried in the same plot as his Father, grave reference H394.

Albert's grave (C Bonnett)

Albert Hodgson is also commemorated on the following memorials.

- Bridlington War Memorial.
- St Mary (The Priory) Parish Church Roll of Honour.
- The Commonwealth War Graves Commission Website.

Sergeant (Air Bomber) KENNETH HERBERT HOGARTH

The Royal Air Force, Service No. 1055990, Bridlington School Old Boy

Kenneth Herbert Hogarth was born in the September quarter of 1921 the youngest son of Thomas Herbert and Violet Rebecca Hogarth (nee Coverdale) of 7 Vernon Road, Bridlington. Kenneth's father was a Chartered Accountant and Kenneth came to Bridlington School in 1932 and left in 1938. On leaving School he became an Articled Accountant with Messrs Foley, Judge and Easton, Accountants of Hull.

Kenneth Hogarth (Bridlington School)

In 1940, 18 year old Kenneth Herbert Hogarth joined the RAF, volunteered for air crew training and was assigned to the Royal Air Force Volunteer Reserve (RAFVR). By 1943 Kenneth was serving as a Sergeant (Air Bomber) with 207 Squadron. 207 Squadron formed in 1918 and was not disbanded at the end of the WW1. In February 1943 it was in 5 Group Bomber Command and stationed at Langar in Nottinghamshire operating the Avro Lancaster heavy bomber.

Lancaster Bomber (F Bull)

Sergeant (Air Bomber) Kenneth Herbert Hogarth was killed in action on the 25th February 1943 aged 21 when his Lancaster ED356 (EM-W) crashed near Ludwigshafen Germany, there were no survivors. Lancaster ED356 (EM-W) had taken off at 7.50 p.m. as part of a force of 337 aircraft on an operation to bomb Nuremberg, Another eight aircraft were lost on this raid. Kenneth Herbert Hogarth was buried in Durnbach Cemetery, Bad Tolz, Bayern, Germany, Collective Grave 1.C.6-9., and he is commemorated on the following memorials.

- Bridlington School Second World War Roll of Honour.
- Bridlington War Memorial.
- St Mary (The Priory) Parish Church Roll of Honour.
- The Commonwealth War Graves Commission Website.

Private TOM CHRISTOPHER HOGGARD

The Green Howards (Alexandra, Princess of Wales's Own Yorkshire Regiment), Service No. 4391385

Tom Christopher Hoggard was born on November 5th 1920 the son of Tom and Annie Elizabeth Hoggard (nee Fenby) of 27 Nelson Street, Bridlington. In WW2 Tom served with the 7th battalion of the Green Howards.

The 7th Battalion served in France and Flanders and was evacuated from Dunkirk. In April 1941 the 7th Green Howards were part of the 69th Brigade, 50th (Northumbrian) Infantry Division, and went to the Middle East as part of the Eighth Army. In May 1942 they took part in the Battle of Gazala and later in the battles for El Alamein They landed in Sicily on the 9th July 1943, the first day of the Allied forces invasion. After Sicily they were one of the units recalled from the 8th Army in Italy to prepare for the invasion of North-West Europe.

The 7th Battalion, Green Howards were part of the D-Day landings, wading ashore on the morning of 6 June 1944. By the evening of the first day they had fought their way seven miles inland, further than any other British or American unit. Then followed the exhaustive battles for Normandy and Operation Market Garden where they continued onward towards Nijmegen and the capture of Bremmel.

On the 1st October 1944 during the capture of Bremmel the 7th battalion Green Howards withstood a terrific German counter-attack in which 23 year old Tom Christopher Hoggard was killed in action.

Tom Christopher Hoggard was buried in Arnhem Oosterbeek War Cemetery, grave reference: 8. C. 10, and he is commemorated on the following memorials.

- Bridlington War Memorial.
- St Mary (The Priory) Parish Church Roll of Honour.
- The Commonwealth War Graves Commission Website.

Flying Officer (Pilot) WILLIAM HENRY HOGGARD

The Royal Air Force, Service No. 115259, Bridlington School Old Boy

William Henry Hoggard was born in the June quarter of 1915 registered at Sculcoates. He was the son of George and Annie Elizabeth Hoggard (nee Gibbon) of 14 Scarborough Road, Bridlington. William Henry came to Bridlington School in 1926 and left in 1934. After leaving school he took up teaching as a career. In the March quarter of 1942 William married Hilda Mary Pate of Braisworth, Suffolk and they came to live at The Old Hall Elmswell Driffield.

William Hoggard (Bridlington School)

On joining the RAF he volunteered for air crew training and was assigned to the Royal Air Force Volunteer Reserve (RAFVR). William was a Sergeant Pilot before being commissioned and by 1943 he was serving as a Spitfire pilot with 130 (Punjab) Squadron RAF. 130 (Punjab) Squadron re-formed in 1941 and by January 1943 it was a fighter squadron equipped with Supermarine Spitfires stationed at Aerranporth, Cornwall and specialising in convoy patrols and fighter sweeps over France.

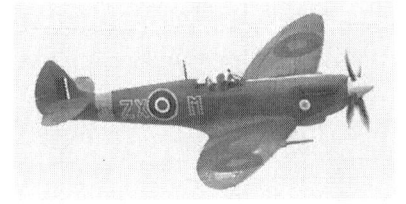

Supermarine Spitfire (F Bull)

On the 26th January 1943 William, aged 27, was the pilot of Spitfire Vc EE632 (PJ-?) and was part of the escort to a group of bombers on an operation to attack the railway viaduct at Morlaix, Brittany, France. He was shot down by a Focke-Wolf Fw 190 near the Ile de Batz while covering a Spitfire that was returning with engine trouble.

Flying Officer (Pilot) William Henry Hoggard has no known grave and is commemorated on Panel 125 of the Royal Air Force Memorial at Runnymede in Surrey. As he was not a Bridlington resident he is not recorded on the Bridlington War Memorial or the Priory Roll of Honour but he is commemorated on the following memorials.

- Bridlington School Second World War Roll of Honour.
- The Commonwealth War Graves Commission Website.

GERTRUDE HOLDEN

Civilian

Gertrude was born in Carnaby village Bridlington in 1885 and was brought up by her Aunt and Uncle Richard and Mary Chaplin (nee Crompton).

Gertrude Chaplin married Thomas William(Willie) Holden in the March quarter of 1909 registered at Bridlington. Thomas was a tobacconist and confectioner in the Promenade and was well known as the organist at the Promenade Methodist Church but sadly died on the 25 August 1937 at the early age of 54.

On the 18th June 1941, an enemy aircraft dropped two parachute mines which exploded in Lamplugh Road and St. Anne's Road. Several houses were completely destroyed and many others were badly damaged.

Lamplugh Road (Bridlington Local Studies Library)

56 year old Gertrude, now a widow, was killed at 'Oak Lodge', 6 Lamplugh Road Bridlington when her house was destroyed.

Gertrude Holden was buried in Bridlington Cemetery on 21 June 1941, grave ref V136 and is commemorated on the following memorials:

- Bridlington War Memorial.
- St Mary (The Priory) Parish Church Roll of Honour.
- The Commonwealth War Graves Commission Website (Civilian War Dead).

Gunner THOMAS CLIVE HOLDERNESS

The Royal Artillery, Service No. 4534941

Thomas Clive Holderness was born in the March quarter of 1914 registerd in Leeds. Thomas was the son of Arthur and Emma Holderness (nee Oglesby) of Leeds. In the March quarter of 1935 Thomas Clive Holderness married Doreen Mary Flinton. Thomas and Doreen lived at Hyde Park Leeds but moved to 50 North Street, Bridlington where Thomas was a Painter and Decorator. They had three children whom they named Arthur, Valerie and Doreen.

In WW2 Thomas was serving as a gunner with the 66th (The Leeds Rifles) HAA Regiment Royal Artillery. In the early months of the war the 66th Heavy Anti-Aircraft Regiment RA (TA) formed part of Home Forces and deployed its anti-aircraft batteries in the Humber and Tees area, the Tyne area, Birmingham, Sheffield and the Orkneys.

The Regiment moved by train to Glasgow in March 1942 and embarked on SS *Orion* to Bombay, India. On arrival in India several weeks were spent at the Barrakpur Racecourse Calcutta, where new equipment was drawn and acclimatisation carried out. 184 Battery was detached for airfield defence in Assam, and the remainder of the Regiment deployed to defend the key steelworks and airfield at Asansol. The Regiment later moved to the Manipur Road base, and six months later, joined the air-defences of the Assam Oil Company refinery at Digboi, and the American air base at Ledo. By 1945 the Japanese air force could no longer threaten key installations in Burma and on the 15th March the Regiment was placed in 'suspended animation' and then split up with all the officers and men being posted to various units.

31 year old Thomas Clive Holderness died on the 18th August 1945 and was buried in Bridlington Cemetery, grave reference Y19.

Grave Y19 in Bridlington Cemetery (C Bonnett)

Thomas Clive Holderness is not recorded on the Bridlington War Memorial or the Priory Roll of Honour but he is commemorated on the following memorial.

- The Commonwealth War Graves Commission Website.

Leading Seaman (Writer) ARTHUR HOLMES

The Royal Navy, Service No. C/JX259666, Bridlington School Old Boy

Arthur Holmes was born in 1914 the son of Arthur and Joan Holmes of 25 Oxford Street; Bridlington. He was educated at Oxford Street School and then went to Bridlington School in 1925 and left in 1930. Arthur was a nephew of Alderman C. H. Holmes, a former School Governor. On leaving School Arthur Holmes joined the staff of the local Rating Department under Mr. T. E. Mott and was a popular and efficient official. He passed his final examination and after several years at Bridlington took up an appointment in the Rating Department at Mitcham and Streatham London in 1934.

Arthur Holmes (Bridlington School)

In the March quarter of 1940 Arthur married Betty Vivienne Dorothy Bate. The marriage was registered in Wandswort District and after their marriage they lived at 33 Briarwood Road Clapham Park London SW 4 where they had one child, a girl whom they named Gillian. In March 1941 Arthur joined the Royal Navy and by 1944 he was a Leading Seaman (Writer) on the Flower Class corvette HMS *Asphodel* (K56).

HMS *Asphodel* (Luis Photos)

On the 3rd February 1943, HMS *Asphodel* had picked up survivors from the torpedoed motor tanker MV *Inverilen* on which fellow Bridlington Old Boy Chief Engineer Fred Ellis had been killed.

On the 9th March 1944 HMS *Asphodel* was torpedoed by U-575 in the Atlantic Ocean off north-west Spain and 30 year old Leading Seaman (Writer) Arthur Holmes was among those killed in action.

Arthur Holmes has no known grave and is commemorated on Panel 74 3 of the Royal Navy Memorial at Chatham in Kent. He is also commemorated on the following memorials.

- Bridlington School Second World War Roll of Honour.
- Bridlington War Memorial.
- St Mary (The Priory) Parish Church Roll of Honour.
- Christ Church Roll of Honour.
- The Commonwealth War Graves Commission Website.

Sergeant FREDERICK WILLIAM HOPE

The Royal Air Force, Service No. 944653

Frederick William Hope was born in the June quarter of 1915, he and his brother Henry were the twin sons of Frederick Beresford Hope and Adelaide Lillian Hope (nee Burton) of North Bierley in West Yorkshire. Frederick was educated at Bingley Grammar School and on leaving school he joined the Merchant Navy. After only one voyage to America he left the MN owing to ill health. He was then apprenticed to a motor firm in Bridlington and then went on to work for Cornelius Parish Ltd in Hull. Frederick married Rita Mosey in the September quarter of 1938 in Hull. They had one son and in 1936 were living at 10 Swanland Avenue in Bridlington. Their address before Frederick enlisted was 'Hadfield' 10 Lambert Road, Bridlington. In WW2 Frederick joined the RAF and was assigned to the Royal Air Force Volunteer Reserve (RAFVR). By 1942 he was serving as a Sergeant with 102 Squadron which was active from the second day of the Second World War and equipped with A. W. Whitley aircraft.

In February 1942 the Whitley's were replaced by the Handley Page Halifax. The squadron continued for the next three years to fly night sorties (including the thousand bomber raids) over Germany. On the 9th of November 1942, two 102 Squadron Halifax bombers took off from RAF Pocklington to bomb Hamburg and did not return.

Halifax Bomber (RAF.mod. uk)

One of those aircraft was Halifax W7864, DY-F, in which Frederick William Hope was the Flight Engineer. The aircraft was shot down over the sea, 40 km west of Wijk aan Zee by Helmut Lent. 27 year old Frederick Hope and the other seven members of the crew were lost without trace. Frederick William Hope has no known grave and he is commemorated on Panel 86 of the Royal Air Force Memorial at Runnymede in Surrey. Frederick is also commemorated on the following memorials.

- Bridlington War Memorial.
- St Mary (The Priory) Parish Church Roll of Honour.
- The Commonwealth War Graves Commission Website.

Lieutenant *AUBREY TREVOR HORNBY*

The York and Lancaster Regiment, Service No. 182360
Bridlington School Old Boy

Aubrey Trevor Hornby was born in the March quarter of 1921 registered in Driffield. Aubrey was the son of Sydney and Margaret Sarah Hornby (nee Smith) of 4 Clarence Avenue, Bridlington. He came to Bridlington School in 1933 and left in 1939. Aubrey joined the Army and first received an officer's commission while serving in the King's Own Yorkshire Light Infantry and then became a Lieutenant with the 7th (Pioneer) Battalion of the York and Lancaster Regiment.

Aubrey Hornby (Bridlington School)

The 7th (Pioneer) Battalion formed in autumn 1940 and was transferred to India on garrison and security duties in October 1941. While in India Aubrey married Clara Ina Williamson in 1942, the marriage being registered by the British India Office in the Presidency of Bengal.

In March 1945 the 7th (Pioneer) Battalion was serving in the 123rd Indian Infantry Brigade of the 5th Indian Infantry Division and took part in the offensive to re-conquer Burma. 24 year old Aubrey Trevor Hornby was killed in action in Burma on the 12th April 1945 while trying to go to the aid of a wounded man.

Aubrey was buried in Taukkyan War Cemetery Burma, (now Myanmar) grave reference 21.A.8.

Taukkyan War Cemetery (CWGC)

Aubrey Trevor Hornby is also commemorated on the following memorials.

- Bridlington School Second World War Roll of Honour.
- Bridlington War Memorial.
- St Mary (The Priory) Parish Church Roll of Honour.
- The Commonwealth War Graves Commission Website.

Flying Officer (Pilot) GRANVILLE HORSAMAN

The Royal Air Force, Service No. 153841, Bridlington School Old Boy

Granville Horsaman was born in the December quarter of 1921 the son of Allan Brown Horsaman and Dora Horsaman (nee Wallis) of Atwick, near Hornsea. Granville came to Bridlington School in 1933 and left in 1939. On leaving School he took up articles in accountancy, but joined the RAF in 1940, volunteered for air crew training and was assigned to the Royal Air Force Volunteer Reserve (RAFVR). Granville spent part of his training in Canada and was also trained in radio location, (Radar).

Granville Horsaman (Bridlington School)

Granville Horsaman married Catharine Mary O'Neil in the December quarter of 1944 registered in Birmingham. After their marriage they lived at Field House Atwick Driffield. Upon qualifying as a pilot Granville was commissioned as a Flying Officer (Pilot) and in 1945 was serving with 138 Squadron which had re-formed in 1941 as the first Special Duty squadron in the RAF specialising in dropping agents and supplies into occupied Europe. In March 1945 138 became a conventional bomber squadron in 3 Group equipped with Avro Lancaster heavy bombers and was stationed at Tuddenham in Suffolk.

On the 14th April 1945 Granville Horsaman was flying Lancaster RF103 (NF-O) as part of a force of 500 aircraft on a mission to bomb Potsdam, Germany. This was the last raid of the war on a German city by a major Bomber Command force. Lancaster RF103 was coned in searchlights and then shot down by a night fighter. There were no survivors and this was the only aircraft to be lost on the operation.

23 year old Granville Horsaman was buried in Berlin Cemetery in Brandenburg Germany, collective grave reference 7.L.22-25.

There is a memorial plaque in his memory inside the church of St. Lawrence in Atwick but as he was not a Bridlington resident he is not recorded on the Bridlington War Memorial or the Priory Roll of Honour but he is commemorated on the following memorials.

- Bridlington School Second World War Roll of Honour.
- The Commonwealth War Graves Commission Website.

Able Seaman JAMES DONALD HOUGHTON

The Royal Navy, Service No. P/JX 151937

James Donald Houghton was born on the 27th February 1922 registered in Knaresborough. He was the only son of Frank and Alice Janet Houghton (nee Barker) and was educated at Gipton School in Leeds. James joined the Royal Navy when he was 15½ and his address before enlistment was 16 St Stephen Road, Bridlington. James married Margaret Ward of Morecambe in the September quarter of 1942, registered in Leeds.

James served on HMS *Hood* and was transferred before her fatal last voyage. He was taken prisoner at Tobruk but escaped. By 1943 James was serving on H.M.S. *Egret*.   HMS *Egret* (Luis Photos)

HMS *Egret* (L75/U75) a Royal Navy sloop built by J. Samuel White at Cowes on the Isle of Wight was part of the 1st Support Group consisting of the sloops *Egret* and *Pelican*, and the frigates *Jed*, *Rother*, *Spey* and *Evenlode*.

On the 27 August 1943 the 1st Support Group relieved the 40th Support Group in the Bay of Biscay. The 1st Support group was then attacked by a squadron of 18 Dornier Do 217 carrying Henschel Hs 293 glider bombs. One of the two covering destroyer HMCS *Athabaskan* was heavily damaged by a bomb and HMS *Egret* was sunk with the loss of 194 of her crew. *Egret* was the first ship ever to be sunk by a guided missile and one of the 194 crew lost on the 27th August 1943 was 24 year old James Donald Houghton.

James has no known grave and is commemorated on Panel 74, Column 3, of the Portsmouth Naval Memorial, his medal entitlement is the 1939/45 Star, the North Africa and Palestine medals. James is also commemorated on the following memorials.

- Bridlington War Memorial.
- St Mary (The Priory) Parish Church Roll of Honour.
- The Commonwealth War Graves Commission Website.

Warrant Officer Class II WILLIAM HENRY HOWES

The Royal Army Ordnance Corps, Service No. 4384572

William Henry Howes was born in the June quarter of 1909 the son of John Thomas and Jane Isobel Howes (nee Durant) of 41 Queensgate Bridlington. William was a soldier for over 20 years and devoted to the Army. He became a Warrant Officer Class II (S.Q.M.S.) with the Royal Army Ordnance Corps.

William Henry Howes married Dorothy Patten on the 15th October 1936 at the Priory Church in Bridlington. After their marriage they lived at 'Northmore' Sewerby Road but during WW2 they lived with his wife's parents at 4 Lawson Road in Bridlington.

In 1939 at the beginning of the war William went to France with the BEF and was evacuated from Brest. He was stationed in Scotland for some time and then moved to Shrewsbury where he became ill with appendicitis.

William died aged 34 in No.111 Military Hospital, Copthorpe Shrewsbury on the 24th February 1944 and was buried in Bridlington Cemetery, grave reference X164.

William Howes grave in Bridlington Cemetery (C Bonnett)

William Henry Howes is also commemorated on the following memorials.
- Bridlington War Memorial.
- St Mary (The Priory) Parish Church Roll of Honour.
- The Commonwealth War Graves Commission Website.

MOLLIE HYLAND

Civilian

Mollie Hyland was born in 1911 the only daughter of Harry and Amy Simpson, of 10 Bridge Street, Bridlington.

Mollie was the wife of Philip John Hyland whom she married in 1935 and they lived at 28 Ellers Avenue, Bessacarr, Doncaster.

On the night of the 8th May 1941 the German Air Force dropped aerial mines (large canisters of explosives hanging from parachutes) on Doncaster. The subsequent blasts resulted in many people killed and injured, and destroyed and damaged many buildings.

30 year old Mollie Hyland was killed at her home during this air raid.

Mollie was buried in Bridlington Cemetery, grave reference X345 on Tuesday the 20th May 1941 following a memorial service at Christ Church, Bridlington.

Mollie Hyland is one of the 67,092 names commemorated in the Civilian War Dead Roll of Honour, near St. George's Chapel in Westminster Abbey, London. She is also commemorated on the following memorials.

- Bridlington War Memorial.
- St Mary (The Priory) Parish Church Roll of Honour*.
- The Commonwealth War Graves Commission Website (Civilian War Dead).

Note: *Recorded as Molly by the Priory.

GEORGE IRELAND

Civilian

George was born in 1891, the youngest son of Joseph and Ellen Ireland (nee Brigham) of 32 West Street, Bridlington. His father Joseph was a Cordwainer (a boot & shoe repairer) in Bridlington.

George married Jane A Miles in the December quarter of 1911, registered at Bridlington. They had one son whom they named Bernard. George Ireland served in the Army in WW1 and afterwards became a member of the British Legion. George was employed as a Driver & Motor Mechanic with the Hull Co-Operative Society. At the outbreak of the war he joined the Home Guard.

On the 17th July 1941, 50 year old George was killed in an air raid at 105 The Promenade where he and his wife lived. Just after midnight a German aircraft dropped four HE's bombs which exploded along the Promenade completely destroying the properties at 101, 103, 105 and 107. The houses hit were occupied by the RAF and at Numbers 103 and 105 twenty two airmen had a miraculous escape. Unfortunately George Ireland and two airmen, George Edwards and Edward Redding were killed in this air raid.

Promenade Air Raid damage
(Bridlington Local Studies Library)

George Ireland was buried in the family grave ref. L55 in Bridlington Cemetery on 21 July 1941. At his funeral his coffin was draped with the Union flag and an escort was provided by the Home Guard.

George's grave (C Bonnett)

George is also commemorated on the following memorials:
- Bridlington War Memorial
- St Mary (the Priory) Parish Church Roll of Honour
- The Commonwealth War Graves Commission website (Civilian War Dead).

Stoker 2nd Class WILLIAM JACKSON

The Royal Navy, Service No. D/KX 162043

William Jackson was the son of Joseph and Francis Jackson of 42 Sewerby Road in Bridlington. In 1943 William was a Stoker 2nd Class serving on HMS *Charybdis* a Dido class light AA cruiser. *Charybdis* joined the Home Fleet followed by Force H at Gibraltar and took part in Operation Pedestal to resupply Malta. In November 1942 she joined the 12th Cruiser Squadron and took part in Operation Torch followed by the Salerno landings after which *Charybdis* returned to the UK.

William Jackson (family archive)

On the 22nd/23rd Oct. 1943 *Charybdis* and the destroyers *Grenville, Rocket, Limbourne, Wensleydale, Talybont* and *Stevenstone* took part in operation 'Tunnel' to intercept the German blockade runner *Münsterland*. The *Münsterland*'s escorts consisted of six minesweepers and five *Elbing* Class torpedo boats. The night interception did not go as planned and *Charybdis* was hit and sunk by at least two torpedoes. HMS *Limbourne* was also hit and had to be sunk by HMS *Rocket*, the German force escaped unharmed. 452 men were lost from *Charybdis* and 42 from *Limbourne*, many of them drowned before they could be rescued from the bitterly cold water. Only four officers and 103 ratings survived from *Charybdis*. Bodies were later washed ashore on the French coast (over 100) and in the Channel Islands of Guernsey (20), Sark (1) and Jersey (38), not all of them were identified and their graves are marked *'A Naval Rating RN Known to God'*.

HMS *Charybdis* (Luis Photos)

Stoker 2nd Class William Jackson has no known grave and he is commemorated on Panel 82 Column 2 of the RN Memorial in Plymouth. William is also commemorated on the following memorials:
- Bridlington War Memorial.
- St Mary (The Priory) Parish Church Roll of Honour.
- The Commonwealth War Graves Commission Website.

Able Seaman FRANK STANLEY JAMES

The Royal Navy, Service No. C/J109512, Bridlington School Old Boy

Frank Stanley James was born in the September quarter of 1907 in Corton Suffolk. Frank was the son of George and Bessie James of Flamborough. He came to Bridlington School in 1921 and left in 1922. Frank came from a seafaring family and was a pre-war Regular having joined the Royal Navy on leaving School. In 1931 Frank married Hannah Leng of Flamborough and their only son entered Bridlington School in September 1943.

Frank James (Bridlington School)

In 1942 Frank James was a member of the crew of HM Submarine *Talisman*, a Trident Class submarine which displaced 1, 575 tons and had a ship's company of 53 officers and men. Her armament consisted of one 4 inch gun and ten 21 inch torpedo tubes.

HM Submarine *Talisman* (Luis Photos)

35 year old Able Seaman Frank Stanley James was believed killed in action on the 18 September 1942, along with all of the ships company, when HMS *Talisman* vanished without trace in the Strait of Sicily.

Frank has no known grave and is commemorated on Panel 54, 3 of the Royal Navy Memorial, Chatham, Kent. As he was not a Bridlington resident he is not recorded on the Bridlington War Memorial or the Priory Roll of Honour but he is commemorated on the following memorials.

- Bridlington School Second World War Roll of Honour.
- The Commonwealth War Graves Commission Website.

Pilot Officer JOHN ERNEST PHILLIP JEFF

The Royal Air Force, Service No. 88034

John Ernest Phillip Jeff was born in 1919 the youngest son of Ernest and Madge Jeff (nee Voase). His parents had several associations with East Yorkshire and resided for a while at Kellythorpe and at 'Helbythorpe' in Summerfield Road in Bridlington. His father Ernest was born in Hull and was an 'Old Hymerian' and a Solicitor in Malaya for 30 years. His mother came from a well-known Holderness family.

John Jeff (Hull Daily Mail)

John was educated at Felsted School in Essex and was the younger brother of Robert (Bobby) Jeff who was killed in action in 1940 while flying with 87 Squadron. At that time John Jeff was undergoing pilot training with the RAF. After completing his training John Ernest Phillip Jeff was posted to 44 Squadron.

No.44 was re-formed at Wyton in March 1937, as a bomber squadron with Hawker Hinds, moving later in the year to Waddington, where it re-equipped with Blenheims and then Hampdens. On the outbreak of the Second World War 44 Squadron was part of No. 5 Group

Handley Page Hampden Mk1 (Wikipedia)

23 year old Pilot Officer John Ernest Phillip Jeff was killed in action over Germany on the 3rd May 1941 while serving with No.44 Squadron.

John Jeff has no known grave and is commemorated on Panel 33 of the Royal Air Force Memorial, Runnymede, Surrey. He is also commemorated on the following memorials:

- Bridlington War Memorial
- St Mary (the Priory) Parish Church Roll of Honour
- The Commonwealth War Graves Commission website.

Flight Lieutenant (Pilot) ROBERT VOASE JEFF DFC and Bar

The Royal Air Force, Service No. 39285

Robert Voase Jeff was born in Kuala Lumpur in 1913 the eldest son of Ernest and Madge Jeff (nee Voase) who had several associations with East Yorkshire and resided for a while at Kellythorpe and at 'Helbythorpe' in Summerfield Road Bridlington. His father Ernest was a Hull man, an 'Old Hymerian' and a Solicitor in Malaya for 30 years. His mother came from a well-known Holderness family.

Robert Jeff (Hull Daily Mail)

Robert (Bobby) Jeff was educated at Cheltenham College and commissioned into the RAF in 1935. He served with 87 (fighter) Squadron and was a member of their aerobatic team. Bobby Jeff was promoted to Flying Officer in 1939 and led his flight of Hawker Hurricanes over to Lille in France just 6 days after war was declared as part of the air element of the BEF. in November 1939 Bobby Jeff became the first British Pilot to shoot down a German bomber in France and also the first WW2 British Officer to be awarded the Croix-de-Guerre. He was also awarded the Distinguished Flying Cross for 'Leadership and Devotion to Duty'.

By the time France fell, Bobby Jeff had shot down nine enemy aircraft and had been awarded a bar to his DFC and promoted to acting Flight Lieutenant. 87 Squadron was forced across the Channel to Debden and then moved north to Yorkshire where it received new aircraft. In July 87 Squadron moved to Exeter to take part in the Battle of Britain. Flight Lieutenant Robert (Bobby) Jeff was killed in action on the 11th August 1940 while attacking 100+ enemy aircraft over the English Channel.

Hurricane Mk IIc (F Bull)

27 year old Robert V. Jeff has no known grave and is commemorated on Panel 4. of the Royal Air Force Memorial, Runnymede, Surrey. He is also commemorated on the following memorials:
- Bridlington War Memorial
- St Mary (the Priory) Parish Church Roll of Honour
- The Commonwealth War Graves Commission website.

Private ALFRED JEFFREY

The Green Howards (Alexandra, Princess of Wales's Own Yorkshire Regiment), Service No. 4387668

Alfred Jeffrey was born in the December quarter of 1913 the son of Tom and Ann Jeffrey (nee Lakes) of 5 Queen Street Driffield. The family moved to Bridlington and by 1937 they were living at Westgate Cottages and later in Dorringtons Yard (Westgate).

In the December quarter of 1936 Alfred Jeffrey married Dorothy Gambles, of Illingworth, Halifax. The marriage was registered in Driffield. Alfred and Dorothy had 2 children, a girl and a boy whom they named Dorothy F. and Alfred I. Jeffrey both births were registered in Buckrose which covers Bridlington.

During WW2 Alfred served with the 5th Territorial Army (TA) Battalion, The Green Howards. The 5th Battalion was part of the 150th Infantry Brigade, 50th (Tyne Tees) Division. This was one of 10 British Army infantry divisions in the British Expeditionary Force which fought in the Battle of France in 1940. The 5th Battalion, Green Howards were among the last British units off the beaches of Dunkirk.

27 year old Alfred Jeffrey was killed between the 29th and 30th May 1940 during the evacuation from Dunkirk. He has no known grave and is commemorated on Column 50 of the Dunkirk Memorial.

The Dunkirk Memorial (CWGC)

When his wife submitted his name to the Bridlington War Memorial Committee Dorothy Jeffrey was at 92 Marton Road Bridlington.

Alfred Jeffrey is commemorated on the following memorials:

- Bridlington War Memorial
- St Mary (the Priory) Parish Church Roll of Honour
- The Commonwealth War Graves Commission website.

Seaman *ARTHUR J. JORDAN*

The Royal Navy, Service No. LT/JX 198815

Arthur J. Jordan was born on the 18th June 1915 the son of Mark and Eva Jordan, of Boynton's Yard, Beck Hill, Bridlington and the older brother of Mark Jordan.

Arthur was the husband of Sarah Ellen (Peggy) Jordan (nee Johnson) and they lived at 9 Applegarth Lane Bridlington with their two children, Ellen and Michael. His wife Sarah Ellen (Peggy) Johnson was the sister of Esther Amelia (Millie) Johnson who married Arthur's brother Mark.

Before joining the Royal Navy Arthur worked as a fisherman on the Bridlington coble *Victory*.

Arthur J. Jordan (family archive0

Arthur Jordan was serving on H.M.M.B. *Cervantes* of the Royal Naval Patrol Service. The motor boat *Cervantes* is believed to be one of the eight motor boats of the Medway Motor Boat Patrol based at Sheerness. Arthur J. Jordan died on the 3rd November 1942 when he and two other seamen drowned while ferrying provisions from one boat to another near Chatham.

26 year old Arthur J. Jordan was buried in Bridlington Cemetery, grave reference S308. A Memorial Service was held for Arthur on Sunday the 15th November 1942 at the Sailors Bethel in Bridlington.

Arthur's grave (C Bonnett)

Seaman Arthur J. Jordan RN is also commemorated on the following memorials:

- Bridlington War Memorial.
- St Mary (the Priory) Parish Church Roll of Honour.
- The Commonwealth War Graves Commission website.

Corporal MARK JORDAN

The Royal Air Force, Service No. 543264

Mark Jordan was born in Bridlington on the 16th June 1917 the son of Mark and Eva Jordan, of Boynton's Yard, Beck Hill, Bridlington and the younger brother of Arthur Jordan.

Mark married Esther Amelia (Millie) Johnson, the sister of Sarah Ellen (Peggy) Johnson who married Mark's brother Arthur.

Mark and Millie lived at 57 St. Albans Road, Bridlington. They had one daughter named Margaret and Mark Jordan worked as a printer with Mr. Grant of Bridlington, Mark was also a keen member of the local cycling club.

Mark Jordan (family archive)

Mark enlisted in the RAF at the outbreak of the war and was assigned to the Royal Air Force Volunteer Reserve (RAFVR).

Mark Jordan was serving at RAF Sutton Bridge, the home of No. 56 Operational Training Unit (OTU) whose role was training fighter pilots. Mark was taken ill and died in Holbeach and District Emergency Hospital of Encephalitis and Tuberculosis on the 8th May 1941. His death was registered at East Elloe, Lincolnshire.

23 year old Mark Jordan was buried in Bridlington Cemetery, grave reference S312, after a funeral service held in the Gospel Hall.

Mark's grave (C Bonnett)

Corporal Mark Jordan, RAFVR, is commemorated on the following memorials:

- Bridlington War Memorial.
- St Mary (the Priory) Parish Church Roll of Honour.
- The Commonwealth War Graves Commission website.

Trooper RONALD HENRY JORDAN

The 23rd Hussars, Service No. 7957901

Ronald Henry Jordan was born on the 8th May 1923 the son of Joseph and Kate Jordan (nee Storry) of 58 Jameson Road, Bridlington, East Yorkshire. He was educated at St Georges Senior Boys School on St. Mary's Walk Bridlington. Prior to joining the Army in 1941 Ronald was employed by Mr. Wells on timber felling at Boynton.

Ronald Henry Jordan joined the army and served with the 23rd Hussars, Royal Armoured Corps. The 23rd Hussars were based in Bridlington in 1944 while training for the invasion of Normandy. Equipped with Sherman tanks they were part of the 29th Armoured Brigade of the 11th (The Black Bull) Armoured Division.

Sherman Firefly in Normandy
(Wikipedia)

The 11th Armoured Division took part in the Battle of Normandy, Operation Epsom, Operation Goodwood, Operation Bluecoat, and the battle of the Falaise pocket. It crossed the Seine on 28th August and liberated Amiens and Antwerp in September.

'Black Bull' Insignia

Trooper Ronald Henry Jordan, of the 23rd Hussars was killed in action on the 10th September 1944 at Helchteren in Belgium.

21 year old Ronald Henry Jordan was buried in Leopoldsburg War Cemetery, Limburg, Belgium, grave reference II. D. 2. He is also commemorated on the following memorials:

- Bridlington War Memorial.
- St Mary (the Priory) Parish Church Roll of Honour.
- The Commonwealth War Graves Commission website.

Note.
Ronald is not recorded on the 23rd Hussars screen in the Priory.

Flight Sergeant (Pilot) JOHN PHILIP REGINALD JULIAN

Royal Air Force, Service No. 1018129, Bridlington School Old Boy

John Philip Reginald Julian was born in the September quarter of 1917 the son of Tom Julian DCM and Gladys Muriel Julian (nee Holdsworth) of Victoria Road in Driffield. He came to Bridlington School in 1928 and left in1934. John was an all-round sportsman and played Hockey, Tennis, Football and Rugby Union in Driffield. On leaving School he went to St. John's College, York and qualified as a teacher. Prior to being called up John was a teacher at Hutton Cranswick Council School.

John Julian (Bridlington School)

John joined the RAF, volunteered for air crew training and was assigned to the Royal Air Force Volunteer Reserve (RAFVR). He served with 34 Squadron that had first formed in WW1 and re-formed in 1935. In September 1939 it was sent to Singapore and from December 1941 it was in action against the Japanese in Malaya, Java and Sumatra where it was destroyed. It was re-formed again in India in April 1942 and deployed in bombing Japanese bases in Malaya with Blenheim IV aircraft.

Bristol Blenheim IV (F Bull)

In August 1942 it was based at Ondal, India where John Philip Reginald Julian was killed in action on the30th August 1942 aged 25. He and his crew went missing on an internal security flight. The wreckage of his aircraft was found in the River Ganges. John Philip Reginald Julian has no known grave and is commemorated on Column 414 of the Singapore Memorial. As he was not a Bridlington resident he is not recorded on the Bridlington War Memorial or the Priory Roll of Honour but he is commemorated on the following memorials.

- Bridlington School Second World War Roll of Honour.
- Bridlington Trinity AFC War Memorial
- The Commonwealth War Graves Commission Website

Lieutenant-Colonel *VINCENT KELLY*

The Royal Artillery, Service No: not known, Bridlington School Old Boy

Vincent Kelly was born on the 9th September 1904 the son of John and Teresa Kelly (nee Shoesmith) of 'Scarcliffe' St John's Avenue, Bridlington. He came to Bridlington School in 1914 and left in 1916. He was one of three brothers who attended the School.

On leaving school he worked as an engineer with the Bridlington Gas Company and then spent ten years in Malaya as manager of the Singapore Municipal Gas Works.

Vincent Kelly (Bridlington School)

He returned to the UK and succeeded his father as manager of the Bridlington Gas Company. He was then an agent for a large London financial concern with interests in Palestine, the USA and Canada.
On the outbreak of war he joined the Royal Artillery and saw service in North Africa and Sicily. In Italy he served with the Allied Control Commission in Rome. His knowledge of Singapore and the local languages led to his transfer to South East Asia Command and he ended his Army career as Deputy Chief Army Administrator for Malaya.

His health was impaired by war service and he died of Illness on the 24 August 1947 aged 42 in a London nursing home.

His requiem mass and funeral service were conducted by his brother, Father Terence Kelly at the Church of Our Lady and St Peter, Bridlington. Vincent Kelly was buried in Bridlington Cemetery grave reference D229

The death of Vincent Kelly is not recorded by the Commonwealth War Graves Commission and as he was not a Bridlington resident he is not recorded on the Bridlington War Memorial or the Priory Roll of Honour but he is commemorated on the following memorial.

- Bridlington School Second World War Roll of Honour.

Flight Lieutenant WILLIAM KENNY

The Royal Air Force, Service No. 102235

William Kenny was born in 1911, the only son of Thomas and Kathleen Kenny who lived at 9 Queensgate in Bridlington.

In the June quarter of 1928 William Kenny married Marion M. Campbell of Cowley Oxford the marriage being registered in Headington Oxfordshire. William joined the RAF in WW2, volunteered for air crew training and was assigned to the Royal Air Force Volunteer Reserve (RAFVR).

William Kenny was killed in action in Italy on the 14th May 1944, age 43, but there are no service details about his squadron or unit on the CWGC so the circumstances surrounding his death have not been determined to date. William was buried in Naples War Cemetery, grave reference II. C. 7.

Naples War Cemetery contains 1,202 Commonwealth burials of the Second World War. The site for the war cemetery was chosen in November 1943 and burials were made in it from the hospitals (the 65th, 67th and 92nd General Hospitals were in Naples), and the garrison. Later graves were brought in from a number of small cemeteries in the immediate vicinity.

Naples War Cemetery   (CWGC)

William Kenny is also commemorated on the following memorials:

- Bridlington War Memorial
- St Mary (The Priory) Parish Church Roll of Honour.
- The Commonwealth War Graves Commission Website

Sergeant ARTHUR WILLIAM KIRBY

The Parachute Regiment, Service No. 4747561

Arthur William Kirby was born in Bridlington the September quarter of 1912 the eldest son of Arthur William and Elsie Kirby (nee Hayes) of 4 The Promenade, Bridlington, East Yorkshire.

In the June quarter of 1941 Arthur William Kirby married Gladys Allen (nee Haw) and they were living at 9 Blackburn Avenue, Bridlington, when Arthur enlisted.

Arthur Kirby joined the York and Lancaster Regiment in early 1939 and fought with them in the Norwegian Campaign. He then transferred to the 12th Battalion the Parachute Regiment, Army Air Corps, (10th Bn. the Green Howards (Yorkshire Regiment.).

Known as the 12th (Yorkshire) Parachute Battalion, the 12th battalion was formed by the conversion of the 10th (East Riding Yeomanry) Battalion, Green Howards to parachute duties in May 1943. They were then assigned to the 5th Parachute Brigade, which was part of the 6th Airborne Division. The battalion took part in Operation Tonga during the Normandy invasion, capturing Ranville which it held against several German counter-attacks.

31 year old Arthur William Kirby was killed on the 12th June 1944 during the battle for Ranville and was buried in Ranville War Cemetery, Calvados, France, grave reference IVA. K. 18.

Arthur William Kirby is also commemorated on the following memorials:

- Bridlington War Memorial
- St Mary (The Priory) Parish Church Roll of Honour.
- The Commonwealth War Graves Commission Website

CHRISTIAN ROGER MICHEL LAFON

Civilian (French National), Bridlington School Old Boy

Christian Roger Michel Lafon was born in France c1923 and entered Bridlington School in 1937 as a boy of fourteen years. He had come from France to spend a year in this country improving his English. Of lively disposition, he quickly made friends and took an active part in all sides of school life, one of his particular interests being the Fencing Club. Christian returned home in 1938.

Christian Lafon (Bridlington School)

When France was occupied in 1940 he made up his mind to join General de Gaulle, he set off on the hazardous journey to England and actually reached the Spanish frontier where he was arrested by the Germans.

He was taken to Germany and interned, spending some time in the notorious concentration camps of Dachau and Buchenwald. Towards the end of the war he was moved to the east and, from that time, news of him is very vague. From time to time information was received encouraging the hope that he might still be alive but, unfortunately, all trace of him has now been lost and the French authorities have regretfully presumed his death.

The Bridlingtonian of April 1950 carried the following:

> "We offer the sincere sympathy of the School and Old Boys to the family of this very gallant gentleman of France."

As he was not a Bridlington resident Christian Roger Michel Lafon is not recorded on the Bridlington War Memorial or the Priory Roll of Honour but he is commemorated on the following memorial.

- Bridlington School Second World War Roll of Honour.

Lieutenant MALCOLM REDFEARN LAMMING

The Green Howards (Alexandra, Princess of Wales's Own Yorkshire Regiment), Service No. 68498, Bridlington School Old Boy

Malcolm Redfearn Lamming was born in 1918 the son of Lieutenant Robert Sydney Lamming and Clara Gertrude Lamming (nee Redfearn). Robert and Clara lived at 'Kantara' Belvedere Parade Bridlington. Malcolm Redfearn Lamming came to Bridlington School in 1927 and left in 1934. Malcolm was a pre-war Territorial, having received his commission in 1936. Upon the expansion of the Territorial Army in 1939, he became the full-time Assistant Adjutant of the 12th Battalion (TA) of the Green Howards.

Malcolm Lamming (Bridlington School)

In April 1941 he married Doris Callow of the Isle of Man. Malcolm was taken ill with tuberculosis shortly afterwards and was invalided out of the Army in July 1941. Malcolm Redfearn Lamming died of his illness on the 20th December 1941 aged 23 at the Vale of Clwyd Sanatorium, Ruthin, Wales which specialised in the treatment of TB.

Malcolm was buried with full military honours in Bridlington Cemetery, grave reference W16.

Malcolm Lamming's grave (C Bonnett)

There was a memorial chair to Malcolm Redfearn Lamming in Bridlington School and he is also commemorated on the following memorials:

- Bridlington School Second World War Roll of Honour.
- Bridlington War Memorial
- St Mary (The Priory) Parish Church Roll of Honour.
- The Commonwealth War Graves Commission Website.

The Bridlington Roll of Honour for the Second World War

Signalman *JAMES WILLIAM LEASON*

The Royal Corps of Signals, Service No. 2356209

James William Leason was born in the September quarter of 1909 registered at Driffield. James was the son of Arthur and Annie Elizabeth Leason (nee Bell). In 1935 James William Leason married Mary Caroline Davis and they lived at 18 Fairfield Road, Bridlington. They had one son and before James joined the Army they had moved to 16 East Road Bridlington and later to York Road in Driffield.

James William Leason served in the Royal Corps of Signals and became a Japanese Prisoner of War. James died in captivity on the 16th November 1943, age 34. Like many POW's held by the Japanese he was not officially declared dead until December 1945.

James William Leason was buried in Thanbyuzayat War Cemetery, Burma. Thanbyuzayat became a prisoner of war administration headquarters and base camp in September 1942. In January 1943 a base hospital was organised for the sick. The camp was close to a railway marshalling yard and workshops, and heavy casualties were sustained among the prisoners during Allied bombing raids between March and June 1943. The camp was then evacuated and the prisoners, including the sick, were marched to camps further along the line where camp hospitals were set up. However, Thanbyuzayat continued to be used as a reception centre for the groups of prisoners arriving to reinforce the work parties on the notorious Burma-Siam railway.

Thanbyuzayat War Cemetery was created by the Army Graves Service who transferred to it all graves along the northern section of the railway, between Moulmein and Nieke.

Thanbyuzayat War Cemetery (CWGC)

James William Leason was buried in Thanbyuzayat War Cemetery, Burma (now Myanmar), grave reference B6. V. 10. and he is also commemorated on the following memorials:

- Bridlington War Memorial.
- St Mary (The Priory) Parish Church Roll of Honour.
- The Commonwealth War Graves Commission Website.

Sergeant (Air Gunner) JOHN WILLIAM LEASON

The Royal Air Force, Service No. 999653

John (Jack) William Leason was born in the December quarter of 1912 the second son of Thomas and Susan Leason (nee Pickering) of 15 St. John Street, Bridlington. John was educated at Oxford Street School and after leaving school he worked for Mr. Limon in his grocery shop and was then employed as a grocer by Mr. Lyon and Burtons stores. In 1934 John William Leason married Enid Rimmington of Hull. After their marriage they lived at 15 St. John Street, Bridlington and had two children, Ann and Jeffrey. John joined the RAF, volunteered for aircrew training and was assigned to the Royal Air Force Volunteer Reserve (RAFVR).

John (Jack) Leason saw war service as a Sergeant (Air Gunner) with 207 Squadron. 207 Squadron reformed on 1 November 1940 as part of Bomber Command's No. 5 Group at RAF Waddington where they introduced the ill-fated Avro Manchester into service. On the 12/13th October 1941, aircraft from 207 Squadron took off from R.A.F. Waddington, Lincolnshire to bomb the synthetic rubber factory at Hüls. 79 Hamden's and 11 Manchester's took part in this operation which turned out to be a very dissatisfactory bombing raid as the target was completely cloud covered and the bombing scattered. One of the aircraft taking part was Manchester I Serial: L7312 Coded EM-L in which Sergeant (Air Gunner) John William Leason was part of the seven man crew. Manchester L7312 was shot down at 04.08 hrs. by Ofw. Paul Gildner flying a Bf110, of 4/NJG1 and the aircraft crashed at Horendonk about 2 km east of Essen. Seven of the crew were killed including Sergeant John William Leason, age 28. John William Leason was buried in a communal grave in Essen (Horendonk) Communal Cemetery. Sergeant John William Leason is also commemorated on the following memorials:

- Bridlington War Memorial.
- St Mary (The Priory) Parish Church Roll of Honour.
- The Commonwealth War Graves Commission Website.

Note: Fl/Sgt. Jack A. Cheeseman survived and became a P.O.W. Ofw. Paul Gildner was killed on the 24/25 February 1943 in a forced landing near Gilze-Rijen airfield after engine failure.

Seaman *JOSEPH PATRICK LEDDY*

The Merchant Navy

Joseph Patrick Leddy was born in Goole in the June quarter of 1903 the son of Peter Michael and Margaret Leddy (nee Leathley), his father Peter was a senior clerk to the customs at Goole. In the June quarter of 1932 Joseph Leddy married Selina Martin and after their marriage they came to Bridlington and lived at Flat Two, 40 The Promenade where they had one child.

Joseph rejoined the Merchant Navy in March 1940 and was making his first sea trip as a member of the crew of the S.S. *Mersey* (Goole). The SS *Mersey* was launched in 1906 and was owned by the Lancashire & Yorkshire Railway. She was used on the route between Goole and Rotterdam until the Second World War when she was sunk in 1940. The report in the Hull Mail of 22nd April 1940 follows:

'Goole Steamer Mined with Loss of 14'
"Three of six survivors in Hospital'. Goole's biggest shipping disaster since the outbreak of war occurred on Saturday, when the 1,037-ton collier Mersey sank off the south-east coast following an explosion, and 14 of her crew of 20 were lost. It is believed that she struck a mine. The ship was only a few miles from the shore at the time of the explosion, and it sank within a few minutes. A man walking on the cliffs at the time said: "I was looking out to sea, and there was suddenly terrific explosion. A column of water shot into the air. The ship I had been looking at a few minutes before had disappeared." With the exception of two men from Hull and Bridlington all the crew belonged to Goole including the master Captain W. Rockett. Joseph Patrick Leddy was the Bridlington crew member and he died in the explosion on the 20th April 1940, age 38.

Joseph has no known grave and is commemorated on Panel 70 of the Merchant Navy Memorial, Tower Hill, London. He is also commemorated on the following memorials:

- Bridlington War Memorial.
- St Mary (The Priory) Parish Church Roll of Honour.
- Christ Church Roll of Honour.
- The Commonwealth War Graves Commission Website.

Sergeant (Observer) GRAHAM DOUGLAS LINDSAY

The Royal Air Force, Service No. 1078148, Bridlington School Old Boy

Graham Douglas Lindsay was born in the December quarter of 1922 registered in Leeds. Graham was the son of Ralph Morgan Lindsay and Margery Lindsay (nee Hesselgrave) of Kirk Ella. He came to Bridlington School in 1931 and left in 1938, while at the School he was awarded his Second XV Colours.

Graham joined the RAF, volunteered for air crew training and was assigned to the Royal Air Force Volunteer Reserve (RAFVR). He saw war service with 21 Operational Training Unit. 21 OTU formed on 21st January 1941 at Moreton-in-Marsh, Gloucestershire to train the crews of Vickers Wellington bombers.

Graham Lindsay (Bridlington School)

Graham Douglas Lindsay, aged 19, was killed in a flying accident on the 14th April 1942 at Wollerton, Shropshire. Graham was part of the crew of Vickers Wellington Mk IC, R1085, of E Flight of 21 OTU which had taken off on a cross-country sortie. A propeller came off and the aircraft stalled and crashed at Wollerton, Shropshire at 3.31 p.m. All six crew members were killed.

Vickers Wellington (RAF.mod.uk)

Graham Douglas Lindsay was buried in Stoke-upon-Tern (St Peter) Church Cemetery, Shropshire, grave reference Row H, Grave 247. As he was not a Bridlington resident he is not recorded on the Bridlington War Memorial or the Priory Roll of Honour but he is commemorated on the following memorials.

- Bridlington School Second World War Roll of Honour.
- The Commonwealth War Graves Commission Website.

Corporal JOHN WILLIAM LINSLEY

The Royal Engineers, Service No. 936824

John William Linsley was born in the September quarter of 1918 the son of Frances Jane Linsley of 40 Milner Road Bridlington. After leaving school John worked for Messer's Boyd, Beesting and Moss of Bridlington as a joiner. He was a member of the Amalgamated Woodworkers Society and an enthusiastic member of the Bridlington Weight Lifting Club.

John Linsley joined the Royal Artillery (Service No. 10159034) on the outbreak of the war but transferred to the Royal Engineers in May 1940. John was assigned to the 97th Bomb Disposal Section of the Royal Engineers when he was killed on the 8th September 1940 in Caterham Reigate Surrey.

John was dangerously wounded along with 5 others whilst endeavoring to immobilise a bomb dropped by enemy aircraft on the Guards Parade Ground, Caterham, during the battle of Britain and he died in hospital the same day

Bomb disposal team in 1940 (Wikipedia)

22 year old Corporal John Linsley was buried in Bridlington Cemetery on Monday the 23rd September 1940, grave reference G232B. His grandparents John Robert and Mary Jane Linsley are buried in the same grave.

The Linsley grave (C Bonnett)

John Linsley is also commemorated on the following memorials:
- Bridlington War Memorial.
- St Mary (The Priory) Parish Church Roll of Honour.
- The Commonwealth War Graves Commission Website.

Captain BRIAN JOHN BARNETT LISTER

The Royal Electrical and Mechanical Engineers, Service No. 303489
Bridlington School Old Boy

Brian John Barnett Lister was born in the December quarter of 1922 in Bridlington. Brian was the eldest son of Major John Barnett Lister TD MA and Winifred Lister (nee Dyson) of 4 Cardigan Road, Bridlington. His father John was a Bridlington School Old Boy (1907-1914; Assistant Master (1919-1950); and Second Master (1950-1956).

Brian Lister came to Bridlington School in 1930 and left in 1940. At School he achieved a high academic standard and gained a reputation for conscientiousness. On leaving School he worked as a trainee engineer at Bridlington Gas Works and then attended Selwyn College, Cambridge, where he gained a BA degree in Engineering. On leaving Cambridge he went to an Officer Cadet Training Unit and was commissioned into The Royal Electrical and Mechanical Engineers (REME) in 1943. The REME formed in 1942 to organise support for the Army's vehicles, guns and technical equipment.

Brian Lister (Bridlington School)

Brian Lister spent a good part of his war service in Burma where he served in a tank recovery unit. At the end of WW2 he was posted to India and never returned home. Brian John Barnett Lister died in the Combined Military Hospital Peshawar India on the 29th November 1946, aged 23, after receiving severe injuries in a road vehicle crash the previous day at Risalpur, North West Frontier Province. India. His remains were later transferred to Karachi Cemetery in Pakistan, grave reference 3.13.9. Brian John Barnett Lister is commemorated on the following memorials:

- Bridlington School Second World War Roll of Honour.
- Bridlington War Memorial.
- St Mary (The Priory) Parish Church Roll of Honour.
- The Commonwealth War Graves Commission Website.

Bombardier CHARLES HELLAWELL LOCKWOOD

The Royal Artillery, Service No. 1620438, Bridlington School Old Boy

Charles Hellawell Lockwood was born in the September quarter of 1908 in Huddersfield. Charles was the son of Lewis Edgar and Lucy Lockwood (nee Hellawell) of Huddersfield. Charles came to Bridlington School in 1920 and left in 1924. On leaving School he was prominent in the Manchester and District Branch of the Old Bridlingtonians' Club. By 1942 his address was 10 Marsh Grove Road Edgerton Huddersfield.

Charles Lockwood (Bridlington School)

Charles saw war Service with the 14th Light Anti-Aircraft Regiment, RA. The Regiment served in North Africa in 1941 in the 8th Army. It was equipped with 48 Bofors anti-aircraft guns.

Whilst on active service in North Africa, Bombardier Charles Hellawell Lookwood contracted Sand Fly Fever, which led to pneumonia, and his health broke down.

He was evacuated to a large military hospital in Durban South Africa but died of Illness on the 8th March 1942 aged 33.

Charles Hellawell Lockwood was buried in Durban (Stellawood) Cemetery, South Africa, grave reference, block F, Grave 265.

Durban (Stellawood) Cemetery (CWGC)

As he was not a Bridlington resident Charles is not recorded on the Bridlington War Memorial or the Priory Roll of Honour but he is commemorated on the following memorials.

- Bridlington School Second World War Roll of Honour.
- The Commonwealth War Graves Commission Website.

Gunner GEORGE HENRY LONGDEN

The Royal Artillery, Service No. 1835189

George Henry Longden was born in the September quarter of 1909 registered in Hunslet. He was the son of George Henry and Emily Longden (nee Gough) who were married at Holy Trinity Church in Bridlington on the 27th December 1902. Emily Goughs parents were boarding house keepers in Bridlington and it can be assumed that Emilys son George would have spent a considerable part of his formative years in Bridlington.

George was a member of the Institute of Bankers and in the September quarter of 1936 he married Nellie Marjorie Sladen, the marriage being registered in North Leeds. By 1943 they were living at The Cottage Beckett Park Leeds

In WW2 George Longden was serving with the 221st Battery (1 West Riding) of the 91st Heavy Anti-Aircraft Regiment of the Royal Artillery.

In September 1939 his Regiment was part of UK Home Forces and by September 1940 they were in 39 AA Brigade, 10 AA Division.

In October 1942 the Regiment was serving in Palestine with the 9th Army. The Ninth Army was formed in the Levant, at the rear of the Eighth Army. It was initially commanded by General Sir Harry M. Wilson who was nicknamed 'Jumbo', hence the elephant on the badge.

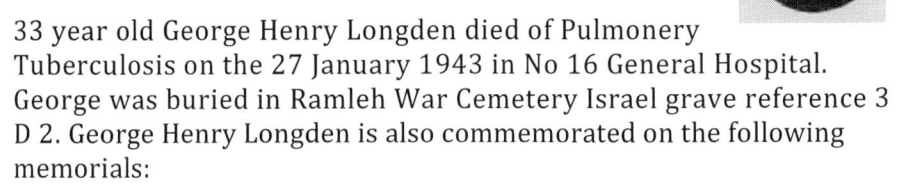

33 year old George Henry Longden died of Pulmonery Tuberculosis on the 27 January 1943 in No 16 General Hospital. George was buried in Ramleh War Cemetery Israel grave reference 3 D 2. George Henry Longden is also commemorated on the following memorials:

- Bridlington War Memorial.
- St Mary (The Priory) Parish Church Roll of Honour.
- The Commonwealth War Graves Commission Website.

ARTHUR LUMB

Civilian, Bridlington School Old Boy

Arthur was born in the March quarter of 1913 the son of Arthur and Lily Sledge Lumb (nee Fox) of 2 Ayresome Avenue Roundhay Leeds. He was one of four brothers who attended Bridlington School and was a Senior Prefect and Captain of Cricket during his time at the School.

Arthur Lumb married Irene Marjorie Houldsworth in the June quarter of 1938, registered at Sheffield. Arthur worked as an inspector for an insurance company and was transferred from London to Bristol. He and Irene lived at Thornwick, Woodleigh Gardens Wells Road Knowle Bristol.

Arthur Lumb (Bridlington School)

At about 11.45 am on the 25 September 1940 a force of 58 Heinkel He 111 bombers of KG55 escorted by Bf109 fighters, evaded the defences and dropped 90 tons of high explosive bombs and 24 oil bombs on and around the Bristol Aero Works at Filton. More than 250 people were killed or injured in the area of the factory and 107 elsewhere. Arthur Lumb was killed while sheltering in an air raid shelter in Lower Maudlin Street Bristol that received a direct hit. Arthur was 27 years old and left a wife and a son called Peter. The CWGC claims he was injured at Bristol Aeroplane Works at Filton and died the same day on the way to Bristol Royal Infirmary.

Arthur Lumb was buried in a Bristol County Borough Cemetery and as he was not a Bridlington resident he is not recorded on the Bridlington War Memorial or the Priory Roll of Honour but he is commemorated on the following memorials.

- Bridlington School Second World War Roll of Honour
- The Commonwealth War Graves Commission Website (Civilian War Dead).

Corporal SIDNEY LYTH

The Royal Army Service Corps, Service No. T/14286268

Sidney Lyth was born in the December quarter of 1922 the son of Charles William and Martha Lyth (nee Holliday), of 58 West Street, Bridlington. In WW2 Sidney was a Corporal in the 780th Company of the RASC and he married Josephine Cairney in the June quarter of 1944 registered in Buckrose which covers Bridlington.

22 year old Corporal Sidney Lyth died on the 22nd June 1946 and was buried in Hamburg Cemetery Germany, Grave Reference 3A. C. 1.

The Commonwealth section of this cemetery contains 1,466 Second World War burials, mostly of servicemen who died with the occupying forces, or airmen lost in bombing raids over Germany. There are also 378 post Second World War graves and 14 war graves of other nationalities.

Hamburg Cemetery (CWGC)

Details of how Sidney Lyth died have not been found and he is commemorated on the following memorials:

- Bridlington War Memorial.
- St Mary (The Priory) Parish Church Roll of Honour.
- The Commonwealth War Graves Commission Website.

Petty Officer EDWARD FRANCIS INKERFIELD MARTIN

The Royal Navy, Service No. P/228794

Edward Francis Inkerfield Martin was born in 1888 in Lifton Devon the son of Edward and Rebecca Martin. Edward joined the Royal Navy and in the 1911 census he was serving aboard HMS *Aboukir* a Cressy Class cruiser in Devonport.

HMS *Aboukir* along with sister ships *Cressy* and *Hogue*, were all torpedoed by the German U-boat U9 on 22nd September 1914. Three cruisers and 1459 men were lost in the space of an hour and a half, one of the worst Royal Navy disasters in WW1.

It is not known if Edward was serving in HMS *Aboukir* at the time but if he was he survived and in the December quarter of 1920 Edward Martin married Annie Myes the marriage being registered in Conway Wales. It is possible that Annie came from Seaford in Sussex.

Edward also served at H.M.S. Excellent a Royal Navy "stone frigate" (shore establishment) sited on Whale Island near Portsmouth in Hampshire. HMS Excellent is itself part of the Maritime Warfare School, with a Headquarters at HMS Collingwood. Although a number of lodger units are resident within the site, the principal of which is the Headquarters of Commander in Chief Fleet (Navy Command Headquarters).

By WW2 Edward Martin was a 'pensioned officer RN' and had retired to 2 Bedford Grove, Bridlington. Edward died on the 16 February 1943, age: 55, and was buried on the 19 February in Bridlington Cemetery, grave reference X62.

Edward Martin's grave
(C Bonnett)

Edward Francis Inkerfield Martin is not recorded on any of the Bridlington war memorials but he is is commemorated on the following memorial:

- The Commonwealth War Graves Commission Website.

Private FRANK MARTINDALE

The Australian Infantry, Service No. VX11702

Frank Martindale was born in the September quarter of 1894 registered at Sculcoates Hull. Frank was the youngest son of Thomas Vessey and Fanny Martindale (nee Batty). By the 1901 census the family were living in St Georges Avenue Bridlington and his father Thomas was a builder. By 1911 they had moved to 'Glencoe' Wellington Road Bridlington and later Thomas V. Martindale became a Bridlington Councillor. Frank Martindale served in the army during WW1, mostly in Salonika where he contracted Malaria and was invalided to Malta. After the end of WW1 he lived in St Georges Avenue and Haslemere Avenue Bridlington for a few years and was employed as a joiner by his brother Fred who had taken over the family building firm after the death of their father Thomas Martindale.

Frank was well known in the building trade and worked in Bridlington and Hull. In 1923 he emigrated to Melbourne, Australia aboard the P&O ship *Borda*, returned to England but went back to Australia in 1933 on the P&O ship *Strathnaver*. On the outbreak of WW2 Frank joined the Australian Imperial Forces and served with the 2/6 Battalion, 17th Brigade of the 6th Australian Division. The Division departed Melbourne for service overseas on 14 April 1940. It arrived in the Middle East on 18 May 1940 and after further training in Palestine and Egypt, embarked on its first campaign, against the Italians in eastern Libya just before Christmas, Its first battle, fought at Bardia between 3 and 5 January 1941, was costly, although the battalion was given a diversionary role, a series of misunderstandings resulted in heavy casualties that included Frank Martindale.

Frank Martindale was killed in action on the 3rd January 1941 during the battle for Bardia and was buried in Halfaya Sollum War Cemetery, Egypt, grave reference 18. H. 3. The CWGC gives his age as 36 but he was actually 46. Frank Martindale is also commemorated on the following memorials

- Bridlington War Memorial.
- St Mary (The Priory) Parish Church Roll of Honour.
- The Commonwealth War Graves Commission Website.

Flight Sergeant (Air Bomber) PETER DRAKE MARTINDALE

The Royal Air Force, Service No. 1437917, Bridlington School Old Boy

Peter Drake Martindale was born in the June quarter of 1921 registered at Knaresborough. Peter was the son of Wilfred and Gertrude Martindale (nee Drake) of Bridlington. He came to Bridlington School in 1930 and left in 1939.

On leaving School he attended Glasgow Veterinary College but interrupted his studies in 1941 and joined the RAF. He volunteered for air crew training and was assigned to the Royal Air Force Volunteer Reserve (RAFVR).

Peter Martindale (Bridlington School)

Peter joined 514 Squadron as a Flight Sergeant (Air Bomber). 514 Squadron formed in September 1943, by January 1944 514 Squadron was in 3 Group, Bomber Command, based at Waterbeach, Cambridgeshire with Avro Lancaster heavy bombers. Peter had flown on 28 operations by the end of January 1944.

Peter Martindale was killed in action on the 30th January 1944, aged 23, when he was one of the crew of Lancaster DS706 (JI-G). His aircraft took off at 5.23 p.m. as part of a force of 534 aircraft on an operation to bomb Berlin. Lancaster DS706 vanished without trace and another 32 aircraft were lost on the same raid.

Peter Drake Martindale has no known grave and is commemorated on Panel 220 of the Royal Air Force Memorial at Runnymede.

He is also commemorated on the following memorials:
- Bridlington School Second World War Roll of Honour.
- Bridlington War Memorial.
- St Mary (The Priory) Parish Church Roll of Honour.
- The Commonwealth War Graves Commission Website.

Squadron Leader (Pilot) LOUIS PATRICK MASSEY DFC & Bar

The Royal Air Force, Service No: 84686, Bridlington School Old Boy

Louis Patrick Massey was born in the June quarter of 1918 registered at Sculcoates Hull. He was the son of Paul and Teresa Massey (nee Connelly) of Cottingham. Louis Massey came to Bridlington School in 1927 and left in 1934. On leaving School he followed a commercial career and then joined the RAF. He volunteered for air crew training and was assigned to the Royal Air Force Volunteer Reserve (RAFVR).

Louis Massey (Bridlington School)

His award of the Distinguished Flying Cross was published in the London Gazette on 12th November 1940 and the citation stated that, `Late in October 1940, this officer was captain of a bomber aircraft engaged in a search for an aircraft believed to be down in the North Sea, when a Heinkel 115 was attacked and shot down. It was due to his skill in handling his aircraft that Pilot Officer Massey was able to press home his attack. In all of his 33 operational flights he has shown an admirable combination of courage and determination'. His award of a Bar to the DFC was published in the London Gazette on 26 May 1942, there was no citation but it is believed he received the Bar for pressing home an attack on a target at Essen, Germany at low level despite his aircraft being hit by anti-aircraft fire. He volunteered for duty in the Far East and by 1943 was serving with 159 Squadron based at Salbani in India. 158 was the first RAF squadron in India to use the American Consolidated B-24 Liberator four-engined bomber for operations against the Japanese in Burma.

Squadron Leader (Pilot) Louis Patrick Massey DFC & Bar was killed in action on the 9th October 1943 aged 25 when his Liberator DZ341 (G) failed to return from a mission to bomb Mingalodon airfield in Burma

He is buried in Rangoon Cemetery Myanmar (formerly Burma) collective grave reference 411-8. As he was not a Bridlington resident he is not recorded on the Bridlington War Memorial or the Priory Roll of Honour but he is commemorated on the following memorials.

- Bridlington School Second World War Roll of Honour.
- The Commonwealth War Graves Commission Website.

Chief Engineer STANLEY MAXWELL MAXWELL

The Merchant Navy, Service No. 119504, Bridlington School Old Boy

Stanley Maxwell Maxwell was born in Leven on the 6th September 1896 the son of Robert Morran Maxwell and Mary Elizabeth Maxwell (nee Calvert). He came to Bridlington School in 1910 and left in 1913. He was the youngest of three brothers who attended the School and Stanley Maxwell was awarded his First XI Colours for Cricket and was a School Prefect. Two of his sisters married Bridlington School Masters, H. W. Male and B. A. Farrow. Stanley served as an engineer in the Merchant Navy during the First World War and afterwards he worked mostly on the India run. In the June quarter of 1928 Stanley married Hannah P. Wolstenholm at Beverley but unfortunately Hannah died in 1930.

Stanley Maxwell (Bridlington School)

Stanley left the Merchant Navy and took up poultry farming in Devon and was then an engineer at the Bristol Aero Works. In the December quarter of 1935 Stanley married Marjorie Willmott Jenkins at Bideford in Devon. Stanley returned to the Merchant Navy just before WW2 and by March 1941 he was Chief Engineer on the steam cargo vessel SS *Royal Crown*. In March 1941 the German battle cruisers *Scharnhorst* and *Gneisenau* were loose in the Atlantic and on the 15/16th March 1941 SS *Royal Crown* was sunk by gunfire from the *Gneisenau*, the crew of 39 were taken from the water and eventually sent to the Merchant Navy and Royal Navy POW Camp at Marlag und Milag Nord near Bremen. In 1945 Stanley had taken part in a notorious forced march in sub-zero conditions as the Allies advanced. Chief Engineer Stanley Maxwell Maxwell died of Illness on the 25th April 1945 aged 48 and was buried in Bideford Public Cemetery Devon, grave reference Section B, Grave 200 but as he was not a Bridlington resident he is not recorded on the Bridlington War Memorial or the Priory Roll of Honour but he is commemorated on the following memorials.

- Bridlington School Second World War Roll of Honour.
- The WW2 Honour Roll in Bideford Church of St. Mary.
- The Commonwealth War Graves Commission Website.

Captain JAMES McALLISTER

The Royal Army Medical Corps, Service No.345603

James McAllister was born in 1910 the son of Mr. and Mrs. A McAllister of Edinburgh, Scotland.

Before WW2 James McAllister L.R.C.P., L.R.C.S. (Edin.), L.R.F.P.S. (Glasgow), was in practice in Bridlington with Dr. J. Harrison Broadbent. During the Second World War James enlisted in the Royal Army Medical Corps (RAMC) and served in India, Singapore and Malaya with the rank of Captain. In 1943 James married Dorothy Joan Blyth and they lived at 'Fairwinds' 19 Harland Road in Bridlington.

During WW2, technology enabled the RAMC greater access to mechanised land and air transport allowing specialists and operating teams to get right to the front-line in an increasingly mobile war. There were major medical developments pioneered by the army, such as the use of penicillin and the development of blood transfusion.

In July 1946 James was returning to England by ship from the Far East when he became ill. After four weeks of illness, 36 year old James McAllister died at sea on the 31 July 1946.

Captain James McAllister has no known grave and is commemorated on Panel 18, Column 1, of the Brookwood Memorial in Surrey which commemorates the men and women of the land forces of the Commonwealth who died during the Second World War and have no known grave, the circumstances of their death being such that they could not appropriately be commemorated on any of the campaign memorials in the various theatres of war.

James McAllister is also commemorated on the following memorials:

- Bridlington War Memorial.
- St Mary (The Priory) Parish Church Roll of Honour.
- The Commonwealth War Graves Commission Website.

Sergeant DAVID McKIRDY

The Parachute Regiment, Service No. 4388377

David McKirdy was born in Glasgow in 1907 the son of David Vincent and Jean McKirdy. David was the husband of Emily McKirdy (nee Pinder), they had three children, Donald, Jean and Ian and lived at 52a Brookland Road in Bridlington. David was a Plasterer with Mr. J. R. Briggs Builders. Before the war David was a member of the local Territorials (the Green Howards) and in WW2 he went to France with the Green Howards as part of the BEF.

David McKirdy (G Colman)

David was wounded in both arms at Dunkirk but was evacuated back to the UK. In 1941 the Green Howards went to the Middle East and in 1942 David was taken prisoner in North Africa. After eighteen months of captivity in an Italian POW camp he escaped on the 20th September 1943 and was mentioned in Despatches for his actions (gazetted 27th April 1944). David then volunteered for the airborne forces and after completing the training course he transferred to the 13th Battalion of the Parachute Regiment (2/4th Bn. the South Lancashire Regiment, Prince of Wales Volunteers) which at that time was part of the Army Air Corps (AAC). On D Day the 6th June 1944, David jumped with his battalion into drop zone N, North of the town of Ranville in Normandy. He came home on leave at the beginning of August and then returned to his unit. Three weeks later on the 23rd August 1944 Sergeant David McKirdy was killed in action by a hidden German Machine gun while leading his men during an assault to capture Pont L' Eveque. David was 37 years old and was buried in Ranville War Cemetery, grave reference VIA B 4. His scroll is shown (right) with permission of the Lords Feoffees of the Manor of Bridlington. Both the scroll and his medals are displayed in the Bayle Museum in Bridlington. David McKirdy is also commemorated on the following memorials:
- Bridlington War Memorial.
- St Mary (The Priory) Parish Church Roll of Honour.
- The Commonwealth War Graves Commission Website.

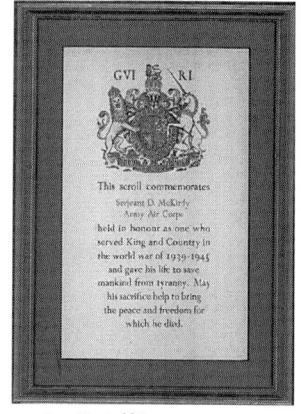

Chief Refrigerator Engineer GEORGE MEGSON

The Merchant Navy, Service No. not known

George Megson was born in the September quarter of 1890 registered at Howden. George was the son of Henry and Clara Ann Megson (nee Clark). George Megson married Grace Hutton Rial and they lived at 25 Harland Road Bridlington.

In WW2 George was serving as a Chief Refrigeration Engineer in the Merchant Navy. On the 2nd December 1940 he was on board the M.V. *Pacific President*. The *Pacific President* was a British Motor Cargo vessel of 7113 tons, built in 1928 and owned by Furness Withy and Company Limited of Liverpool.

George Megson (find my past)

MV *Pacific President*
(www.UBoat.net)
(City of Vancouver Archives, CVA 447-2545)

MV *Pacific President* (Master James Smith Stuart) sailed from Leith in ballast to join Convoy OB-251 from Liverpool to New York. While sailing in Convoy OB-251 she was hit by two torpedoes from U-43 and sank fast by the bow in the Atlantic Ocean west-southwest of Rockall at 09.01 hours on the 2nd December 1940. The master, one gunner and 50 crew members, including 50 year old George Megson, were lost.

George Megson has no known grave and is commemorated on Panel 79 of the Merchant Navy Memorial Tower Hill London. George is also commemorated on the following memorials:

- Bridlington War Memorial.
- St Mary (The Priory) Parish Church Roll of Honour.
- The Commonwealth War Graves Commission Website.

Note U-43 was sunk by a Fido homing torpedo from an Avenger aircraft of the US escort carrier USS *Santee* on 30th July 1943 south-west of the Azores, all 55 crew of U-43 died.

Lieutenant JOHN WILFRED MILLARD

The Royal Sussex Regiment, Service No. 233263,
Bridlington School Old Boy

John Wilfred Millard was born in the September quarter of 1921 the only son of Wilfred and Gladys Mary Millard (nee Bate) of Carlton Street in Bridlington. His father Wilfred was the assistant manager of the Bridlington Gas Company. John went to Bridlington School in 1931 and left in 1939. He was awarded a State Scholarship for Classics and went to Oriel College, Oxford where he gained a First Class BA degree in 1941 by which time the family had moved to live in Chelmsford in Essex.

John Millard (Bridlington School)

John Millard initially saw war service with the 10th Battalion the Royal Sussex Regiment which formed in 1939 and was a relatively short-lived home defence formation which belonged to the 10th Independent Beach Brigade on the Sussex and Kent beaches. John was then seconded to the 1st Battalion, Duke of Wellington's (West Riding) Regiment, a Regular battalion that had returned from Dunkirk and then went to North Africa as part of the 3rd Infantry Brigade of the 1st Infantry Division. The 'Dukes' fought in the North Africa Campaign, fighting with distinction in a number of actions and gaining several Battle Honours. By mid-April 1943, the Axis forces were hemmed into a small corner of north-eastern Tunisia and the Allies were grouped for their final offensive. John Millard was killed in action in Tunisia on the 6th May 1943 aged 21 during the final breakthrough which led to the defeat of the Axis forces in North Africa. Lieutenant John Wilfred Millard was buried in Massicault Cemetery Tunisia, grave reference 11117. He is also commemorated on the following memorials:

- Bridlington School Second World War Roll of Honour.
- Bridlington War Memorial.
- St Mary (The Priory) Parish Church Roll of Honour.
- The Commonwealth War Graves Commission Website.

Note: In 1945 the Millard Memorial Prize for History was endowed by his parents in his memory and was awarded in the Sixth Form.

Captain *JAMES FRANCIS DAWSON MILLS*

The Royal Artillery, Service No: 73787, Bridlington School Old Boy

James Francis Dawson Mills was born in the March quarter of 1915 the only child of Francis and Annie Mills (nee Smith) of 22 York Road, Beverley. He came to Bridlington School in 1923 and left in 1928. On leaving School he became a solicitor in the family practice of Crust, Todd, Mills and Co. of 34 Lairgate Beverley. James saw war service with the 77th Heavy Anti-Aircraft Regiment, Royal Artillery. The 77th was equipped with twenty-four 3.7 inch anti-aircraft guns and left the UK in December 1941 and arrived in Java in February 1942. On 12 March 1942 the unit was captured by the Japanese and the surviving personnel all became POW's.

James Mills (Bridlington School)

The Hull Daily Mail of 16th April 1945 carried the following bequest of his Grandfather James Willis Mills of Abbeyville Beverley.

"£100 to James Francis Dawson Mills now a prisoner of war in Borneo in acknowledgement of his gallant conduct in volunteering for service in the Far East during the present war".

Captain James Francis Dawson Mills died in a Japanese prisoner of war camp on the 3 July 1945, aged 30. He has no known grave and is commemorated on Column 2 of the Kranji Memorial in Singapore.

The Kranji Memorial Singapore (CWGC)

As he was not a Bridlington resident James Mills is not recorded on the Bridlington War Memorial or the Priory Roll of Honour but he is commemorated on the following memorials.

- Bridlington School Second World War Roll of Honour.
- The Commonwealth War Graves Commission Website.

Merchant Navy Apprentice CHARLES WHITEHEAD MILNER

The Merchant Navy, Service No. not known

Charles (Charlie) Whitehead Milner was born in the September quarter 1922 at Bilton, Doncaster, the birth being registered in Thorne. He was the son of Cyril and Laura Agnes Milner (nee Whitehead) and the brother of Margaret Milner who was born in 1921. The family lived at 'Ewbank' 7 Wellington Road, Bridlington, for several years and Charles was a member of the Christ Church Company of the Church Lads Brigade.

He joined the Merchant Navy as an apprentice and in 1939 was in the crew of a merchant vessel sailing to the USA. In July 1940 he was on the SS *Clan Macfarlane*. The *Clan MacFarlane* was a steam cargo ship of just over 6000 tons, she was built in 1922 by the Ayrshire Dockyard Co. Ltd., Irvine Scotland, for Clan Line Steamers Ltd.

On the 17 July 1940 the SS *Clan Macfarlane* sank after a collision with the British steamer *Ganges* 250 miles SE of Cape Gardafui in the Red Sea. Of her crew of 87, her master, Captain F J Houghton, and 46 crew survived, 41 crew died including merchant navy apprentice Charles Whitehead Milner.

SS *Clan Macfarlane* (unknown)

18 year old Charles Whitehead Milner has no known grave and is commemorated on Panel 30, of the Merchant Navy Memorial at Tower Hill, London. He is also commemorated on the following memorials:

- Bridlington War Memorial.
- Christ Church Roll of Honour.
- The Commonwealth War Graves Commission Website.

Note: Charles is not listed on the Priory Church Roll of Honour, His parents moved to Crowle but the CWGC lists their address as Countesthorpe in Leicestershire.

Lance Corporal HAROLD MITCHELL

The Durham Light Infantry, Service No. 4469577

Harold Mitchell was born in the December quarter of 1919 the son of John and Agnes Maude Mitchell (nee Winder) of 176 Sewerby Road in Bridlington.

In WW2 Harold was serving with 'C' Company of the 16th Battalion of the Durham Light Infantry.

The 16th Battalion DLI formed in Edinburgh, Scotland in early July 1940 and sailed away to war on Christmas Day 1942 from Liverpool aboard the MV *Staffordshire*, as part of 139 Brigade of the 46th Infantry Division of the British First Army. Entering the frontline in the Green Hill sector of Northern Tunisia on January 17th 1943, the 16th DLI suffered grievous losses in the Battle of Sedjenane, which began for the Durham's on the morning of February 27th 1943.

On the 2nd March 1943, 16 DLI attacked both Hill 231 and the village of Dejebel Guerba but the attacks failed at the cost of many casualties. 23 year old Lance Corporal Harold Mitchell was reported 'missing presumed killed in action' during the Battle of Sedjanane and is now known to have died on the 2nd March 1943.

Harold Mitchell has no known grave and is commemorated on face 28 of the Medjez-El-Bab Memorial in Tunisia.

The Medjez-El-Bab Memorial (CWGC)

Harold is also commemorated on the following memorials:
- Bridlington War Memorial.
- St Mary (The Priory) Parish Church Roll of Honour.
- The Commonwealth War Graves Commission Website.

Leading Aircraftman RICHARD DOUGLAS MOLLETT

The Royal Air Force, Service No. 1151230, Bridlington School Old Boy

Richard Douglas Mollett was born in Huddersfield in the June quarter of 1917 the son of William Ernest and Jane Mollett (nee Jackson) of Colchester in Essex. He came to Bridlington School in 1932 and was awarded his First XV Colours for Rugby. He left the School in 1934. On leaving School he went into farming and joined the staff of the Land Settlement Association. In 1939 at the age of 22 he became Chief Assistant to the Regional Administrator.

Richard Mollett (Bridlington School)

In WW2 Richard joined the RAF, volunteered for air crew training, and was assigned to the Royal Air Force Volunteer Reserve (RAFVR). He was sent to No1 British Flying Training School at Terrell, Kaufman County, Texas, USA, (the unit formed on 19 August 1941 before the USA was in the war).

AT-6C Texan/Harvard (F Bull)

While under training, 24 year old Richard Douglas Mollett was killed in a flying accident on the 30 November 1941. His aircraft, a North American Aviation AT-6A Texan, single-engine advanced trainer crashed just after take-off. It was believed that he had been distracted temporarily while asking the control tower for his time of take-off. Richard Douglas Mollett was buried in Terrell (Oakland) Memorial Park, Texas, USA, grave reference RAF Plot, Grave 4.

The grave of Richard Mollett (Ancestry.co.uk)

As he was not a Bridlington resident Richard is not recorded on the Bridlington War Memorial or the Priory Roll of Honour but he is commemorated on the following memorials.

- Bridlington School Second World War Roll of Honour.
- The Commonwealth War Graves Commission Website.

Boy 1st Class JOHN WILLIAM MORRIS

The Royal Navy, Service No, C/JX 170982

John William 'Jack' Morris was born in Hull in 1923 the son of Walter and Ethel Morris (nee Hallatt). His father Walter was a Railway Porter at Bridlington and had served in WW1 with the NER Railway Battalion of the Northumberland Fusiliers and he later transferred to the 18 Battalion of the York and Lancaster Regiment.

'Jack' Morris was one of five children, his siblings being Joan, Frederick, Audrey and Roy. In 1935 his mother Ethel died and was buried in Bridlington Cemetery, The family were living at 13 New Burlington Road in Bridlington and Jack was a member of the Christ Church Lads Brigade. John William 'Jack' Morris joined the Royal Navy and was serving as a Boy 1st Class on HMS *Orion*, a Leander-class light cruiser commissioned in January 1934. HMS *Orion* served with distinction in World War II where she received 13 battle honours, a record only exceeded by HMS *Warspite*, and matched by two others. In the early part of 1941 she was in the Crete and Aegean areas and was also at the Battle of Cape Matapan in March 1941.

On 29 May 1941, during the evacuation of Crete, *Orion* was bombed and badly damaged while transporting 1900 evacuated troops. Around 360 lives were lost, of whom 100 were soldiers. After extensive damage control had been undertaken she limped to Alexandria at 12 knots, providing a spectacular sight in the harbour with the mast wedged into the ship's funnel and significant battle damage.

One of those killed in action during the evacuation from Crete on the 29 May was Boy 1st Class John William 'Jack' Morris. He has no known grave and is commemorated on Panel 48, 2, of the Chatham Naval Memorial in Kent.

Chatham Naval Memorial (CWGC)
Jack Morris is also commemorated on the following memorials:
- Bridlington War Memorial.
- St Mary (The Priory) Parish Church Roll of Honour.
- Christ Church Roll of Honour
- The Commonwealth War Graves Commission Website

Leading Aircraftman ROBERT MACLEAN MURRAY

The Royal Air Force, Service No. 1090336

Robert Maclean Murray was born in the June quarter of 1922 the eldest son of David and Ruth Murray (nee Lyon) of 33 Jameson Road Bridlington.

Robert joined the RAF and was assigned to the Royal Air Force Volunteer Reserve (RAFVR).

Robert died in Raywell Sanatorium Cottingham on the 4th September 1945 age 23 from an illness he contracted in Italy during the war.

Leading Aircraftman Robert Murray was buried in Bridlington Cemetery, grave reference W43.

The grave of Robert Murray
(C Bonnett)

Robert Murray is also commemorated on the following memorials:
- Bridlington War Memorial.
- St Mary (The Priory) Parish Church Roll of Honour.
- The Commonwealth War Graves Commission Website.

Note: The CWGC does not record which unit or squadron Robert Maclean Murray was serving with when he died.

Sergeant (Pilot) CLAUDE LAMBERT NAYLOR

The Royal Air Force, Service No: 101204, Bridlington School Old Boy

Claude Lambert Naylor was born in the June quarter of 1922 the son of Henry (Harry) and Lizzie Isabel Naylor (nee Robinson) of Holly Bank York Road Driffield. His father was a Flight Lieutenant with the RFC in WW1. Claude was educated at Driffield Church of England School and then came to Bridlington School in 1934 and left in 1939. On leaving School Claude worked at Priestmans of Kingston upon Hull an engineering company that manufactured diggers, dredgers, cranes, industrial machinery and the Priestman Oil Engine.

Claude Naylor (Bridlington School)

Claude, joined the RAF in 1940, volunteered for air crew training and was assigned to the Royal Air Force Volunteer Reserve (RAFVR). In 1941 Claude was training at No. 7 Air Gunners School which formed on the 7th June 1941 at Stormy Down near Porthcawl Glamorgan Wales. Claude was awarded his pilots wings when he was barely 19 years of age.

Claude Naylor died in a flying accident on the 31st August 1941, aged 19, when his aircraft came down into the sea while on a training flight.

Claude Lambert Naylor has no known grave and is commemorated on Panel 49 of the Royal Air Force Memorial, Runnymede Surrey.

Royal Air Force Memorial (CWGC)

As Claude was not a Bridlington resident he is not recorded on the Bridlington War Memorial or the Priory Roll of Honour but he is commemorated on the following memorials.

- Bridlington School Second World War Roll of Honour.
- The Commonwealth War Graves Commission Website.

Sergeant ALBERT LESLIE NEAL

The Green Howards (Alexandra, Princess of Wales's Own Yorkshire Regiment). Service No. 4391067, Bridlington School Old Boy

Albert Leslie Neal was born in Bridlington the June quarter of 1914. He was the son of Ernest Broadwell Neal and Sarah Ann Neal (nee Cooper) of 12 Blackburn Avenue. Albert came to Bridlington School in 1925 and left in 1931. As a boy he was a member of the Christ Church Choir. On leaving School he became a director of Neal's Furnishers of Bridlington of which his father was the head. He also became a member of the Yorkshire Yacht Club, Bridlington Motor Club and Flamborough Golf Club. Before enlistment Albert lived at 7 Quay Road in Bridlington.

Albert Neal (Bridlington School)

Albert was one of the first recruits to the 7th battalion (TA) the Green Howards in 1939. The 7th and 6th Battalions Green Howards together with the 5th Battalion, The East Yorkshire Regiment formed the 69th Infantry Brigade, a Territorial Army unit that fought during the Battle of France and was among the last British units off the beaches of Dunkirk. One of those rescued was Albert Leslie Neal. In April 1941 the 69th Brigade, as part of 50th (Northumbrian) Infantry Division, was dispatched to the Middle East via Cyprus, Iraq, Syria, Egypt and then into Libya as part of XIII Corps in the Eighth Army. In 1942 Sergeant Albert Leslie Neal aged 27 was due to be transferred to an Officer Cadet Training Unit but on the 19 March 1942 during a period of offensive patrolling in Libya he was wounded in the head and legs and died of his wounds while being transported to a field hospital. Albert Leslie Neal was buried in Knightsbridge, Acroma, War Cemetery Libya, grave reference 8.E.13. He is also commemorated on the following memorials:

- Bridlington School Second World War Roll of Honour.
- Bridlington War Memorial.
- St Mary (The Priory) Parish Church Roll of Honour.
- Christ Church Roll of Honour.
- The Commonwealth War Graves Commission Website.

Note Albert's uncle, Lt. Harry Beecroft Neal, Machine Gun Corps is included on Bridlington School's First World War Roll of Honour.

Sergeant GEORGE STEPHENSON (Gus) NEEDLER

The Royal Air Force, Service No. 920736, Bridlington School Old Boy

George Stephenson (Gus) Needler was born in the December quarter of 1915. He was the son of Wilfred Stephenson Needler and Muriel Elizabeth Needler (nee Consitt) of 'Kendal' Queensgate, Bridlington and later of Hull. He was one of three brothers who attended Bridlington School. In the September quarter of 1940 Gus married Nancy (Anne) Watson, the marriage being registered in Winchester. After their marriage they are believed to have lived in the Regent's Park area of London.

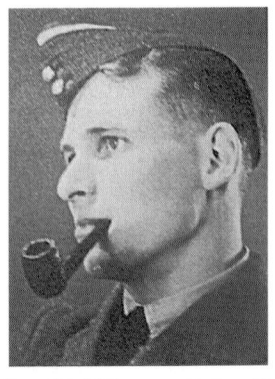

George Needler (Bridlington School)

Gus Needler joined the RAF, volunteered for air crew training and was assigned to the Royal Air Force Volunteer Reserve (RAFVR). By 1941 Gus was serving with 226 Squadron. 226 Squadron had re-formed in 1937 and in October 1941 was part of 2 Group, Bomber Command stationed at Wattisham, Suffolk and equipped with Bristol Blenheim IV twin engine light bombers. George (Gus) Needler was killed in action on the 15th October 1941 aged 25 when his Blenheim IV Z7494 (MQ-Z) was lost without trace and was believed to have been shot down by enemy fighters. His aircraft had taken off from Tangmere, Sussex at 1.46 pm. as part of a force of 12 aircraft, escorted by fighters to bomb the docks at Le Havre, France.

Blenheim IV (F Bull)

George Stephenson (Gus) Needler has no known grave and is commemorated on Panel 49 of the Royal Air Force Memorial at Runnymede in Surrey. As he was not a Bridlington resident he is not recorded on the Bridlington War Memorial or the Priory Roll of Honour but he is commemorated on the following memorials.

- Bridlington School Second World War Roll of Honour.
- The Commonwealth War Graves Commission Website.

Leading Aircraftman KENNETH ERIC NEW

The Royal Air Force, Service No. 567295

Kenneth Eric New was born in the March quarter of 1919 registered in Cardiff. He was the son of William Arthur and Concepcion New (nee Romero). In the December quarter of 1939 Kenneth Eric New married Dorothy Coates, the marriage was registered in Buckrose district which includes Bridlington. After their marriage they lived at 29 Eighth Avenue in Bridlington.

In 1940 Kenneth New was serving in the Royal Air Force as a leading aircraftman with No. 77 Squadron at RAF Driffield. At that time RAF Driffield was home to the only two bomber squadrons based in East Yorkshire, No's 77 and 102 Squadrons equipped with the Armstrong Whitworth Whitley V.

On the 15th August 1940 the radar operators at Staxton Wold picked up a large number of aircraft approaching the Yorkshire coast from the North Sea. The 50+ Ju88's of KG30 were intercepted and combat extended over Filey Bay and Bridlington Bay The attackers split up with the main body heading for its primary target of RAF Driffield. At least 17 aircraft dropped bombs on RAF Driffield and other enemy aircraft were engaged in strafing attacks. Four of the five hangers were badly damaged as well as several other buildings. One civilian and thirteen service personnel were killed, including 21 year old leading aircraftman Kenneth Eric New of 77 Squadron.

Kenneth Eric New was buried with full military honours in Bridlington Cemetery, grave reference W72.

Kenneth's grave (C Bonnett)

Kenneth is also commemorated on the following memorials:

- Bridlington War Memorial.
- St Mary (The Priory) Parish Church Roll of Honour.
- The Commonwealth War Graves Commission Website.

JANE NEWTON

Civilian

Jane Newton was born in 1872, the daughter of Robert and Catherine Stephenson of Day Street, Hull. She married Master Mariner Capt. Edward Newton in the June quarter of 1890, registered in Hull. Capt. Edward Newton died in 1922 aged 61. In 1941 Jane, now a widow was living at 7 Lamplugh Road with her daughter Elsie Gertrude Chatterton, also a widow.

On the 18th June 1941, 69 year old widow Jane Newton was killed, together with her 49 year old daughter Elsie Chatterton, in an air raid which destroyed 7 Lamplugh Road where they were both living.

Lamplugh Road   (Bridlington Local Studies Library)

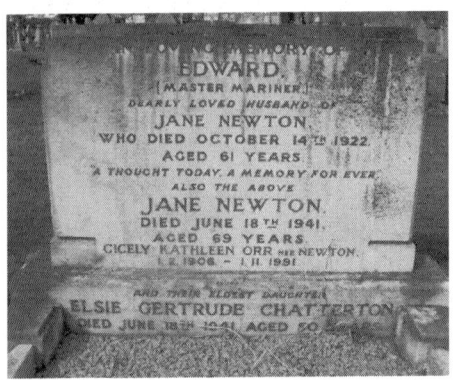

Jane Newton and Elsie Chatterton were buried together in the Newton family grave, ref. J213, in Bridlington Cemetery on 22 June 1941.

The Newton family grave (C Bonnett)

Jane Newton is also commemorated on the following memorials:

- Bridlington War Memorial.
- St Mary (the Priory) Parish Church Roll of Honour.
- The Commonwealth War Graves Commission Website (Civilian War Dead).

Flying Officer (Pilot) THOMAS ARTHUR NEWTON AFM

The Royal Air Force, Service No. 46505, Bridlington School Old Boy

Thomas Arthur Newton was born in Scotland in 1906 the second son of Richard and Jessie Newton. By 1911 the family were living at 15 Thorpe Street, Bridlington. Thomas came to Bridlington School in 1918 and left in 1922. He was a Governors' Scholar and one of four brothers who attended the School, their father Richard was a retired professional soldier who was the School Attendance Officer for Bridlington Corporation. On leaving School Thomas became a pre-war Regular in the RAF and was awarded the Air Force Medal (AFM) in 1931 for *'courage and devotion to duty' in Iraq, Cyprus and the Sudan.* The award was announced in the 1932 New Year Honours List to Sgt. 302547 Thomas Arthur Newton. By 1942 Thomas had taken a commission and also held the RAF Long Service and Good Conduct Medals.

Thomas Newton (Bridlington School)

In 1942 Thomas was an instructor at 22 Service Flying Training School (SFTS) at Thornhill, Gwelo in Southern Rhodesia. 22 SFTS opened in September 1940 as part of the British Commonwealth Air Training Plan which in turn was part of the Joint Air Training Scheme for training South African Air Force, Royal Air Force and Allied air crews during World War 2. The SFTS provided advanced pilot training for fighter and multi-engine aircraft and No 22 SFTS was equipped with Harvard and Oxford aircraft. Thomas Newton of 98 St. John's Avenue visited Bridlington School while on leave in April/May 1942 and revealed that his work involved training night fighter crews.

Thomas Arthur Newton AFM died on the 28th May 1942 in Southern Rhodesia (presumably in a training accident), He was 36, unmarried and was buried in Gweru Cemetery in Southern Rhodesia (now Zimbabwe) grave reference Plot 3, Row A, Grave 9. There was a Memorial Chair in Bridlington School and he is commemorated on the following memorials.
- Bridlington School Second World War Roll of Honour.
- Bridlington War Memorial.
- St Mary (The Priory) Parish Church Roll of Honour.
- The Commonwealth War Graves Commission Website.

AGNES ANNIE NICHOLSON

Civilian

Agnes was born in 1896 at Welton, East Yorkshire, the daughter of George Frederick and Jane Annie Nicholson (nee Potter).

Agnes was unmarried and had lived in Bridlington from about 1920. Her father died in Bridlington in 1936 and by 1940 Agnes was living with her widowed mother Jane and sister Mary Elizabeth at 9 South Back Lane Bridlington.

On the 11 July 1940 Agnes, a 44 year old spinster, was in Hilderthorpe Road when a lone enemy aircraft dropped a stick of high explosive bombs between Bridlington Railway Station and Hilderthorpe Road. Agnes, three other civilians and a soldier were killed outright and another civilian was fatally injured in this air raid which devastated Hilderthorpe Road.

Hilderthorpe Road. (Bridlington Local Studies Library)

Agnes Annie Nicholson was buried in Bridlington Cemetery on 15 July 1940, grave ref V198 and is commemorated on the following memorials:

- Bridlington War Memorial
- St Mary (the Priory) Parish Church Roll of Honour
- The Commonwealth War Graves Commission Website (Civilian War Dead).

Driver BEN NICHOLSON

The Royal Army Service Corps, Service No. T/136624
Bridlington School Old Boy

Ben Nicholson was born in Bridlington in the December quarter of 1919 the youngest son of Ryby and Norah Isobel Nicholson (nee Clarke) of 63 the Promenade, his father Ryby was a builder. Ben came to Bridlington School in 1933 and left in 1936. On leaving School Ben was employed by Mr R. Oyston who was a wholesale tobacconist. Ben enlisted in 1939 and became a driver with the Troops Company, Royal Army Service Corps (RASC) in the 18th Infantry Division.

Ben Nicholson (Bridlington School)
The 18th was a Second Line Territorial Army Division that was made up mostly of units from East Anglia. The 18th Infantry Division's sign represented a windmill, in association with East Anglia where it was raised.

In late 1941 the division sailed for India but was diverted to Malaya. The main part of the division landed at Singapore a few weeks before the fall of the island. After the violent week long Battle of Singapore, General Arthur Percival, commander of the Singapore garrison, surrendered to the Japanese on the 15th February 1942. The 18th Division was not reformed after its surrender in Singapore and all the surviving personnel of the 18th Division, including Ben Nicholson, went into Japanese POW camps.

Driver 'Ben' Nicholson, aged 23, died of beri-beri in a Japanese prisoner of war camp on the 24th November 1943. The beri-beri was caused by vitamin deficiency in a rice diet. He was buried in Thanbyuzayat War Cemetery, Burma (now Myanmar), grave reference B4. V. 8. He was not officially declared dead until December 1945 and he is commemorated on the following memorials.

- Bridlington School Second World War Roll of Honour.
- Bridlington War Memorial.
- St Mary (The Priory) Parish Church Roll of Honour.
- The Commonwealth War Graves Commission Website.

Corporal PATRICK JAMES NICHOLSON

The Royal Northumberland Fusiliers, Service No. 4273666
Bridlington School Old Boy

Patrick James Nicholson was born in the 3rd quarter of 1913 the son of Captain Edward James Nicholson AVC and Edith Nicholson (nee Stubbings) of 5 Swanland Avenue in Bridlington. He came to Bridlington School in 1925 and left in 1931. Patrick took up banking on leaving Bridlington School and in the December quarter of 1939 he married Margaret Winifred Lilley at Sedbergh and after their marriage they lived at 'Ackworth' Station Road in Sedbergh. Before he enlisted James worked as a Clerk with the Midland Bank in Northumberland.

Patrick Nicholson (Bridlington School)

James joined the Army in September 1939 and became a Corporal in the 4th Battalion Royal Northumberland Fusiliers (50th Regiment Reconnaissance Corps). The 4th Northumberland Fusiliers was a Territorial Army battalion that was re-formed in 1939 as the Motor Cycle Battalion of the 50th (Northumbrian) Division, serving in France and Belgium in 1940. James was evacuated from Dunkirk and his battalion was later expanded into a regiment and in April 1941 it became the 50th Regiment, Reconnaissance Corps. The Reconnaissance Corps was raised in 1941 and disbanded in 1946. In 1941 James went to North Africa with his regiment and early in 1942 the regiment was transferred to the 1st Armoured Division in the North African campaign.

Corporal Patrick James Nicholson was taken prisoner in North Africa in June 1942 and was transferred to a prisoner of war camp in Italy. After several months he became seriously ill and died after a year in captivity on the 8th June 1943 aged 30 in a civilian hospital at Caserta, Italy. Patrick James Nicholson was buried in Ancona, Marche, Cemetery, Italy, grave reference III.B.13. He is also commemorated on the following memorials:

- Bridlington School Second World War Roll of Honour.
- Bridlington War Memorial.
- St Mary (The Priory) Parish Church Roll of Honour.
- The Commonwealth War Graves Commission Website.

Signalman STANLEY WILLIAM NIXON

The Royal Corps of Signals, Service No. 2380858

Stanley William Nixon was born in 1918 the eldest son of William Alfred and Emma Nixon (nee Aveyard) of 4 Hermitage Road Bridlington. Stanley worked as a plumber / electrician after serving his apprenticeship with Messrs Snowden and Siddall, plumbers and electricians of Bridlington. He joined the army in early 1941 and became a wireless operator. Stanley was the husband of Mary Nixon (nee Papworth) of Stainforth, Doncaster, and they had one child, a boy.

In WW2 Stanley was serving in the Royal Corps of Signals as a Signalman attached to the 51st (Highland) Division. The 51st (Highland) Division had surrendered in France in 1940 and a new Division was formed in Scotland by re-numbering the 9th (Scottish) Division as the 51st (Highland) Division.

The 51st Highland Division sailed to Egypt in June 1942, landing at Port Tewfik, at the Suez Canal, in August. In September the Division moved to the front line of the British 8th Army. The Division included the Royal Corps of Signals Divisional unit in which Stanley Nixon was serving. As the North Africa campaign was coming to an end the Division was on the Algerian coast making preparation for Operation Husky, the invasion of Sicily.

The Division formed part of 30 Corps and landed near Pachino on 10 July. By the end of July after heavy fighting they were at the Sferro Hills. Signalman Stanley William Nixon died from wounds received in action on the 30th July 1943 during the battle for Sicily He was 25 years old and was buried in Catania War Cemetery Sicily, plot IV, grave H32. He is also commemorated on the following memorials:

- Bridlington War Memorial.
- St Mary (The Priory) Parish Church Roll of Honour.
- The Commonwealth War Graves Commission Website

Lieutenant SIDNEY NIELSEN ORUM DSC

The Royal Navy, Service No. not known

Sidney Nielsen Orum was born in the September quarter of 1919, the third son of Niels Sorjn Nielsen and Eva Orum. His Father Niels was born in Denmark about 1887 and became a Master Mariner who settled in Hull and married Eva Emily Oakes in the September quarter of 1912. Niels Sorjn Nielsen Orum became naturalized English on the 18th October 1920 when he and his family were living at 20 Curzon Street, Hull. During WW2 Niels and Eva lived at 27 East Road Bridlington. Sidney Nielsen Orum married Joan Leathley in the March quarter of 1941 in Hull and they lived at 10 Kings Garden, Goddard Avenue in Hull. In WW2 Sidney served in the Royal Navy where he rose to the rank of Lieutenant RNVR. He took part in the D-Day landings where he won the DSC *"For gallantry, skill, determination and undaunted devotion to duty during the landing of allied forces on the coast of Normandy"*.

Sidney Orum (Hull Daily Mail)

25 year old Sidney Nielsen Orum was killed in action on the 1st November 1944 while on H.M. Landing Craft Flak (Large) No 310 (H.M.L.C.F. (L.).310, during the assault on Walcheren in Holland.

Mrs. Joan Orum with Niels and Eva Orum colleting Sidney's DSC at Buckingham Palace (Hull Daily Mail)

Sidney was awarded a posthumous Mention in Despatches for *"Gallantry and great devotion to duty in the assault on Walcherin in which operation they lost their lives"*.

Sidney Nielsen Orum has no known grave and is commemorated on panel 79, 2. of the Chatham Naval Memorial and also on the following memorials.

- Bridlington War Memorial.
- St Mary (The Priory) Parish Church Roll of Honour.
- The Commonwealth War Graves Commission Website.

Sergeant (Pilot) JOHN MARTIN OXTOBY

The Royal Air Force, Service No. 754620, Bridlington School Old Boy

John Martin Oxtoby was born in the March quarter of 1920 the son of Christopher and Blanche Oxtoby (nee Martin) of Runner End, Holme-on-Spalding-Moor.

He came to Bridlington School in 1930 and left in 1938. John was a senior prefect for part of his last year at School and qualified for a County Major Scholarship, tenable at a university, but he chose to enter the Civil Service.

John Oxtoby (Bridlington School)

At the start of WW2 John Oxtoby joined the RAF and after volunteering for air crew training he was assigned to the Royal Air Force Volunteer Reserve (RAFVR). In August 1940 John was undergoing pilot training at No.5 Operational Training Unit in Gloucestershire. No 5 OTU had formed on the 6th March 1940 to train fighter pilots and was based at Aston Down, Gloucestershire.

On the 10th August 1940 Blenheim L6799 and Spitfire L1063 collided on the ground at Aston Down airfield and all three crew members were killed. Sergeant (Pilot) John Martin Oxtoby aged 20 was a pupil on board the Blenheim and he died just two weeks after being awarded his Pilot's 'wings'.

John Martin Oxtoby was buried in Holme-on-Spalding-Moor (All Saints) Churchyard, grave reference C77. As he was not a Bridlington resident he is not recorded on the Bridlington War Memorial or the Priory Roll of Honour but he is commemorated on the following memorials.

- Bridlington School Second World War Roll of Honour.
- Holme on Spalding Moor War Memorial.
- Holme on Spalding Moor Church Lych-gate.
- The Commonwealth War Graves Commission Website.

Leading Seaman EDWARD GRANT PARISH

The Royal Navy, Service No. C/JX 151616

Edward Grant Parish was born in the June quarter of 1921 the only son of Cyril Grant and Kate Parish (nee Meddick) of Bury St. Edmunds. The family were living in Bridlington when his mother Kate died in 1937. Edward was educated at Burlington School and was a member of the Priory Church Scout Group from 1932 to 1935. He was a very good swimmer and joined the Royal Navy soon after leaving school.

In WW2 Edward was serving on H.M.S. *Juno*. HMS *Juno* (F 46) was a J class Destroyer Built by Fairfield Shipbuilding & Engineering Co. (Govan, Scotland) and commissioned on the 24 August 1939. She took part in several sea battles and escorted many convoys. In 1940 *Juno* transferred to the 14th Destroyer Flotilla in the Mediterranean Fleet.

HMS *Juno* (Luis Photos)

In May 1941 HMS *Juno* deployed from Alexandria with other destroyers and some cruisers to intercept enemy invasion craft on passage to Crete to carry out landings. On the 21st May 1941 The ships came under high level bombing attack by five CANT Z1007 aircraft from the 50th gr. about 30 nautical miles south-east off Crete. HMS *Juno* was hit by three bombs which split the ship in two aft of the bridge structure sinking her in less than two minutes.

116 of ship's company lost their lives including leading seaman Edward Grant Parish who was manning a 'pom-pom' gun. 96 survivors were rescued, by HMS *Kingston, Kandahar* and *Nubian*, Five of those rescued later died.

19 year old Edward Grant Parish has no known grave and is commemorated on Panel 42, 1 of the Chatham Naval Memorial, Kent. He is also commemorated on the following memorials:

- Bridlington War Memorial.
- St Mary (The Priory) Parish Church Roll of Honour.
- The Commonwealth War Graves Commission Website.

EVELYN PARKIN

Civilian

Evelyn was the adopted daughter of Mr. George Thomas (Tom) Foley and Mrs. Violet Annie Foley, of 52 Kingsgate, Bridlington. Tom Foley was the founder of Foley's Cafe and Restaurant at 12-13 Prince Street and had been in business in the town for over 38 years.

Evelyn Foley married Walter Parkin in the September quarter of 1935, registered at Sculcoates, Hull and they lived above Foley's Cafe along with Dorothy and James Watson to whom they were related.

On Friday, 23rd August 1940, a lone German bomber made a low level attack on Bridlington Harbour dropping four high explosive bombs. The third bomb completely wrecked Foley's Cafe and Restaurant next to the harbour and killed Evelyn Parkin and three other people in the Cafe. Evelyn left a daughter Josephine, age 4.

Evelyn's husband Walter Parkin was brought out alive from the wreckage by the ARP Rescue Team and eventually recovered from his serious injuries.

Foley's Café (Bridlington Local Studies Library)

39 year old Evelyn Parkin was buried in Bridlington Cemetery on the 27 Aug 1940, grave ref X57.

Evelyn's grave (C Bonnett)

Evelyn is commemorated on the on the following memorials:

- Bridlington War Memorial.
- St Mary (The Priory) Parish Church Roll of Honour.
- The Commonwealth War Graves Commission website (Civilian War Dead).

Private WILLIAM PARKINSON

The East Yorkshire Regiment (The Duke of Yorks Own)
Service No: 4341211

William Parkinson was born in the March quarter of 1914 registered in Bakewell Derbyshire. He was the son of Benjamin and Susan Eliza Parkinson (nee Fox) of 31 Lambert Road, Bridlington, William was one of four 'Parkinson' brothers who served in WW2, Thomas and Ben in the RAF and Charles and William in the Army. Williams's sister in law, Nora Parkinson, was injured in the bombing of Eight Avenue in Bridlington on the 18th June 1941 and died of her injuries 12 months later.

William served with the 5th Battalion the East Yorkshire Regiment. The 5th battalion saw action on D-Day where the battalion suffered heavy losses in the assault but secured its objectives. Then they fought in the battles for Normandy followed by the rapid advance through Holland as part of Operation Market Garden. This was followed by the battle for the town of Arnhem itself which stopped a furious assault by German tanks and artillery designed to recapture the bridges.

William Parkinson (family archive)

In late October, 1944 as the Allies tried to move forward from their stalled positions in the Netherlands and towards the Rhine. The East Yorkshire Regiment took part in the Battle of Venray. The advance on Venray resulted in heavy losses, especially around a flooded small river that was swollen after heavy autumn rains and the area mined by the Germans. The village of Overloon was destroyed in the fighting and about 2,500 soldiers were killed, making it one of the bloodiest battles in the Netherlands during the Second World War.

William Parkinson was killed whilst on patrol on the 31st October 1944 during the battles for Venray and Overloon. Private William Parkinson was buried in Arnhem Oosterbeek War Cemetery, grave reference 7. B. 19. He is commemorated on the following memorials:

- Bridlington War Memorial.
- St Mary (The Priory) Parish Church Roll of Honour.
- The Commonwealth War Graves Commission Website.

Flight Sergeant (WOP/AG) ERIC HENRY PEACE

The Royal Air Force, Service No. 1434302, Bridlington School Old Boy

Eric Henry Peace was born in the December quarter of 1922 registered in Edmonton Middlesex. Eric was the son of Ernest and Ethel Maud Peace (nee Howard) of 23 Wigginton Road in York.

Eric came to Bridlington School in 1934 and left in 1940.

Eric Peace (Bridlington School)

After leaving School Eric joined the RAF, volunteered for air crew training and was assigned to the Royal Air Force Volunteer Reserve (RAFVR). By 1944 Eric was serving with 97 (Straits Settlements) Squadron as a Flight Sergeant (Wireless Operator/Air Gunner). 97 (Straits Settlements) Squadron had re-formed in 1935. In June 1944 it was in 5 Group, Bomber Command and stationed at Coningsby, Lincolnshire equipped with Avro Lancaster heavy bombers.

On the 23rd June 1944, 21 year old Eric Henry Peace who had completed 22 operational flights, was killed in a flying accident when Lancaster III ME625 (OF-?) collided with another 97 Squadron Lancaster. Both aircraft were engaged in formation flying training and the two aircraft crashed at Cloor House Farm Deeping Fen Cambridgeshire. There was only one survivor from each aircraft.

Eric Henry Peace was buried in Cambridge (City) Cemetery, grave reference 14366.

The grave of Eric Peace (Ancestry.co.uk)

As he was not a Bridlington resident Eric is not recorded on the Bridlington War Memorial or the Priory Roll of Honour but he is commemorated on the following memorials.

- Bridlington School Second World War Roll of Honour.
- The Commonwealth War Graves Commission Website.

PERCIVAL GEORGE PERKINS

Civilian

Percival George Perkins was the son of William and Elizabeth Addison Perkins (nee Dale).

Percy married Enid M Julian in the September quarter of 1927, registered in Driffield.

Percy served in WW1 as a motor mechanic in the Motor Section of the RASC. After WW1 he was employed as a motor engineer by Messrs. Aldreds of Driffield and about 1928 he joined Messrs. Holtby, White & Company. On the outbreak of WW2 he joined the Home Guard as a corporal.

On the 10 April 1941 bombs were dropped on Bridlington and several houses received direct hits, a builder's merchant's showroom was also destroyed.

47 year old Percy of 25 Hamilton Road was fatally injured at home during this air raid and later died in Lloyd Hospital Bridlington.
Percy left a widow and a 9 year old daughter.

Hamilton Road
(Bridlington Local Studies Library

Corporal Percival George Perkins was buried in Bridlington Cemetery on the 14 April 1941, grave ref Y23. Members of the Home Guard formed a guard of honour and acted as bearers at his funeral.

Percival George Perkins is commemorated on the following memorials:
- Bridlington War Memorial.
- St Mary (The Priory) Parish Church Roll of Honour.
- The Commonwealth War Graves Commission Website (Civilian War Dead).

Flight Lieutenant (Pilot) HAROLD CASS (Ben) PEXTON DFC

The Royal Air Force, Service No. 81650, Bridlington School Old Boy

Harold Cass (Ben) Pexton was born in the March quarter of 1912 registered at Great Ouseburn. Ben was the son of Reginald and Marion Pexton (nee Dunn) of Wixley Grange in York in 1911 and later of Watton Abbey. Ben came to Bridlington School in 1922 and left in 1924. On leaving School he took up banking. His hobby was flying and he joined the RAF, volunteered for air crew training and was assigned to the RAFVR. Ben Pexton had completed his first tour of operations by 1941 and twice his aircraft crash-landed when returning from operations and he twice collided with fighters; an enemy fighter over Essen, Germany and an RAF fighter over the UK. He was injured in the second incident and was posted to Canada as an instructor.

Ben Pexton (Bridlington School)

Ben returned to the UK and by July 1943 he was a Flight Lieutenant (Pilot) with No. 35 (Madras Presidency) Squadron. No. 35 Squadron became a Pathfinder squadron in August 1942 and was operating the Handley Page Halifax heavy bomber. By 1943 it was based at Graveley in Cambridgeshire. On the 30th July 1943 Harold Cass (Ben) Pexton aged 31 was killed in action when his aircraft Halifax HR851 (TL-T) was shot down by a combination of anti-aircraft fire and a night fighter. Five crew members were killed and two were taken prisoner. Ben's aircraft was part of a force of 777 aircraft on an operation to bomb Hamburg and another 27 aircraft were lost. Ben Pexton was on his 52nd operational mission and was awarded a posthumous Distinguished Flying Cross; the award was published in the London Gazette on 28 July 1944 with effect from 28 July 1943. Harold Cass (Ben) Pexton has no known grave and is commemorated on Panel 120 of the Royal Air Force Memorial at Runnymede in Surrey. As Ben was not a Bridlington resident he is not recorded on the Bridlington War Memorial or the Priory Roll of Honour but he is commemorated on the following memorials.

- Bridlington School Second World War Roll of Honour.
- The Commonwealth War Graves Commission Website.

Note in 1946 his father presented two stained glass windows to St. Mary's Church, Watton in memory of his son.

Warrant Telegraphist HARRY PINDER

The Royal Navy, Service No. not known

Harry Pinder was born on the 27th March 1901 the son of George and Jemima Pinder (nee Spavin) of 63 Queensgate, Bridlington. Harry married Mary Jane Wimbles and they lived at 57 Hilderthorpe Road in Bridlington where they had two children, both girls, whom they named Mary and Betty. In July 1943 Harry Pinder was serving in the Royal Navy as a Warrant Telegraphist at Delta W/T station HMS *Nile* the Royal Navy shore base at Alexandria in Egypt.

Harry Pinder (family archive)

Harry was killed on active service in an aircraft accident on the 4th July 1943 whilst returning to England for his daughter Mary's wedding. This was no ordinary accident and it involved the death of General Wladyslaw Sikorski and is still described by some historians as mysterious. The B24 Liberator II serial AL 523, crashed into the sea 16 seconds after taking off from Gibraltar Airport at 23:07 hours. The plane's pilot was the only survivor. Sikorski, his daughter, his Chief of Staff, and seven others including 42 year old Harry Pinder were killed. The catastrophe, while officially classified as an accident, has led to several conspiracy theories that persist to this day, and often propose that the crash was an assassination, which has variously been blamed on the Soviets, British or even a dissenting Polish faction. A Memorial plaque dedicated to Sikorski is located at the end of the Great Siege Tunnels in Gibraltar. The plaque notes that *"the cause of this mysterious accident has never been ascertained; a fact which has given rise to many speculations, doubts and rumors."*

Harry Pinder has no known grave and is commemorated on Panel 73, Column 1 of the Portsmouth Naval Memorial in Hampshire and on the following memorials.
- Bridlington War Memorial.
- St Mary (The Priory) Parish Church Roll of Honour.
- Christ Church Roll of Honour.
- The Commonwealth War Graves Commission Website.

Private GEORGE OLAF PINKNEY

The West Yorkshire Regiment (The Prince of Wales's Own)
Service No: 4395077

George Olaf Pinkney's birth was registered in the March quarter of 1915 in Bridlington. He was the son of George and Olufine (Ena) Pinkney (nee Hopland) of 14 Portland Place in Bridlington. His father George died in December 1914 while serving with the Yorkshire Regiment in WW1 and his mother remarried in the December quarter of 1921 to Ernest A Brunton. George and his stepfather ran a woodyard in Fairfield Road and in the June quarter of 1936 George married Anne Partland in Bridlington.

George and Anne Pinkney had two children whom they named George and Josephine. Before enlisting George was working as a taxi driver.

George Olaf Pinkney saw war service with the West Yorkshire Regiment (The Prince of Wales's Own).

George Pinkney (family archive)

28 year old George Olaf Pinkney died suddenly in Leeds on the 6th December 1943. George was buried in Bridlington Cemetery, grave reference Z9, following a requiem mass on Friday the 10th of December at the Catholic Church in Bridlington,

The grave of George Olaf Pinkney (C Bonnett)

George Olaf Pinkney is not recorded on the Bridlington War Memorial or the Priory Roll of Honour but he is commemorated on the following memorial:

- The Commonwealth War Graves Commission Website.

Lance Corporal FRANCIS HAROLD POLLARD

The Royal Electrical and Mechanical Engineers, Service No. 7628025

Francis (Frank) Harold Pollard was born in Bridlington in the December quarter of 1914. Frank was the youngest son of George William and Mary Pollard(nee Wrides) of The 'Barn' Bempton. Frank Pollard was educated at Bempton School and before enlisting he was employed as a motor mechanic by Messrs. Holtby, White Ltd., garage proprietors of Bridlington.

Frank married Florence (Florrie) Patricia Jackson in Leeds in 1942 and they were living at 23 Haselmere Avenue Bridlington when Frank enlisted. Frank Pollard saw war service with the Royal Electrical and Mechanical Engineers (REME), In 1942 his REME unit was attached to the 6th Battalion. Queens Own Royal West Kent Regiment. The 6th Battalion was reconstituted in 1940 and by November 1942 it was part of the 78th Infantry Division and played a major role in 'Operation Torch', the Anglo-American invasion of French Algeria. 78th Division, which included the 6th Battalion moved swiftly east towards Tunis. They distinguished themselves by holding the cross roads at Djebel Aboid for four days against an armoured column. After this successful defence the advance continued only to be halted on November 30th at Green Hill (Djebel Azzag). It was during the advance to Tunisia that Francis (Frank) Harold Pollard was killed in action on the 17th November 1942 Age 28.

Lance Corporal Francis Harold Pollard was buried in Tabarka Ras Rajel War Cemetery, Tunisia, grave reference3. D. 25.

Tabarka Ras Rajel War Cemetery (CWGC)

Francis (Frank) Harold Pollard is also commemorated on the following memorials:

- Bridlington War Memorial.
- St Mary (The Priory) Parish Church Roll of Honour.
- The Commonwealth War Graves Commission Website.

Flight Sergeant (Air Gunner) DENNIS KILVINGTON POTTER

The Royal Air Force, Service No. 628018

Dennis Kilvingon Potter was born in Driffield in 1921 the son of Eric and Doris Potter (nee Bromley) and the elder brother of Nancy E. K. Potter who was born in Bridlington in 1930. Dennis received his general education at Oxford Street School in Bridlington and then went to Thomas Commercial School in Bridlington. He was a member of the Priory Church Scout Group, the Church Lads Brigade and later joined the TA battalion of the Green Howards.

In WW2 Dennis was serving as a Flight Sergeant (Air Gunner) with 207 Squadron. 207 Squadron origins lay with No. 7 Squadron RNAS formed in 1916. It became No. 207 Squadron, on the formation of the Royal Air Force in 1918. By 1938 it was equipped with Fairey Battles as an Operational Training Unit based at RAF Cottesmore, Leicestershire. In 1940 207 Squadron reformed as part of Bomber Command's No. 5 Group at RAF Waddington, operating Avro Manchester's. It moved to RAF Bottesford where it re-equipped with Avro Lancaster Bombers and in September 1942 the Squadron was based at Langar Nottinghamshire.

Dennis Kilvingon Potter age 21 was killed in action on the 24 October 1942 when his Lancaster W4121 coded EM-B Crashed in the sea off Blainville sur Mer France while on a daylight raid on Milan.

Lancaster Bomber (F Bull)

Dennis was posted missing and eventually his body was washed ashore and he was buried in Cherbourg Old Communal Cemetery, Manche, France, grave reference Plot 6, Row D, Grave 13.

Dennis is also commemorated on the following memorials:

- Bridlington War Memorial.
- St Mary (The Priory) Parish Church Roll of Honour.
- The Commonwealth War Graves Commission Website.

MABEL POTTER

Civilian

Mabel Potter was born in the December quarter of 1921, the daughter of Richard and Ellen Potter (nee Hornby) of Fern View, Beeford, Driffield.

In 1940, 19 year old Mabel was living at 85 Hilderthorpe Road, Bridlington and on the 11 July 1940, a lone German aircraft on a hit and run raid, dropped a stick of high explosive bombs between Bridlington Railway Station and Hilderthorpe Road. Mabel and three other civilians and a soldier were killed outright and another civilian, was fatally injured and died later. This air raid caused severe damage to people and property in Hilderthorpe Road.

Mabel Potter was buried in the churchyard of St Leonard's Church Beeford and is the only civilian commemorated on the Beeford War Memorial.

Mabel Potter's grave (J Bull)

St Leonard's Church Beeford (J Bull)
(The white stone War Memorial topped with a cross is on the left}.

Mabel Potter is also commemorated on the following memorial:

- The Commonwealth War Graves Commission website (Civilian War Dead).

Flight Sergeant (WOP/AG) FRANK POWLS

The Royal Air Force, Service No. 1452097

Frank Powls was born in the March quarter of 1923 the youngest son of William and Elsie Jane Powls (nee Mainprize) of 38 Jameson Road, Bridlington. Frank went to the Baptist Church in Quay Road and after leaving school Frank was employed in the outfitting department of Carlton Ltd in King Street Bridlington.

In 1941 Frank joined the RAF, volunteered for air crew and was assigned to the Royal Air Force Volunteer Reserve (RAFVR). After pilot training with the US Navy in Pensacola Florida he gained his wings as a Sergeant Pilot on the 9th February 1943.

Frank Powls and his Certificate (family archive)

Frank joined 172 Squadron RAF as a Flight Sergeant (Wireless Operator / Air Gunner). 172 Squadron was a anti-submarine (a/s) squadron that operated the Vickers Wellington equipped with the Leigh Light and was part of 19 Group, Coastal Command. The squadron was the first to attack a U-Boat at night using the combination of ASV and the Leigh Light. Before D Day the squadron was on a/s operations and on the 24th May 1944 Frank Powls was the second Pilot in the 6 man crew of Wellington Mk.XIV, s/n NB 802 that took off from Chivenor at 2226 hours on 23 May 1944 to carry out an a/s patrol in the Bay of Biscay. Nothing further was heard from the aircraft after take-off and it did not return. After the war all the crew was recorded as 'missing, lost at sea'. Frank Powls has no known grave and is commemorated on Panel 221 of the Air Forces Memorial at Runnymede near Windsor. Frank Powls is also commemorated on the following memorials:

- Bridlington War Memorial.
- St Mary (The Priory) Parish Church Roll of Honour.
- The Commonwealth War Graves Commission Website.

Sergeant (Pilot) JOHN KIRKWOOD PURDON

The Royal Air Force, Service No. 745547, Bridlington School Old Boy

John Kirkwood Purdon was born in Bridlington in the June quarter of 1920 the youngest son of Francis Kenneth and Kate (Kitty) Alice Purdon (nee Kirkwood) of 69 Cardigan Road, Bridlington. John came to Bridlington School in 1929 and left in 1934. His father was a Bridlington School Old Boy (1906 - 1909) and from being a Cabinet Maker in 1911 he rose to become a Auctioneer and Valuer by WW2 and also a Vice-Chairman of the School Governors. John's older brother Peter was also a Bridlington School Old Boy (1926 - 1932) and was also killed in WW2.

John Purdon (Bridlington School)

John Purdon left Bridlington School aged 14 and went to Worksop College. He passed the intermediate examination of the Auctioneers and Estate Agents Institute joined the well-known firm of F. Purdon and Son, estate agents of Bridlington and Driffield, with which his father and grandfather were associated. He was a keen Rugby player, amateur boxer, golfer and a member of the Bridlington RUFC. Before he enlisted his address was 86 Cardigan Road, Bridlington. John joined the RAF before the war and became a Sergeant (Pilot) RAFVR with No. 51 Squadron. 51 Squadron re-formed in 1937 and by April 1941 it was equipped with Armstrong Whitworth Whitley bombers in 4 Group, Bomber Command and was stationed at Dishforth in Yorkshire.

John Kirkwood Purdon was killed in action on the 4th April 1941 aged 20. His aircraft, Whitley V Z6556 (MH-Q), took off at 6.56 p.m. as part of a force of 90 aircraft on an operation to bomb enemy warships in the port of Brest, France. A bearing was obtained whilst over the English Channel but the aircraft subsequently crashed at Trebeurden in France, about 8 km south-west of Lannion. There were no survivors. Two other aircraft were also lost. John Kirkwood Purdon was buried in Trebeurden Communal Cemetery Cotes-d'Armor France, grave reference 1and he is also commemorated on the following memorials.

- Bridlington School Second World War Roll of Honour.
- Bridlington War Memorial.
- St Mary (The Priory) Parish Church Roll of Honour.
- The Commonwealth War Graves Commission Website.

Sergeant (Pilot) PETER DAVID KIRKWOOD PURDON

The Royal Air Force, Service No. 740295, Bridlington School Old Boy

Peter David Kirkwood Purdon was born in Patrington in the December quarter of 1918 the eldest son of Francis Kenneth and Kate (Kitty) Alice Purdon (nee Kirkwood) of 69 Cardigan Road, Bridlington. He came to Bridlington School in 1926 and left in 1932. His father was a Bridlington School Old Boy (1906 - 1909) and from being a Cabinet Maker in 1911 he rose to become a Auctioneer and Valuer by WW2 and also a Vice-Chairman of the School Governors. Peter's younger brother John was also a Bridlington School Old Boy (1929 - 1934) and was also killed in WW2.

Peter Purdon (Bridlington School)

Peter Purdon left Bridlington School aged 14 for Barnard Castle School and then joined Messrs. E. B. Bradshaw and Sons, flour millers of Driffield He later went to Messrs. Townrowe, flour millers of Gainsborough in Lincolnshire and passed the final examinations of the Flour Milling Institute concerned with the technical side of the industry. He was a keen sportsman, playing Rugby for Bridlington RUFC and was a capable amateur boxer and a member of the Royal Yorkshire Yacht Club. Peter joined the RAFVR in 1937 and amassed about 2,000 flying hours as a pilot. On the outbreak of war he became a flying instructor and by 1941 was based at RAF Bobbington, (later Halfpenny Green), the home of No.3 Air Observer & Navigator School. On the 30th June 1941 Peter Purdon aged 22 was killed in a flying accident at Enville in Staffordshire when an aircraft piloted by him crashed. Peter was buried with full military honours in Bridlington Cemetery grave reference W25. Bridlington School was represented at his funeral by the Headmaster and several Masters.

Peter's grave (C Bonnett)

Peter D. K. Purdon is also commemorated on the following memorials.
- Bridlington School Second World War Roll of Honour.
- Bridlington War Memorial.
- St Mary (The Priory) Parish Church Roll of Honour.
- The Commonwealth War Graves Commission Website.

Aircraftman 2nd Class EDWARD STANLEY REDDING

The Royal Air Force, Service No. 1061485

Edward Stanley Redding was born in the March quarter of 1922 registered in Glanford Brigg district. Edward was the son of Henry James and Florence Redding (nee Beadle) of The Cottage, Wawne Lodge, near Hull. Edward joined the RAF in WW2 and was assigned to the Royal Air Force Volunteer Reserve (RAFVR).

In 1941 Edward was billeted at 105 the Promenade, Bridlington and just after midnight on Thursday the 17th July 1941 a German aircraft dropped four HE's bombs which exploded along the Promenade completely destroying the properties at 101, 103, 105 and 107. The houses hit were occupied by the RAF and at Numbers 103 and 105 twenty two airmen had a miraculous escape. Edward Redding was not so lucky and he and fellow airman George Edwards were killed in this air raid together with civilian George Ireland who also lived at 105 the Promenade.

Promenade Air Raid damage
(Bridlington Local Studies Library)

19 year old Edward Stanley Redding was buried in Bridlington Cemetery, grave reference W24,

Edwards grave (C Bonnett)

The CWGC does not record which unit or squadron Edward was serving with when he died and he is not recorded on the Bridlington War Memorial.

Edward Stanley Redding is commemorated on the following memorials:

- St Mary (The Priory) Parish Church Roll of Honour.
- The Commonwealth War Graves Commission Website.

Private THOMAS RENNOLDSON

The Green Howards (Alexandra, Princess of Wales's Own Yorkshire Regiment), Service No: 4033031

Thomas Rennoldson was born in the December quarter of 1911 the son of George Aynsley and Margaret Rennoldson (nee Moore) of 49 Wood Street Benfieldside Consett. Thomas married Jessie Wright of Beeford and they lived at 2 Marton Avenue Bridlington and had one child. Thomas joined the Army in 1932 and was a regular soldier for 14 years with the Green Howards and spent 5 years in India before WW2. In WW2 Thomas was appointed driver & batman to the famous Yorkshire and England cricketer Captain Hedley Verity of the 1st Green Howards.

The 1st Battalion went to France in 1939 and then to Norway. In 1942 they sailed to India and in 1943 they were part of the 15th Brigade. They invaded Sicily on the 10th July 1943. During the heavy fighting in Sicily, Captain Verity led his company in an attack on a farmhouse at one end of a fortified ridge in Catania. *"They crawled on their bellies through the cornfield while the tracer bullets flew overhead. The moon at their backs was outshone by the flares and mortar explosions. We were up against it and we went right into it,"* remembered Rennoldson. *"They set the corn alight and gave us everything they had got, we were trapped. Keep going"* Verity urged *"Keep going and get them out of that farmhouse."* Those were his last words to his men as a bullet hit Verity in the chest. They had to pull back leaving Rennoldson tending to Verity's wounds in the cornfield where they were both taken prisoner. Hedley Verity was taken to Naples and then Caserta where he died from his injuries. Thomas Rennoldson was sent to an Italian POW camp and then to Stalag XVIII-A, a German POW camp in Wolfsberg Austria. Thomas was released in 1945 and returned to 2 Marton Avenue before moving to 17 Trinity Road, Bridlington. In 1946 Thomas went into Sutton Annex (Hospital) and died on the 31st December 1946, age 35, as a result of his privations as a POW.

Thomas Rennoldson was buried in Consett Blackhill and Blackhill old Cemetery, Durham, grave ref, sec. 16, new ground, Grave 241. He is commemorated on the following memorials:
- Bridlington War Memorial.
- St Mary (The Priory) Parish Church Roll of Honour.
- The Commonwealth War Graves Commission Website.

NORAH RILEY

Civilian

Norah Riley (nee Pounder) was born in Leeds in 1872, the daughter of Charles Hezmelhalc and Mary Elizabeth Pounder. She married Thomas Charles Riley in the September quarter of 1896, registered at Leeds.

By the 1911 Census Nora, Thomas and their four children were living in Northampton and they all stated that they were born in Leeds.

On the 15th August 1940 a large number of enemy aircraft mounted an air raid on RAF Driffield and were intercepted approaching the Yorkshire coast The attackers split up and one aircraft dropped four HE bombs over the Byass Avenue - St Alban Road area of Bridlington. This caused considerable damage to property and people had remarkable escapes but one civilian, 68 year old Norah Riley of 37 St. Cuthbert Road, Bridlington, was killed when her house received a direct hit from a 250kg high explosive bomb. The force of the explosion was such that the body of Nora Riley was never found and there was no subsequent burial or a record of any funeral service.

It is thought that Nora's husband was not in the house at the time and he left Bridlington soon after the end of WW2. A probable match for his death is that of a 'Thomas C Riley, age 79, who died in the March quarter of 1950, registered at Newcastle'.

Norah Riley is commemorated on the following memorials:

- Bridlington War Memorial.
- St Mary (the Priory) Parish Church Roll of Honour.
- The Commonwealth War Graves Commission Website (Civilian War Dead).

Seaman RICHARD JAMES RIPLEY

The Royal Navy, Service No. LT/X 19603A

Richard James Ripley was born in Bridlington his birth being registered in the June quarter of 1915. Richard was the son of Matthew and Jean Elizabeth Ripley (nee Webster) of 7 Jubilee Avenue Sewerby Road, Bridlington.

After leaving school Richard worked as a fisherman on the Bridlington motor cobles *Irene* and *Primrose*.

Richard was a Royal Navy Reservist from 1936 and was called up on the outbreak of WW2.and served with the Royal Naval Reserve (Patrol Service). In 1940 Richard was part of the crew of H.M. Trawler *Benvolio*.

HMT *Benvolio* was a fishing trawler of 352 gross tons, built by Cochrane's of Selby and launched in 1930. In 1939, *Benvolio* appears to have been sold or transferred to Shire Trawlers Ltd (W. A. Bennett) of Grimsby and re-registered GY183. *Benvolio* was requisitioned in 1939 and converted to a minesweeper.

Benvolio H347 (not recorded)

HMT *Benvolio* had been damaged by mines and her luck ran out on the 23rd February 1940 when she was destroyed by a mine off the Humber. All 10 members of her crew were lost including 24 year old Richard James Ripley.

Richard James Ripley has no known grave and is commemorated on Panel 2, Column 3 of the Royal Navy Memorial in Lowestoft Suffolk. He is also commemorated on the following memorials:

- Bridlington War Memorial.
- St Mary (The Priory) Parish Church Roll of Honour.
- The Commonwealth War Graves Commission Website.

Lance Corporal *JOSEPH ROBINSON*

The Green Howards (Alexandra, Princess of Wales's Own Yorkshire Regiment), Service No. 4390630, Bridlington School Old Boy

Joseph Robinson was born in the December quarter of 1919 registered in Scarborough district. Joseph was the son of Joseph Walter and Margaret Frances Robinson (nee Atkinson) of Filey. He came to Bridlington School in 1931 and left in 1939. Joseph served in the 5th Battalion (Territorial Army) of the Green Howards. The 5th Battalion formed in 1938 as a Territorial Force battalion and was part of the British Expeditionary Force (BEF) in 1939/1940.

Joseph Robinson (Bridlington School)

The 5th Battalion served in 150th Brigade, 50th (Northumbrian) Division in France and Flanders. The BEF was involved in the later stages of the defence of Belgium following the German invasion in May 1940 and suffered many casualties in covering the withdrawal to Dunkirk.

20 year old Lance Corporal Joseph Robinson was killed in action on the 26th May 1940 while taking part in the heavy fighting in the defence of Ypres. A number of those killed during the battle were originally buried where they died, but in 1941 they were brought in for reburial in Bus House Cemetery in West-Vlaanderen in Belgium. This cemetery stands behind a farm-house that was called 'Bus House'

Bus House Cemetery (CWGC)

Lance Corporal Joseph Robinson is in buried in grave reference AA-9 and as he was not a Bridlington resident he is not recorded on the Bridlington War Memorial or the Priory Roll of Honour but he is commemorated on the following memorials.

- Bridlington School Second World War Roll of Honour.
- The Commonwealth War Graves Commission Website.

Flight Lieutenant (Navigator) JOHN HENRY ROBSON DFC.

The Royal Air Force, Service No. 121950, Bridlington School Old Boy

John Henry Robson was born in Bridlington on the 25th May 1920. He was the only son of Thomas Henry (Harry) and Annie Robson (nee Woodcock) of the Promenade Bridlington. His father was a grocer and John came to Bridlington School in 1931 and left in 1939. He joined the RAFVR in 1940 and became an observer based at Kinross. In February 1942 John married Miss Betty Arlene Jackson of Halifax whom he met while she was serving in the Women's Auxiliary Air Force in Bridlington.

John Robson (Bridlington School)

After their marriage they lived at 99 the Promenade in Bridlington. John rose to the rank of Flight Lieutenant (Navigator) with 139 Pathfinder Squadron equipped with De Haviland Mosquitoes. By January 1945 the squadron was stationed at Upwood in Cambridgeshire. John's award of the Distinguished Flying Cross was for *'devotion to duty'* after completing over 100 operational flights over enemy occupied Europe. The award was published in the London Gazette on 14 November 1944.

John Henry Robson was killed in action on the 15th January 1945 aged 24. His aircraft Mosquito XVI MM132 (XD-?) took off at 9.05 p.m. as part of a diversionary operation to Berlin while the Main Force attacked a synthetic oil plant. Bad weather set in on the return journey and while making a beam-guided approach to Little Staughton airfield the aircraft crashed into a tree about one mile short of the runway. In November 1946 John's widow and his mother collected his DFC from HM the King at Buckingham Palace. John Henry Robson was buried in Bridlington Cemetery, grave reference W34.   John Robson's grave (C Bonnett)

John Robson is also commemorated on the following memorials.
- Bridlington School Second World War Roll of Honour.
- Bridlington War Memorial.
- St Mary (The Priory) Parish Church Roll of Honour.
- The Commonwealth War Graves Commission Website.

Gunner NORMAN COOKE ROBSON

The Royal Artillery, Service No. 1764990

Norman Robson was born in the March quarter of 1905 the son of James Harold and Maud Maria Robson (nee Cooke) of 93 Hilderthorpe Road. His father died in 1911 and they moved in with his mother's father and brother at 67 Nelson Street Bridlington. Norman was educated at Hilderthorpe School and was a member of the Church Lads Brigade and was a chorister at Emmanuel Church. After leaving school Norman worked as a painter and decorator with Robsons of High Street Bridlington. In the March quarter of 1928 Norman married Elisabeth Broumpton at the Priory Church in Bridlington.

Norman and Elisabeth lived at 16 Scarborough Road in Bridlington and had two sons whom they named Norman and Brian. In WW2 Norman Robson was serving in the Eighth Army as a Gunner with 118 Battery 30th Regiment L.A.A. Royal Artillery. At the beginning of November 1942 the Eighth Army defeated Rommel in the decisive Second Battle of El Alamein, pursuing the defeated Axis army across Libya.

38 year old Norman was wounded at the second battle of El Alamein and died of his wounds in Egypt on the 3rd April 1943 just before the Axis forces in North Africa surrendered in May 1943.

Norman Robson (family archive)

Norman Robson was buried in Heliopolis War Cemetery, Egypt, grave reference 3. B. 33.

Norman's grave (family archive)

Norman is also commemorated on the following memorials:
- Bridlington War Memorial.
- St Mary (The Priory) Parish Church Roll of Honour.
- Christ Church Roll of Honour.
- The Commonwealth War Graves Commission Website.

Major HAROLD DENNIS ROGERS

The Parachute Regiment, Service No. 153174,
Bridlington School Old Boy

Harold Dennis Rogers was born in Yate Gloucestershire in December 1910. He was the son of Cyril Evelyn and Amy Florence Rogers (nee Edwards). Harold came to Bridlington School in 1923 and left in 1927. On leaving School he developed a successful building business in Springfield Avenue in Bridlington and in 1935 he married Doris Elizabeth Sugden and they lived at 26 Kingsgate in Bridlington where they had one daughter called Jill in 1937.

Harold Rogers (Bridlington School)

Harold was prominent in the Bridlington Rugby Club, the Londesborough Lodge of Freemasons and the Royal Yorkshire Yacht Club where he was part owner of the yacht *Avis*. Harold was also one of the first recruits to the 7th Battalion (TA), The Green Howards and as Sergeant Harold Rogers was mobilized on the outbreak of the war and went to France with the BEF. He was evacuated from Dunkirk and later commissioned and transferred to the 10th Green Howards. As Major Harold Rogers he remained with the battalion when it was transferred to the Parachute Regiment in May 1943 as its 12th (Yorkshire) Battalion. In June 1944 the 12th Battalion was in the 5th Airborne Brigade, 6th Airborne Division and was dropped into Normandy in the early hours of D-Day (6 June 1944) with Major Harold Rogers in command of `B' Co. On 12 June the seriously depleted battalion attacked and cleared the enemy out of Breville and was then subjected to enemy mortar fire and shelling plus misdirected Allied fire. 33 year old Harold Rogers was killed in action while ordering his men to dig in and was buried in Ranville War Cemetery in Calvados, France, grave reference IVA J 17. He is also commemorated on the following memorials:

- Bridlington School Second World War Roll of Honour.
- Bridlington War Memorial.
- St Mary (The Priory) Parish Church Roll of Honour.
- The Commonwealth War Graves Commission Website. (He is recorded as Harry by the CWGC)

Gunner PERCY ROGERS

The Royal Artillery, Service No. 901398

Percy Rogers was born in the March quarter of 1918 in Wrexham Denbighshire. He was the son of William and Bessie Rogers (nee Edwards). In WW2 Percy was serving as a Gunner with 61 (The Denbighshire Yeomanry) Medium Regiment RA. The Denbighshire Yeomanry was one of the Yeomanry Regiments that were re-roled as Royal Artillery units. It was amalgamated with the 61st Medium Brigade Royal Garrison Artillery (the former Carnarvonshire Artillery Volunteers), to form 61 Medium Regiment R.A. (Caernarvon and Denbigh Yeomanry) which saw service in France during 1939-1940) and returned to the UK after the Dunkirk evacuation. In July 1940 Percy Rogers was in Bridlington.

On the 11 July 1940, a lone Ju88 of KG 30 on a hit and run raid on Bridlington dropped a stick of high explosive bombs between Bridlington Railway Station and Hilderthorpe Road. Gunner Percy Rogers R.A. and five civilians were killed in this Air Raid that devastated Hilderthorpe Road.

Hilderthorpe Road
(Bridlington Local Studies Library)

Percy Rogers was buried in Coedpoeth Cemetery and Memorial Garden, Denbighshire, Wales, grave reference Sec. D. Grave 1872.

As he was not a Bridlington Resident Percy is not recorded on the Bridlington War Memorial but he is commemorated on the following memorials:

- St Mary (The Priory) Parish Church Roll of Honour.
- The Commonwealth War Graves Commission Website.

Second Lieutenant RONALD HOSKINS ROMYN
The Royal Sussex Regiment, Service No. 137321

Ronald Hoskins Romyn was born in Sussex in the March quarter of 1908 the youngest son of John Richard Dickson and Mabel Eleanor Romyn (nee Selwyn) of 12 Cardigan Road Bridlington. Ronald was a well known local golfer and won "The Bystander" golf trophy in 1937 and 1939. In the December quarter of 1939 Ronald married Dorothy May Pentith in Buckrose district which covers Bridlington. When Ronald enlisted they were living at 10 Belvedere Parade in Bridlington.

At the beginning of WW2 Ronald joined the Green Howards but later transferred to the Royal Sussex Regiment where he served as a Second Lieutenant with the 9th Battalion. The 9th Battalion was raised by Lt. Col. (later Field Marshal) Gerald Templer in the aftermath of Dunkirk and was initially on coastal defence duties.

33 year old Ronald Hoskins Romyn died on the 13th November 1940. Initial confirmation was received that he died of a revolver accident in Swansea. The subsequent inquest by the Swansea Borough Coroner revealed that he had been found dead, in the room of a house in which he was billeted, with a pistol shot through the head.

The Coroner remarked on the absence of a motive for the act and a verdict was returned that death was due to a wound in the brain caused by shooting himself whilst the balance of his mind was disturbed.

Second Lieutenant Ronald Hoskins Romyn was buried in Swansea (Oystermouth) Cemetery Wales grave reference Section N Grave 15.

Ronald's grave (Ancestry.co.uk)

Ronald is also commemorated on the following memorials:

- Bridlington War Memorial.
- St Mary (The Priory) Parish Church Roll of Honour.
- The Commonwealth War Graves Commission Website.

Sergeant (Air Bomber) JOHN RAYMOND ROUNDING

The Royal Air Force, Service No. 1239106, Bridlington School Old Boy

John Raymond Rounding was born in Bridlington in the December quarter of 1922 the only son of Robert and Mary Rounding (nee Baker) of Moor Croft Farm, Harpham. John came to Bridlington School in 1930 and left in 1938. On leaving School he worked as a newspaper reporter and then joined his father on the farm. Despite being in a reserved occupation, in 1942 he volunteered for aircrew duties in the RAF and was assigned to the RAFVR. John Rounding was serving as a Sergeant (Air Bomber) with 550 Squadron that formed in 1943.

John Rounding (Bridlington School)

In 1944 550 Squadron was serving in No. 1 Group, Bomber Command, stationed at Waltham, Lincolnshire and equipped with the Avro Lancaster heavy bomber.

On the 2nd January 1944 his aircraft, Lancaster DV345 (BQ-?), took off at five minutes past midnight as part of a force of 383 aircraft on an operation to bomb Berlin. John Raymond Rounding aged 21 was killed in action when on its return the aircraft crashed at 7.08 am. at Whaplode Drove, 8 miles south-east of Spalding in Lincolnshire. There were no other survivors and another 37 aircraft were lost on the same raid.

Sergeant (Air Bomber) John Raymond Rounding was buried in Harpham (St. John of Beverley) churchyard, grave reference D 6. There was a Memorial Chair to him in Bridlington School but as he was not a Bridlington resident he is not recorded on the Bridlington War Memorial or the Priory Roll of Honour but he is commemorated on the following memorials.

John Rounding's grave (C Bonnett)

- Bridlington School Second World War Roll of Honour.
- The Commonwealth War Graves Commission Website.

Fireman and Trimmer GEORGE ELLIOTT ROUTLEDGE

The Merchant Navy, Service No. not known

George Elliott Routledge was born in Newcastle on Tyne in the March quarter of 1898 the son of George and Rebecca Routledge. In the March quarter of 1921 George Elliott Routledge married Mary E. Goodwill in Newcastle on Tyne and they lived at 4 Grenford Road Newcastle. When WW2 started George was serving as a fireman and trimmer in the Merchant Navy.

In January 1940 George was a member of the crew of the coal cargo ship S.S. *Stanburn* (London). The S.S. *Stanburn* was built in 1924 as the SS *Hebburn* and renamed *Stanburn* in 1938 when purchased from W.A. Souter & Co., Newcastle by the Stanhope Steam Ship Company of London.

SS Stanburn (wrecksite.eu)

On the 29th January 1940 'SS *Stanburn* (2,881t) was bombed and sunk off Flamborough Head by German aircraft, probably by Heinkel He111 bombers from X Fliegerkorps. Captain Lewis and twenty-five of her crew were killed in the attack, there were only three survivors. Unfortunately George Elliott Routledge was one of those killed.

George Elliott Routledge age 42 of 4 Greenford Road Newcastle was found drowned off Bridlington and was buried in Bridlington Cemetery, grave reference W 23.

The grave of George Routledge (C Bonnett)

George is not recorded on the Bridlington War Memorial or the Priory Roll of Honour. Other than his burial in Bridlington he is not believed to have any connection to the Town. George Elliott Routledge is also commemorated on the following memorial.

- The Commonwealth War Graves Commission Website.

Sergeant (WOP/AG) JOSEPH PETER ROWLEY

The Royal Air Force, Service No. 1579631, Bridlington School Old Boy

Joseph Peter Rowley was born in Derby in the June quarter of 1922 the son of Joseph and Kate Stafford Rowley (nee Sharpe) of 91 Headlands Kettering, Northamptonshire. He came to Bridlington School in 1933 and left in 1938. While at Bridlington School he was awarded his Cricket Colours. During WW2 Joseph Peter Rowley joined the RAF, volunteered for air crew training and was assigned to the Royal Air Force Volunteer Reserve (RAFVR). Joseph served as a Sergeant (Wireless Operator/Air Gunner) with 101 Sqn.

Joseph Rowley (Bridlington School)

101 Squadron re-formed in 1928. In August 1944 it was stationed at Ludford Magna, Leicestershire in 1 Group, Bomber Command and was equipped with Avro Lancaster heavy bombers. Some aircraft carried special equipment to jam enemy radio frequencies, and also German speaking wireless operators to confuse enemy night fighter crews and their controllers.

Joseph Peter Rowley was killed in action on the 26th August 1944 aged 22. His aircraft Lancaster NN705 (SR-O) had taken off at 8.32 p.m. as part of a force of 412 aircraft on an operation to bomb the Opel motor factory at Russelsheim, Germany. Lancaster NN705 (SR-O) crashed in France, one crew member evaded capture but the rest of the crew were killed. The aircraft was carrying nine crew, instead of the more usual seven crew. The extra two men were probably operating jamming equipment. Another 14 aircraft were lost on the same raid.

Sergeant Joseph Peter Rowley was buried in Choloy War Cemetery, Meurthe-et-Moselle in France grave reference 1.D.5. As he was not a Bridlington resident he is not recorded on the Bridlington War Memorial or the Priory Roll of Honour but he is commemorated on the following memorials.

- Bridlington School Second World War Roll of Honour.
- The Commonwealth War Graves Commission Website.

FRANK LINCOLN RUSSELL

Civilian, Bridlington School Old Boy

Frank Lincoln Russell was born in the September quarter of 1909 registered in Stafford district. He was the son of the Reverend William Ernest Russell, a Wesleyn Methodist minister, and Martha Russell (nee Fox). Frank was a pupil at Bridlington School from 1918 to1921 and later attended London University, where he was awarded a BA degree.

Frank Russell (Bridlington School)

His mother Martha died in 1929 at Fareham Hampshire and in the December quarter of 1931 his father married Adelade Ellen Day at Fareham.

On the 11 September 1942, Frank Russell of 14 Lee Street, Louth in Lincolnshire, was visiting his father and step mother who lived at 'Wilmar'11 Marlborough Road, Parkstone Dorset when an air raid took place and Frank and his father (now a retired minister) were both killed.

33 year old Frank Lincoln Russell was buried at a Cemetery in Poole, Dorset. Frank was not a Bridlington resident so he is not recorded on the Bridlington War Memorial or the Priory Roll of Honour but he is commemorated on the following memorials.

- Bridlington School Second World War Roll of Honour.
- The Commonwealth War Graves Commission Website (Civilian War Dead).

Pioneer JOSEPH SAMPSON

The Pioneer Corps, Service No. 13005630

Joseph Sampson was born in Bridlington in the October quarter of 1902, the son of Joseph and Maria Jane Sampson (nee Carr).

Joseph married Edith May Danby in the September quarter of 1928 in Bridlington. Joseph and May had two daughters, Annie and Dorothy and they all lived at 32 St. John Street in Bridlington. Joseph was a Greengrocer.

Joseph Sampson
(via Steve Adamson)

In WW2 Joseph served from the 5 January 1940 to the 28 June 1943 in the Pioneer Corps. The Royal Pioneer Corps was a British Army combatant corps used for light engineering tasks. It was formed in 1939 and Pioneer units performed a wide variety of tasks in all theatres of war, handling all types of stores, laying prefabricated track on the beaches and stretcher-bearing, constructed airfields, roads and erected bridges. A large number of Pioneers served in France with the British Expeditionary Force.

Joseph died on the 12th November 1943 at 38 West Street Bridlington from a bronchial illness caused by wounds from his war service.

Joseph Sampson was buried in Bridlington Cemetery, grave reference Q104 and he is also commemorated on the following memorials.

- Bridlington War Memorial.
- St Mary (The Priory) Parish Church Roll of Honour.

Note. Joseph Sampson is not listed on the Commonwealth War Graves Commission Website.

Sergeant (WOP/AG) GERALD SANDERSON

The Royal Air Force, Service No. 1589903, Bridlington School Old Boy

Gerald Sanderson was born in the March quarter of 1912 registered in Sculcoates. Gerald was the son of Herbert and Florence Sanderson (nee Davis) of Bridlington. He came to Bridlington School in 1924 and left in 1927. On leaving School he went into business as a builder and in the December quarter of 1941 Gerald married Nancy Honorah Hair the marriage being registered in Hull. Gerald and Nancy lived at 19 George Street Bridlington and they had one son whom they named Gerald R. Sanderson.

Gerald Sanderson (Bridlington School)

In WW2 Gerald joined the RAF, volunteered for air crew training and was assigned to the Royal Air Force Volunteer Reserve (RAFVR). While on deferred service, he trained with the Bridlington squadron of the Air Training Corps. By 1945 he was serving as a Sergeant (Wireless Operator/Air Gunner) with 115 Squadron. 115 Squadron re-formed in 1937 and served in 3 Group, Bomber Command. In February 1945 it was stationed at Witchford, Cambridgeshire and equipped with Avro Lancaster heavy bombers.

33 year old Sergeant Gerald Sanderson was killed in action on the 15th February 1945 when his Lancaster III LM725 (KO-X) crashed at Haveluy, France, about 9 km west-south-west of Valenciennes. There were no survivors and Gerald was killed on his first operation. Another 12 aircraft were lost out of the 717 aircraft sent to bomb industrial targets at Chemnitz in Germany.

Gerald Sanderson was buried in Haveluy Communal Cemetery, Nord, France, collective Grave No. 7. He is commemorated on the following memorials:

- Bridlington School Second World War Roll of Honour.
- Bridlington War Memorial.
- St Mary (The Priory) Parish Church Roll of Honour.
- The Commonwealth War Graves Commission Website.

Trooper KEITH SANGWIN

The Fife and Forfar Yeomanry, Service No: 7916751
Bridlington School Old Boy

Keith Sangwin was born in 1914 the son of Joseph Buck Sangwin and Florence Elizabeth Sangwin (nee Stephenson) of 336 Beverley Road, Hull. Keith Sangwin came to Bridlington School in 1927 and left in 1930.

Keith followed a commercial career after leaving school and was a popular member of the Bridlington Rugby Union Football Club. He married Miss Dorothea Mary Seeley Matthews, daughter of the Vicar of Holy Trinity Church, Bridlington. Their daughter was three months old when her father was killed and he never saw her.

Keith Sangwin (Bridlington School)

Keith Sangwin served as a Trooper with the 2nd Fife and Forfar Yeomanry, Royal Armoured Corps. The 2nd Fife and Forfar Yeomanry had formed in 1939 as a duplicate of the 1st Regiment which was a Territorial unit. It joined the 29th Armoured Brigade, 11th Armoured Division in 1941 and on the 13th June 1944 it landed in Normandy. The 2nd Fife and Forfar Yeomanry was equipped with Sherman tanks and took part in the battles of the Odon, Bourgebus Ridge, Mont Pincon and the capture of Antwerp.

Trooper Keith Sangwin aged 30, died of wounds on the 16th December 1944 in Belgium and was buried in Schoonselhof Cemetery, Antwerp, grave reference I. C. 33. He is commemorated on the following memorials:

- Bridlington School Second World War Roll of Honour.
- Bridlington War Memorial.
- St Mary (The Priory) Parish Church Roll of Honour.
- The Commonwealth War Graves Commission Website.

Gunner CHARLES SAWDEN

The Royal Artillery, Service No. 1784746

Charles Sawden was born on the 2nd July 1906 the fifth son of James and Jane Annie Sawden (nee Claxton). In 1911 the family lived at 2 Rope Walk in Bridlington. Before enlistment in WW2 Charles worked at the Cliff Café in Sewerby and lived at 3 Jubilee Avenue in Bridlington.

Charles Sawden served with No. 6 Battery, 3 Maritime A.A. Regiment Royal Artillery. No. 3 Maritime A.A. Regiment had its headquarters at Thornbury and No. 6 Battery covered South Devon, South Wales and the Severn Estuary.

The Maritime RA had its beginnings in the early part of the war when the Admiralty requested the RA to provide 500, 2 man Light Machine Gun (LMG) teams to provide AA defence on merchant coasters.

With the increase in attacks on shipping, the Maritime Anti-Aircraft Regiment RA was formed in 1941, initially with 3 LMG Regiments and 1 Bofors 40mm Regiment.

In January 1943 the regiment was re-titled Maritime Royal Artillery.

Gunner Charles Sawden, age 35, was wounded while serving in West Africa and was brought back to Hairmyers Military Hospital, East Kilburn, Lanarkshire Scotland where he died on the 12th March 1942.

Charles was brought home from Scotland and was buried in Bridlington Cemetery, grave reference W 33.

The grave of Charles Sawden (C Bonnett)

Charles Sawden is also commemorated on the following memorials:

- Bridlington War Memorial.
- St Mary (The Priory) Parish Church Roll of Honour.
- The Commonwealth War Graves Commission Website.

Staff Sergeant *JOHN BENNETT SAWDON*

The Royal Engineers, Service No. 7393581, Bridlington School Old Boy

John Bennett Sawdon was born in the June quarter of 1905 registered in Pickering. John was the son of Richard and Alice Sawdon (nee Bennett) and he came to Bridlington School in 1919 and left in 1921. On leaving School John worked in the building trade and was employed by his uncle, John Sawdon of Filey.

In the September quarter of 1930 John Bennett Sawdon married Rachel Wright of Filey and they had two daughters.

John Sawdon (Bridlington School)

Although in a reserved occupation, John Bennett Sawdon volunteered in 1942 and joined the Royal Engineers and spent most of his service in Northern Ireland attached to the 28th Field Hygiene Section, Royal Army Medical Corps.

40 year old Staff Sergeant John Bennett Sawdon collapsed and died suddenly of a previously undiagnosed heart disease on the 25th June 1945 the death being registered at Haverford West Pembroke Wales. At the time of his death John Sawdon was in charge of a platoon that was assisting a farmer in haymaking,

John Sawdon was buried in Bridlington Cemetery, grave reference M 131.

John Bennett Sawdon's grave (C Bonnett)

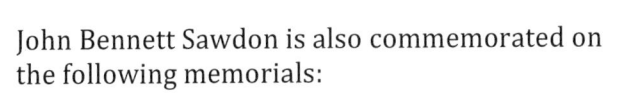

John Bennett Sawdon is also commemorated on the following memorials:

- Bridlington School Second World War Roll of Honour.
- Bridlington War Memorial.
- St Mary (The Priory) Parish Church Roll of Honour.
- The Commonwealth War Graves Commission Website.

ESTHER SHAW

Civilian

Esther Shaw was born in 1915, the daughter of Mr. and Mrs. John Grantham Shaw of 49 Eighteenth Avenue, North Hull Estate, Hull.

25 year old Esther Shaw of 7 Oxford Street, Bridlington was working as an hotel maid at the Britannia Hotel in Prince Street in 1940.

On Wednesday the 21 August 1940, at about 15.30 hours, a lone bomber made an attack on the harbour but missed and the four high explosive 250kg bombs landed in the town. One bomb hit the Britannia Hotel where Esther was working on the top floor, half of the hotel was destroyed and Esther and a soldier, Gunner Edmund R Beecroft, were both killed.

The Britannia Hotel (Bridlington Local Studies Library)

Esther Shaw was buried in Bridlington Cemetery on the 24 August 1940, grave reference W55 and is commemorated on the following memorials:

- Bridlington War Memorial.
- St Mary (the Priory) Parish Church Roll of Honour.
- The Commonwealth War Graves Commission Website (Civilian War Dead).

This largely undamaged teapot was found in the rubble of the Britannia Hotel on the morning of Thursday 22nd August after the raid was over and was given to Pat Keane who has kindly allowed us to photograph it for inclusion in this book.

Private JOHN J. SHAW

The West Yorkshire Regiment (Prince of Wales's Own)
Service No: 2344628

John J Shaw was born in 1914 the son of Mr. and Mrs. J. Shaw, of Bridlington. John was the husband of Edith Mary Shaw and they lived at 7 Oxford Street, Bridlington..

In WW2 John served with the 1st Battalion the West Yorkshire Regiment.

When the War commenced in 1939, the 1st West Yorkshire were in India performing the normal Imperial garrison duties, but were moved by sea to Rangoon immediately following the Japanese Invasion. Joining the battle at Pegu, the battalion was constantly involved in heavy fighting throughout the terrible retreat from Burma, but gained a formidable reputation which was to remain for the rest of the war. They returned to the Assam front in 1943, and were severely tested the following year in the desperate battles around Imphal.

Private John J Shaw died on the 24th May 1944, age 30, and was buried in Maynamati War Cemetery Bangladesh, grave reference1. E. 10,

The cemetery is dominated by a small flat-topped hill crowned with indigenous flowering and evergreen trees. On a terrace about half-way up the hill, facing the entrance, stands the Cross of Sacrifice.

Maynamati War Cemetery (CWGC)

John J Shaw is also commemorated on the following memorials:
- Bridlington War Memorial.
- St Mary (The Priory) Parish Church Roll of Honour.
- Christ Church Roll of Honour
- The Commonwealth War Graves Commission Website.

Corporal HARRY SHIPPEY

The Green Howards, (Alexandra, Princess of Wales's Own Yorkshire Regiment), Service No. 4389438

Harry Shippey was born in Bridlington on the 8th July 1917 the son of John William and Kate Shippey (nee Bishop) of 132 Hilderthorpe Road. Harry worked as a bricklayer with Messrs C. Grant & Co of Bridlington and in the December quarter of 1939 Harry married Gladys Victoria May Thompson and they had a daughter whom they named Hazel.

Harry served with the 1st Battalion, Green Howards (Yorkshire Regiment) and before he enlisted his address was 17 Fairfield Road, Bridlington. The 1st Battalion Green Howards went over to France in 1939 as part of the British Expeditionary Force. They were brought back to England before the Dunkirk evacuation and sailed to Norway to try and hold back the German invasion. They took part in the battle of Otta where for 24 hours the Green Howards held back 7 German battalions, Stuka dive bombers and heavy artillery. As Norway fell the British troops sailed back to Britain.

After a couple of years on the Home Front, the 1st Battalion sailed to India in 1942. By the start of 1943 the 1st Battalion of the Green Howards were making progress in their epic journey as part of the 15th Brigade from India through Persia, and Syria, towards Egypt. They arrived on the shores of occupied Sicily on the 10th July 1943. 26 year old Corporal Harry Shippey was killed in action on the 11th August 1943 during the heavy fighting in Sicily and was buried in Catania War Cemetery, Sicily, grave reference IV. A. 29.

Catania War Cemetery (CWGC)

Harry Shippey is also commemorated on the following memorials:

- Bridlington War Memorial.
- St Mary (The Priory) Parish Church Roll of Honour.
- Christ Church Roll of Honour
- The Commonwealth War Graves Commission Website.

Lieutenant BERNARD SIMPSON

The Royal Navy, Service No. not known

Bernard Simpson was born in the June quarter of 1909 registered in the Sculcoates district of Hull. Bernard was the youngest son of Herbert and Amelia Simpson (nee Smith) who were living in Tennyson Avenue Bridlington in 1928. After leaving school Bernard joined the Merchant Navy where he gained his Masters Ticket. As a qualified Master he was also in the Royal Naval Reserve (RNR). When the Royal Naval Reserve was called up for war service Bernard served as a Lieutenant. In 1940 he married Ellen Riordan in Portsmouth Hampshire and they lived in Hendon Middlesex and they had one daughter.

By 1942 Bernard was an officer on H.M.S. *Hollyhock* (K64), a Flower Class Corvette built by John Crown & Sons Ltd of Sunderland in 1939. H.M.S. *Hollyhock* operated with the 3rd Escort Group in Western Approaches Command and was later based in Iceland escorting Atlantic convoys. In November 1941 HMS *Hollyhock* transferred to a South African Flotilla based at Freetown and in March 1942 she moved to Colombo for convoy escort duties in the Indian Ocean. In early April 1942, HMS *Hollyhock* was the escort of the Fleet Support Tanker SS *Athelstane* during fleet operations searching the Indian Ocean for Japanese forces. The Japanese found them first and on the 9th April 1942 HMS *Hollyhock* was bombed and sunk by Japanese aircraft from the carrier *Soryu* 30 miles SSE of Batticaloa, Ceylon with the loss of 53 of the ship's company. Also sunk that day were the aircraft carrier *Hermes*, the Australian destroyer *Vampire*, SS *Athelstane* and another tanker.

HMS *Hollyhock* (Luis Photos)

32 year old Lieutenant Bernard Simpson died in action on the 9th April 1942 when *Hollyhock* was sunk. Bernard has no known grave and is commemorated on Panel 71, Column 1, of the Portsmouth Naval Memorial. Bernard is also commemorated on the following memorials:

- Bridlington War Memorial.
- St Mary (The Priory) Parish Church Roll of Honour.
- Christ Church Roll of Honour
- The Commonwealth War Graves Commission Website.

Gunner NORMAN SIMPSON

The Royal Artillery, Service Number. 803249

Norman Simpson was born on the 12th December 1907 in Walkington, Yorkshire. He was the son of Norman and Clara Simpson (nee Tyson) of 27 Westbourne Avenue Bridlington. His father Norman was a builder.

Norman never married and became a bricklayer until he joined the Army on the 7th July 1930 and became a gunner in the Royal Horse Artillery, (D Battery, RHA, Aldershot in 1930).

In 1934 Norman was thrown from a horse and was in Broadgates Hospital, Beverley until he died from his injuries on the 3rd April 1941.

Norman Simpson was buried on the 8th April 1941 in Queensgate Cemetery, Beverley, plot D28, but his grave has no headstone or Cross.

Norman is commemorated on the following memorials:

- Bridlington War Memorial.
- St Mary (The Priory) Parish Church Roll of Honour.
- The Commonwealth War Graves Commission Website.

Private STANLEY SIMPSON

The South Staffordshire Regiment, Service No. 4342573

Stanley Simpson was the youngest son of Norman and Clara Simpson (nee Tyson) of 27 Westbourne Avenue Bridlington. Stanley was born in 1914 in Hull and never married. His father was a builder and he was the younger brother of Norman Simpson. Stanley joined the Army in 1932 and served in India for nine years with the East Yorkshire Regiment.

Stanley Simpson (D Flower)

In July 1944 Stanley transferred to the 1/6th Battalion of the South Staffordshire Regiment. The 1st/6th Battalion, South Staffordshire Regiment were part of 177 Brigade, 59th Division and landed on Juno Beach in Normandy on June 25th. During July they took part in Operation Charnwood and Pomegranate. From August 6th-to the 14th they took part in the battle for the Orne River. 177 Brigade was ordered to secure the right flank of the division, and press south toward Thury-Harcourt. They encountered strong defensive positions on the Fresnay-Martinbeau ridge and the Division came under repeated attacks by combined Panzer and Panzer-Grenadiers at le Bas (today called Grimbosq Halte) as the Division advanced towards Thury-Harcourt, the enemy was still resisting strongly on all brigade fronts but Thury-Harcourt was taken on the 14th August 1944.

Private Stanley Simpson was killed on the 12th August 1944 during the final stages of the Orne River battle and was buried in Bayeux War Cemetery, Calvados, France, grave reference XXIII. C. 2.

Bayeux War Cemetery (CWGC)

Stanley Simpson is also commemorated on the following memorials:
- Bridlington War Memorial.
- St Mary (The Priory) Parish Church Roll of Honour.
- The Commonwealth War Graves Commission Website.

Lieutenant HENRY JAMES SLAUGHTER

The Royal Navy, Service No. J104138

Henry James Slaughter was born on the 5th March 1906 in Chatham Kent, the son of James Henry and Edith Mary Slaughter (nee Sutcliffe). By the 1911 Census the family was living at 47 Upper Luton Road, Chatham Kent and his father James (Jas) Henry was a Sergeant in the Royal Marine Light Infantry (RMLI). Henry James Slaughter married Ellen Emily Bannister (nee Bushan) in the September quarter of 1938 registered in Buckrose district which included Bridlington.

In WW2 Henry James Slaughter was a lieutenant Observer with No. 813 squadron FAA on the aircraft carrier HMS *Eagle*. *Eagle* spent the first nine months of World War II in the Indian Ocean and then the Mediterranean in May 1940, where she escorted multiple convoys to Malta and Greece and attacked Italian shipping, naval units and bases in the Eastern Mediterranean and participated in the Battle of Calabria in July.

HMS *Eagle* (Luis Photos)

On 11 November 1940 HMS *Eagle* took part in one of the most memorable Fleet Air Arm events in history when five of her aircraft were embarked in HMS *Illustrious* and took part in the attack on Italian battleships at Taranto where the Italian battleships *Cavour, Littorio* and *Duilio* were successfully torpedoed. Lieutenant Henry James Slaughter was the Observer on one of the Swordfish aircraft that was shot down by gunfire in the second wave and failed to return. Henry James Slaughter and his pilot Gerald W. Bayley were both killed.

After his death on the 11th November 1940, Henry James Slaughter was awarded a Mentioned in Despatches in January and May 1941. Henry is commemorated on Bay 1, Panel 2 of the FAA Lee-on-Solent Memorial. He is also commemorated on the following memorials:

- Bridlington War Memorial.
- St Mary (The Priory) Parish Church Roll of Honour.
- The Commonwealth War Graves Commission Website.

Group Captain BRIAN ARNOLD SMITH OBE (Military)

The Royal Air Force, Service No. not known, Bridlington School Old Boy

Brian Arnold Smith was born in 1889 the son of William Foster Smith and his wife Janet Maria (nee Lebbon) of 1 St. Johns Villas Filey. Brian came to Bridlington School in 1903 and left in 1907. While at the School he was awarded his Colours for Cricket and Football and was Captain of Cricket in 1906 and 1907. He was a School Prefect and was awarded an Open Scholarship in Science, a County Major Scholarship and an Ann Watson Exhibition.

Brian Smith (Bridlington School)

On leaving School Brian studied Science at Trinity College, Cambridge, and was awarded a First Class Degree. He became Science Master at Bridlington School for one term in 1911 and then moved to Tonbridge School, Kent. During the First World War Brian served in the Army and was mentioned in Despatches (MiD).

Brian Arnold Smith married Gladys Evnor Edwards on the 5th February 1918 at All Saints Church Hampstead London.

Brian joined the RAF after WW1 and became a lecturer at the RAF College Cranwell. In 1944 he became Deputy Director of Education at the Air Ministry and was appointed as an Officer of the Order of the British Empire (Military Division) in 1945.

57 years old Group Captain Bryan Arnold Smith OBE (Military) died of illness on the 9th May 1946 at 4 Randolph Gardens London NW6 the strain of the war years having contributed towards his death.

Brian's death is not recorded by the Commonwealth War Graves Commission and he was not a Bridlington resident so he is not recorded on the Bridlington War Memorial or the Priory Roll of Honour but he is commemorated on the following memorial.

- Bridlington School Second World War Roll of Honour.

Corporal MALCOLM BOSTON SMITH

The East Yorkshire Regiment (Duke of York's Own), Service No. 4344752, Bridlington School Old Boy

Malcolm Boston Smith was born in the December quarter of 1920 registered in Skirlaugh district. Malcolm was the son of Arnold Boston and Sarah Ellen Smith (nee Thompson) of Leys House Atwick Road Hornsea. He came to Bridlington School in 1934 and left in 1937, being one of four brothers who attended the School. During WW2 Malcolm served with the 5th Battalion (Territorial Army) of the East Yorkshire Regiment (Duke of York's Own).

Malcolm Smith (Bridlington School)

The Regiment was reformed in April 1939 under the plan to double the size of the Territorial Army. It served in the 69th Brigade, 23rd (2nd Northumbrian) Division which moved to France in April 1940, thus being caught up in the Dunkirk evacuation and in July 1940 the 69th Brigade was transferred to the 50th (Northumbrian) Division which moved to the Middle East in 1941.

Malcolm Boston Smith was killed in action on the 25 October 1942 during the Battle of Alamein when his battalion mounted a night attack against elements of the Italian Folgore Parachute Division. They encountered heavy small arms and mortar fire and more casualties were caused when the British artillery barrage fell short. The 22 year old Corporal was buried in El Alamein Cemetery, grave reference XX.B.6. There was a Memorial Chair to him in Bridlington School and in 1947 his father Arnold Boston Smith presented an oak table to St. Nicholas Church Hornsea in memory of his wife and two of his four sons (Paul and Malcolm) who died during the war. In 1959 the Hornsea WW2 Book of Remembrance was placed in a case upon the oak table. Malcolm was not a Bridlington resident so he is not recorded on the Bridlington War Memorial or the Priory Roll of Honour but he is commemorated on the following memorials.

- Bridlington School Second World War Roll of Honour.
- The Commonwealth War Graves Commission Website.

Marine PAUL BOSTON SMITH

The Royal Marines, Service No. PO/X104773
Bridlington School Old Boy

Paul Boston Smith was born in Cottingham in the June quarter of 1909 the son of Arnold Boston and Sarah Ellen Smith (nee Thompson) who were living at Holly House Hallgate Cottingham in 1911 and later at Leys House Atwick Road Hornsea. He came to Bridlington School in 1923 and left in 1926 and was one of four brothers who attended the School. Paul joined the Royal Marines in March 1941 and served for two years with a radio location (Radar) unit in the West Country.

Paul Smith (Bridlington School)

Paul contracted a severe illness and spent some time in hospital, after which he was placed on light duties. Marine Paul Boston Smith, aged 35, died of Illness in a Royal Naval hospital on the 31st December 1944. His death was registered in the Crosby, Liverpool Registration District.

Paul Boston Smith was buried in Hornsea (Southgate) Cemetery, grave reference A.AT.28 and there was a Memorial Chair to him in Bridlington School. In 1947 his father Arnold Boston Smith presented an oak table to St. Nicholas Church Hornsea in memory of his wife and two of his four sons (Paul and Malcolm) who died during the war. In 1959 the Hornsea WW2 Book of Remembrance was placed in a case upon the oak table.

The grave of Paul B Smith (C Bonnett)

Paul was not a Bridlington resident so he is not recorded on the Bridlington War Memorial or the Priory Roll of Honour but he is commemorated on the following memorials

- Bridlington School Second World War Roll of Honour.
- The Commonwealth War Graves Commission Website.

Private ROBERT SMITH

The Queen's Own Cameron Highlanders, Service No.4541510

Robert Smith was born in Bridlington in the June quarter of 1914 the son of Arthur and Margaret Isabel Smith (nee Mallory). In 1911 they were living at 91 St. John Street and later at 27 Victoria Road in Bridlington. Robert was educated at Burlington School and afterwards he served an apprenticeship as a bricklayer with Messrs. Smallwood (Builders). Robert was the husband of Minnie Smith of Hull.

Robert joined the Army in 1940 and served as a Private in the 2nd Battalion of the Queen's Own Cameron Highlanders in the Middle East.

In June 1941 the 2nd Queen's Own Cameron Highlanders along with C Squadron, 4Royal Tank Regiment formed the Halfaya Group of the Coast Force for Operation Battleaxes, a British Army operation to clear eastern Cyrenaica of German and Italian forces. The battle started on the 15 June 1941with Coast Force moving to capture Halfaya Pass. The attack began without artillery support for the Halfaya Group due to the artillery becoming bogged down in soft sand. Within a few hours all but two tanks from the 4RTR had been destroyed, The Cameron Highlanders continued their advance but were driven back by German armoured cars and motorised infantry.

Private Robert Smith, age 27, was killed in action on the 15 June 1941, the first day of the failed attack on Halfaya Pass. He is commemorated on Column 72 of the Land Forces panels of the Alamein Memorial.

Alamein Memorial (CWGC)

This memorial forms the entrance to Alamein War Cemetery and commemorates more than 8,500 soldiers of the Commonwealth who died in the campaigns in Egypt and Libya, and who have no known grave. Robert is also commemorated on the following memorials.

- Bridlington War Memorial.
- St Mary (The Priory) Parish Church Roll of Honour.
- The Commonwealth War Graves Commission Website.

BETTY SPEAR

Civilian

Betty Spear was born in Sculcoates in 1922, the daughter of Harold Whiting and Ada L Spear (nee Parkin) who married in Grimsby in 1915.

In 1940 Harold and Ada were living at 75 St. Columba Road and 19 year old Betty was at 49 Cardigan Road. Betty was working as a waitress at Foley's Cafe and Restaurant, 13 Prince Street, Bridlington.

On the 23rd August 1940 a lone Ju88 made a low level attack on Bridlington Harbour dropping four high explosive bombs. The third bomb completely wrecked Foley's Cafe and Restaurant, killed Betty Spear and three other civilians.

Foley's Café after the raid
(Bridlington Local Studies Library)

Betty Spear, who was 19 and unmarried, was buried in Bridlington Cemetery on 30 August 1940, grave ref X56.

Betty is commemorated on the following memorials:

- Bridlington War Memorial.
- St Mary (the Priory) Parish Church Roll of Honour.
- The Commonwealth War Graves Commission Website (Civilian War Dead).

Third Radio Officer GEORGE ALEXANDER STOREY

The Merchant Navy, Service No. not known, Bridlington School Old Boy

George Alexander Storey was born in the September quarter of 1921 registered in Morecombe. He was the son of James and Ethel Storey (of Bridlington). He came to Bridlington School in 1933 and left in 1938. George was the husband of E. Storey and they lived at 20 Wellington Road, Bridlington. George joined the Merchant Navy and in 1942 he was the Third Radio Officer on SS *Hartlebury*.

George Storey (Bridlington School)

The London registered SS *Hartlebury* displaced 5,082 tons and had a crew of 45 seamen and 11 gunners. In June 1942 she was bound from Sunderland to Archangelsk, Russia, with a cargo of 6 vehicles, 36 tanks 7 aircraft and 2,409 tons of military stores. SS *Hartlebury* joined the soon to be infamous Convoy PQ 17 at Reykjavik, Iceland.

The convoy of 57 ships, including escorts, set off on 27 June 1942. On the 4th July 1942, as the result of imprecise intelligence regarding the whereabouts of enemy heavy warships, including *Tirpitz, Hipper, Admiral Scheer* and *Lutzow*, the Royal Navy escort was withdrawn.

The convoy was ordered to scatter and this left the 34 merchant ships prey to attacks from about 200 enemy aircraft and nine U-boats. 23 vessels were sunk, including. SS *Hartlebury* on the 7th July, torpedoed by U-355 seventeen miles south of the lighthouse at Britvin, Novaya Zemlya at about 70° 17' north by 56° 10' east in the Barents Sea.

38 of the crew of SS *Hartlebury* were lost including 20 year old George Alexander Storey. He has no known grave and is commemorated on Panel 55 of the Merchant Navy Memorial, Tower Hill, London. George Alexander Storey is also commemorated on the following memorials:

- Bridlington School Second World War Roll of Honour.
- Bridlington War Memorial.
- St Mary (The Priory) Parish Church Roll of Honour.
- The Commonwealth War Graves Commission Website.

Private FRANK STUBBS

The York and Lancaster Regiment, Service No. 1134437

Frank Stubbs was born in the March quarter of 1918 registered in Doncaster. Frank was the son of Thorpe Person Stubbs and Hannah Stubbs (nee Simpson) of Postill Square Bridlington.

Frank saw war service with the 5th Battalion, the York and Lancaster Regiment. The 5th Battalion was a 1st Line Territorial Army unit that converted to the 67th Heavy Anti-Aircraft Regiment, RA in 1936.

The 67th (Y & L) HAA Regiment, Royal Artillery, served in the North African Campaign in 1941 before being transferred to India and then Burma where they were prominent at Imphal, and later at Mandalay. From October 1944 to January 1945 the regiment served as infantry due to the shortage of manpower. In 1946 Frank was serving in Victoria Barracks Beverley and on the 22 June 1946 28 year old Frank Stubbs was found hanging from a tree in Fishpond Wood near Walkington. At the subsequent inquest the Medical Officer at Victoria Barracks said that Frank had complained of headaches and arrangements had been made for him to visit a psychiatrist. In summing up the coroner said *"Undoubtedly his Service experiences in North Africa and elsewhere contributed to his death. What he had gone through was enough to disturb anyone"*. He recorded a verdict that Stubbs took his own life while the balance of his mind was disturbed.

Private Frank Stubbs was buried in Bridlington Cemetery, grave reference J298.

Frank's grave (C Bonnett)

Frank Stubbs is not recorded on the Bridlington or Priory memorials but he is commemorated on the following memorial:

- The Commonwealth War Graves Commission Website.

Note: The Bridlington Burial Book states that Frank Stubbs died at the Camp Reception Station (CRS) Red House, Beverley (the High Hall PoW Camp at Bishop Burton). No information has been found to support this statement.

Private ERNEST EDWARD STURGEON

The Green Howards (Alexandra, Princess of Wales's Own Yorkshire Regiment), Service No. 4389608

Ernest Edward Sturgeon was born in the second quarter of 1920 the son of Walter and Maud Sturgeon (nee Waites) of Bridlington. In the 1911 census his father was a Waggoner at Bessingby.

Before he enlisted Ernest was living at 34 Queensgate Square, Bridlington. Ernest served with the 6th Battalion the Green Howards. The 6th and 7th Battalions were formed as duplicates of the 4th and 5th Territorial Army (TA) Battalions when the TA was doubled in size in 1939.

The 6th Battalion, Green Howards, was in the 69th Infantry Brigade and fought in the Battle of France with the British 23rd (Northumbrian) Division. In April 1941 the 69th Brigade, as part of 50th (Northumbrian) Infantry Division, was dispatched to the Middle East as part of XIII Corps in the Eighth Army. In May 1942 the 69th Brigade took part in the Battle of Gazala where they escaped with the remaining units of 50th Northumbrian Division and eventually reached the El Alamein line by 1 July. On the 23/24 October 1942 the 6th Battalion, Green Howards took part in the 2nd Battle of El Alamein where 69th Brigade, 50th (Northumbrian) Infantry Division initially deployed in the south to attack the Italian 185th Parachute Division 'Folgore'. It was then transferred north to take part in Operation 'Supercharge'. The final victory at the Second Battle of El Alamein in October 1942 was a turning point in the Desert War but one of the many casualties was Private Ernest Edward Sturgeon who died on the 26 October 1942 age 22 years.

Ernest was buried in El Alamein War Cemetery, plot XXIX, grave D7.
He is also commemorated on the following memorials:

El Alamein War Cemetery (CWGC)

- Bridlington War Memorial.
- St Mary (The Priory) Parish Church Roll of Honour.
- The Commonwealth War Graves Commission Website.

Aircraftman 2nd Class ERIC TAYLOR

The Royal Air Force, Service No.1437143

Eric Taylor was probably born as James Eric Tayor in the June quarter of 1922 the son of Joseph and Gladys Taylor (nee Dixon) of 11a Sands Lane, Bridlington. It appears that he never used the name James and was always known as Eric Taylor.

Before he enlisted Eric was living at 112 Queensgate, Bridlington. He was serving as an Aircraftman 2nd Class with the Royal Air Force Volunteer Reserve and died in the Middlesex Hospital in London on the 17 November 1941 as a result of an injection he had been given shortly after joining up.

Eric was 19 years old and the CWGC has not recorded the unit or Squadron to which he was attached.

Eric Taylor was buried in Newbold (St John the Evangelist) Churchyard, Chesterfield Derbyshire on the 22 November 1941 grave reference sec. A new row 14 grave 8.

Eric is also commemorated on the following memorials:

- Bridlington War Memorial.
- St Mary (The Priory) Parish Church Roll of Honour.
- The Commonwealth War Graves Commission Website.

Second Watchkeeper CHARLES HENRY TEMPLE

The Merchant Navy, Service No. not known

Charles Henry Temple was born on the 21 September 1905 at Hunmanby, the son of Harry and Eliza Margaret Temple (nee Deighton). His father Harry worked at Hunmanby as a plate layer on the (NER) railway and in the 1911 census the family were living at the Railway Cottages in Bessingby Road Bridlington. Charles was the younger brother of Edward Wilson Temple and the husband of Ada Temple (nee Price) whom he married in 1933. They had two children named Diane and James and lived at 1 Fairfield Road, Bridlington.

Charles Temple (G Temple)

Like most of the family Charles started going to sea on the Hull Trawlers and then changed to tugs. It is said that in WW2 he went out to HMS *Kelly*, commanded by Lord Mountbatten. This would be in 1940 when HMS *Kelly* was severely damaged in Norway and had to be towed home. Captain James Richardson, Master of the United Towing Tug *Brahman* (renamed *Bat* by the RN) was awarded an MID and MBE for helping to bring *Kelly* safely into harbour.

In August 1941 Charles was Second Watchkeeper on the S.S. *Empire Oak*, an ocean going steam tug, built by the Goole Shipbuilding & Repairing Co. Ltd., for the Ministry of War Transport and operated by the United Towing Co Ltd, Hull. It had been decided that a rescue tug should go with most convoys and *Empire Oak*, on her first voyage, sailed from Oban on 15 August 1941 and joined Convoy OG 71. During the voyage to Gibraltar she picked up survivors from *Aguila* and *Alva*. On the night of Friday, 22 August 1941 *Empire Oak* was torpedoed by U-564 (sunk by the RAF on 14 June 1943). *Empire Oak* sank within seconds and only the master, 3 crew and 4 gunners together with 7 survivors from *Alva* were rescued. 13 crew members from *Empire Oak* were lost including 35 year old Charles Henry Temple. Charles has no known grave and is commemorated on Panel 44 of the Merchant Navy Memorial in London and on the following memorials:
- Bridlington War Memorial.
- St Mary (The Priory) Parish Church Roll of Honour.
- The Commonwealth War Graves Commission Website.

Skipper EDWARD WILSON TEMPLE

The Royal Navy, Service No. JX215676

Edward (Ted) Wilson Temple was born at Reighton on 20th October 1903 the son of Harry and Eliza Margaret Temple (nee Deighton). His father Harry worked at Hunmanby as a plate layer on the (NER) railway and in the 1911 census the family were living at the Railway Cottages in Bessingby Road Bridlington. Ted Temple married Minnie Rose Tindall in 1925, registered at Glanford Brigg in Lincolnshire. They had three children named Jean, Winnie and Gordon and lived at 54 Queensgate Square in Bridlington. Ted joined the Royal Naval Patrol Service on the 28th August 1940 and was promoted to Skipper on the 1st April 1941. Ted transferred from Invergordon to Lowestoft and on the way thought he would call at home and arrived on the 10th April 1941 just after his family had been bombed out of New Burlington Road.

Edward Wilson Temple (G Temple)

Ted was the Executive Officer and 2nd Skipper of H.M. Trawler *Orfasy* and it was his job to see that the ship was ready for sea. HMT *Orfasy* (T204) was a Royal Navy 'Isles' Class armed trawler fitted for minesweeping and anti-submarine duties.

HMT *Orfasy* (IWM FL10665)

On the 21 Oct 1943 the tanker *Litiopa* from Lagos to Freetown heard depth charges being dropped twice by her sole escort, HMT *Orfasy*. Then a heavy explosion shook the tanker. *Orfasy* had been hit by one torpedo from U-68 and she exploded and sank with the loss of all 30 crew 185 miles SE of Freetown.

40 year old Edward (Ted) Wilson Temple has no known grave and is commemorated on Panel 11, Column 1, of the Lowestoft Naval Memorial in Suffolk and on the following memorials:
- Bridlington War Memorial.
- St Mary (The Priory) Parish Church Roll of Honour.
- The Commonwealth War Graves Commission Website.

Note U-68 was sunk 6 months later on 10/04/1944 by aircraft from USS *Guadalcanal*.

Lieutenant EDWARD DEREK THACKERAY

The Royal Artillery, Service No. 177385, Bridlington School Old Boy

Edward Derek Thackeray was born in Hull in the December quarter of 1918, the son of Percy and Grace Thackeray (nee Haller). His father was the Foundry Manager of Geo Clark Jnr. and Co., Ltd., Brass Founders of Neptune Street Hull. The family moved to 3 Swanland Avenue Bridlington but his father died age 40 in June 1923 and was buried in Bridlington Cemetery grave ref. L6. After his father's death his mother re-married at Bridlington in 1930 to Mr. Harold V. Jervis, French Master at Bridlington School from 1915 to1947.

Edward Thackeray (Bridlington School)

Edward Derek Thackeray came to Bridlington School from Pocklington Grammar School in 1931 and he left the School in 1935. Edward was one of the best sporting 'all-rounders' to be at the School before the Second World War and excelled at Rugby, Cricket, Gymnastics and Running (winning the Norfolk Cup two years in succession). After leaving school Edward took up a business appointment at Norwich and subsequently played scrum half for Norfolk County Rugby team and Eastern Counties Rugby team. Edward joined the TA in 1938 and in 1940 served with the 76th Anti-Tank Regiment (TA), Royal Artillery. The 76th was attached to the 1st Armoured Division and saw action in France and Flanders in 1940. Edward was one of those evacuated from Dunkirk and in early 1941 he married Barbara Marjorie Havercroft and they lived at Lavenbar New Road, Puddletown in Dorset. By November 1942 the 1st Armoured Division was taking part in the Battles at El Alamein and on the 3rd November 1942 Edward Derek Thackeray aged 24 was killed in action during the closing stages of the Battle. He has no known grave and is commemorated on Column 31 of the El Alamein Memorial, on his father's grave in Bridlington Cemetery and on the following memorials.

- Bridlington School Second World War Roll of Honour.
- Bridlington War Memorial.
- St Mary (The Priory) Parish Church Roll of Honour.
- The Commonwealth War Graves Commission Website.

Cadet RONALD THOMAS

The Merchant Navy, Service No. not known, Bridlington School Old Boy

Ronald Thomas was born in the June quarter of 1924 registered in Bradford. Ronald was the son of Alfred and Annie Thomas (nee Wells) who later lived in Bridlington. Ronald came to Bridlington School in 1937 and left in 1940. At School he was awarded his First XV Rugby Colours.

Ronald Thomas (Bridlington School)

He joined the Merchant Navy as a cadet and in 1942 was on the SS *Observer*, registered in Liverpool. SS *Observer* displaced 5,881 tons and had a crew of 72 seamen and nine gunners. On the 16th December 1942 SS *Observer* was bound independently from Mersin, Turkey via Cape Town, South Africa to Baltimore USA with a cargo of 3,000 tons of chrome ore. SS *Observer* was torpedoed by U-176 about 350 miles east of Cabo Sao Roque in Brazil

58 crew and 8 gunners were lost including 18 year old Cadet Ronald Thomas.

Ronald Thomas has no known grave and is commemorated on Panel 45 of the Merchant Navy Memorial Tower Hill in London.

SS Observer (uboat.net)

Ronald is also commemorated on the following memorials.
- Bridlington School Second World War Roll of Honour.
- Bridlington War Memorial.
- St Mary (The Priory) Parish Church Roll of Honour.
- The Commonwealth War Graves Commission Website.

Note:
U-176 was sunk on the 15 May 1943 north-east of Havana by depth charges from the Cuban patrol boat CS 13. 53 dead (all hands lost).

Driver ARTHUR THOMPSON

The Royal Army Service Corps, Service No. T/234388

Arthur Thompson was born in Howden in the December quarter of 1913. He was the son of John and Ada Alice Thompson (nee Jackson) who married in Howden in 1901. The family lived in Springfield Avenue in Bridlington.

Arthur married Kathleen May Jenkinson, daughter of Mr. and Mrs. J. W. Jenkinson of Bridlington. Arthur and Kathleen lived at 21 Holyrood Avenue in Bridlington. Before WW2 Arthur was employed by Messrs Strides, butchers of Lansdowne Road in Bridlington.

Arthur enlisted in the Army in October 1940 and became a driver with 200 Field Ambulance, Royal Army Service Corps (RASC). The 200 Field Ambulance were part of the Eighth Army in Egypt. In February 1942 Rommel had regrouped his forces sufficiently to push the over-extended Eighth Army back to the Gazala line, just west of Tobruk.

Arthur Thompson died on the 4th February 1942 age: 28 during the retreat to Tobruk and was buried in Halfaya Sollum War Cemetery Egypt, grave reference 4. C. 8.

Halfaya Sollum War Cemetery (CWGC)

Arthur is also commemorated on the following memorials:

- Bridlington War Memorial.
- St Mary (The Priory) Parish Church Roll of Honour.
- The Commonwealth War Graves Commission Website.

Sergeant (Flt. Engineer) STANLEY WILLIAM THOMPSON

The Royal Air Force, Service No. 1019644

Stanley William Thompson was born in Shrewsbury in the June quarter of 1912. He was the youngest son of William and Jane Ann Thompson (nee Barker). The family moved to Bridlington in 1914 where his father became the Bridlington Borough Waterworks Engineer.

On the 2nd November 1939 Stanley married Edith Mary Duck at Christ Church in Bridlington. After their marriage they lived at 200 Marton Road in Bridlington and had one child, a daughter whom they named Sylvia. Before enlistment Stanley worked for the Prudential Assurance Company in Beverley and was a member of Bridlington Rugby Union Football Club.

Stanley joined the RAF in 1940, volunteered for air crew training and was assigned to the Royal Air Force Volunteer Reserve (RAFVR). He trained in Canada and saw war service with 570 Squadron RAF. 570 Squadron was formed at Hurn in Dorset on the 15th November 1943, equipped with Albemarle's as part of No. 38 Group RAF engaged in supply dropping missions to French resistance units, training paratroops and glider-towing. In March 1944 the squadron moved to RAF Harwell, Berkshire and on the eve of 'D-Day' they provided 12 aircraft (2 aircraft towing gliders) dropping the first troops of the invasion into Normandy, 10 more aircraft took off with supporting glider-borne troops. On 'D Day' 20 more aircraft followed up with the towing and release of glider-borne troops in the Caen area. Secret operations did not stop and, on 7th June, 2 aircraft took off to drop SAS troops in the Brest Peninsular. On 1st July 1944 the Squadron converted to Stirling IV aircraft and commenced SOE operations with them on 27 July. Sadly on 29 July, Stirling LK133 did not return and came down near Orleans with the loss of all its crew including 32 year old Stanley William Thompson.

Stanley was buried in Orleans Main Cemetery, France, grave reference Plot 2. Row A. Collective grave 14-16. Stanley is commemorated on the following memorials:

- Bridlington War Memorial.
- St Mary (The Priory) Parish Church Roll of Honour.
- The Commonwealth War Graves Commission Website.

Private ERIC ARTHUR THWAITES

The Green Howards (Alexandra, Princess of Wales's Own Yorkshire Regiment), Service No. 4394437

Eric Arthur Thwaites was born in the March quarter of 1920 registered in North Bierley. Eric was the son of Thomas William and Elizabeth A. Thwaites (nee Goodacre) of 43 Horsforth Avenue, Bridlington. Eric worked as a painter and decorator for his father.

In WW2 Eric served in the 1st Battalion Green Howards. The 1st Battalion went over to France in 1939 as part of the British Expeditionary Force. They were brought back to England before the evacuation of Dunkirk and sailed to Norway as part of a taskforce to hold back the German invasion. A famous battle took place at Otta where for 24 hours the Green Howards held back 7 German battalions, Stuka dive bombers and heavy artillery. As Norway fell the British troops sailed back to Britain. After a couple of years on the Home Front, the 1st Battalion set sail to India in 1942 as part of the 15th Brigade. By this time Eric was serving with the Headquarters Company carrier platoon.

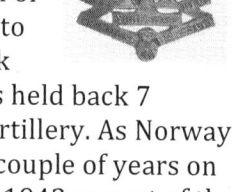

22 year old Private Eric Arthur Thwaites died of heart failure on the 10th June 1942 and was buried in Ranchi War Cemetery India, grave reference 4. F. 9.

Ranchi War Cemetery India (CWGC)

Eric is also commemorated on the following memorials:
- Bridlington War Memorial.
- St Mary (The Priory) Parish Church Roll of Honour.
- The Commonwealth War Graves Commission Website.

Flight Sergeant (Air Gunner) CHRISTOPHER DANBY TOWSE DFM

The Royal Air Force, Service No. 1237476, Bridlington School Old Boy

Christopher Danby Towse was born in Driffield in 1923 the son of John Henry and Marjorie Cordiner Towse (nee Danby). His father Henry was a farmer and in 1913 had been showing horses at the Hornsea Horse Show. Christopher came to Bridlington School in 1937 and left in 1939. He worked on his father's farm, Skerne Grange Farm at Driffield before joining the RAF in 1941. By 1944 Christopher was a Flight Sergeant (Air Gunner) RAFVR with 83 Squadron that had re-formed in 1936 and in 1944 it was a Pathfinder sqn.

Christopher Towse (Bridlington School)

83 Squadron was stationed at Coningsby in Lincolnshire and equipped with Avro Lancaster heavy bombers. Christopher's award of the Distinguished Flying Medal was published in the London Gazette on 14 September 1943. The brief citation stated that the medal had been awarded for *'gallantry and devotion to duty in the execution of air operations'*. The Bridlington Free Press reported that on one occasion he assisted the Pilot to bring the aircraft back safely after the Navigator had been killed by anti-aircraft fire. 20 year old Christopher Danby Towse was killed in action on the 10th May 1944. His aircraft Lancaster III ND494 (OL-G) took off as part of a force of 64 aircraft on an operation to bomb the Gnome-Rhone Works at Gennevilliers in France. The aircraft was hit by anti-aircraft fire while flying low near Rouen and crash-landed on a hillside near Balleul-la-Vallee, Eure in France. Three crew, including Christopher, were killed and four were taken prisoner. Four other aircraft were lost on the same raid. Christopher Danby Towse was buried in Evreux Cemetery in France, grave reference Row B, Grave 14. There is a memorial plaque in Kilham Church but as he was not a Bridlington resident he is not recorded on the Bridlington War Memorial or the Priory Roll of Honour but he is commemorated on the following memorials.

- Bridlington School Second World War Roll of Honour.
- The Commonwealth War Graves Commission Website.

Captain ARTHUR TRUELOVE

The Royal Engineers, Service No. 41553, Bridlington School Old Boy

Arthur Truelove was born in the December quarter of 1908, the son of Joseph Arthur and Martha Jane Truelove (nee Nixon) of Eccleshall Bierlow, Sheffield. Arthur came to Bridlington School in 1917 and left in 1927. Prior to the Second World War his was the most frequent name on the School's athletics and games honours boards. He won the Norfolk's' Cup for the Mile on several occasions. In 1927 his father presented the Truelove Cup to the School to mark his son's achievements. The Cup was awarded to the winner of the Open Quarter Mile.

Arthur Truelove (Bridlington School)

On leaving School he became a Regular soldier in the Royal Engineers. Arthur Truelove was also a founder member of the Sheffield Branch of the Old Bridlingtonians' Club. In 1936 Arthur married Jean Marie Osborn(e) at Chapel-en le Frith Derbyshire and they had a son and daughter. Captain Arthur Truelove was killed in action on the 14th May 1940 aged 31 in Norway. He was killed when the transport MV *Chrobny*, (a former Polish liner), was bombed and set on fire by German aircraft in Vest Fjord, near Narvik. He was the first Old Boy to be killed in action in the Second World War.

Brookwood Memorial (CWGC)

Arthur Truelove has no known grave and is commemorated on Panel 4, Column 3 of the Brookwood Memorial in Surrey. Arthur was not a Bridlington resident so he is not recorded on the Bridlington War Memorial or the Priory Roll of Honour but he is commemorated on the following memorials.

- Bridlington School Second World War Roll of Honour.
- The Commonwealth War Graves Commission Website.

Chief Petty Officer (Pilot) PETER EVERATT TURNER

The Royal Navy, Service No: FX668837

Peter Everatt Turner was born in the December quarter of 1922 registered in Goole. He was the son of Fred and Gertrude Alice Turner (nee Bramhill) of 9 Hustler Road in Bridlington. His father Fred was a grocer.

Peter was a Chief Petty Officer Pilot at H.M.S. *Valluru*, a Royal Naval Air station at Tambaram Madras. With the fall of Singapore in Feb 1942 and the subsequent air strikes by the Japanese on Ceylon (now Sri Lanka) in April 1942, the British set in motion a massive programme of creating naval aviation facilities in India. The role of these facilities was to provide training and support for the squadrons which had disembarked from aircraft carriers of the Eastern and East Indies Fleet.

HMS *Valluru* was commissioned at Tambaram on 1 July 1944 as a 'Double Aircraft Repair Yard' as well as a frontline air station for 6 squadrons and 72 reserve aircraft. A Fleet Requirement Unit 722 squadron operated a variety of aircraft from Tambaram during April 1944 to March 1945 when the squadron shifted to Santa Cruz (Bombay).

Peter Everatt Turner was killed in Madras on the 4th August 1945 age 23 and was buried in Madras (St. Mary's) Cemetery Chennai grave reference: Plot 19 grave 114. Details of how he died have not been found but it is probable that he was involved in a plane crash.

Madras Cemetery (CWGC)

Peter is also commemorated on the following memorials:

- Bridlington War Memorial.
- St Mary (The Priory) Parish Church Roll of Honour.
- The Commonwealth War Graves Commission Website.

Lance Sergeant DONALD FREDERICK TWIDDY

The Royal Corps of Signals, Service No. 2321865

Donald F Twiddy was born on the 2 December 1913 in Jalapahar, Bengal, India. He was the son of George William and Rosamund Laura Twiddy (nee Burton) who married in Madras, India in 1901. Donald's father George William Twiddy was a Major in the Indian Army. When his father retired from the Indian Army the family lived at 'Lynwood' Lansdowne Crescent in Bridlington.

Donald became a regular soldier in the Royal Corps of Signals and in 1938 he married Eileen Vandervelden in Karachi, Bombay, India. In WW2 Donald was posted to the Singapore 'Fortress Signals', Singapore, Malaya. 'Fortress Signals' were responsible for all communications inside the Island.

Singapore finally surrendered in February1942 and Donald Frederick Twiddy became a PoW. He escaped to Sumatra and was re-captured when Sumatra fell on the 26 June 1944. Donald, age 30, was reported as being among the PoW's lost when their prison ships were sunk. This was probably the *Harukiku Maru*, (former-Dutch ship *Van Warweijk)*, that was sunk by HMS *Truculent* on 26 June 1944. 180 of 720 POWs and 27 of 55 Japanese troops on board were killed.

Donald has no known grave and is commemorated on Column 42 of the Singapore Memorial.

The Singapore Memorial is within Kranji War Cemetery and bears the names of over 24,000 casualties of the Commonwealth land and air forces who have no known grave.

The Singapore Memorial (CWGC)

Donald F Twiddy is also commemorated on the following memorials:

- Bridlington War Memorial.
- St Mary (The Priory) Parish Church Roll of Honour.
- The Christ Church Roll of Honour.
- The Commonwealth War Graves Commission Website.

Leading Aircraftman ERNEST ROBSON UNDERWOOD

The Royal Air Force, Service No. 1379081

Ernest Robson Underwood was born in 1911, the son of William and Annie Maria Underwood (nee Williamson) of 9 Trinity Road, Bridlington. His father William was a cinematograph Picture Theatre Proprietor.

In the early 1930's Ernest trained as a solicitor, articled to his grandfather Joseph John Underwood of Messrs. Underwood and Robson, solicitors of Hull and later Bridlington. Ernest then became a solicitor with the family firm. In 1935 Ernest Robson Underwood married Mabel Milner at Christ Church in Bridlington. Afterwards they lived at 'Thalassa' Fortyfoot, Bridlington where they had a daughter whom they named Judith.

In WW2 Ernest was a Leading Aircraftman in the Royal Air Force Volunteer Reserve and was serving with 243 Squadron in Singapore. No.243 had reformed on the 12 March 1941 at Kallang as a fighter squadron for the defence of Singapore with Brewster Buffaloe aircraft. The squadron suffered heavy losses and by the end of January 1942 was operating its surviving aircraft as part of a mixed force and its identity was gradually lost. By the time all fighters were withdrawn from Singapore, it no longer existed as a unit.

243 Squadron Buffaloe (Wikipedia)

Ernest Robson Underwood died on the Sunday 15th February 1942 aged 31, the same day that Singapore surrendered.
Ernest is commemorated on Column 417 of the Singapore Memorial which bears the names of over 24,000 casualties of the Commonwealth land and air forces who have no known grave. Ernest Robson Underwood is also commemorated on the following memorials:

- Bridlington War Memorial.
- St Mary (The Priory) Parish Church Roll of Honour.
- The Commonwealth War Graves Commission Website.

Second Lieutenant GEOFFREY FREDERICK USHER MM.

The Green Howards (Alexandra, Princess of Wales's Own Yorkshire Regiment), Service No. 285744, Bridlington School Old Boy

Geoffrey Frederick Usher was born in Bridlington in the September quarter of 1918 the eldest son of W. Frederick and Hannah Beaumont Usher (nee Marsh) of 8 Summerfield Road, Bridlington. Geoffrey came to Bridlington School in 1927 and he was the eldest of three brothers who all attended the School. Geoffrey left Bridlington School in 1935 and was employed by J. H. Licence and sons (Accountants) on Wellington Road. He was also the Secretary and a player with Bridlington Rugby Club.

Geoffrey Usher (Bridlington School)

Geoffrey was one of the first recruits to the 7th Battalion (TA) the Green Howards, having joined a few months before the war. He was called up when hostilities started, went to France and was evacuated from Dunkirk. He served as a Sergeant in the Carrier Platoon in North Africa from 1941. His award of the Military Medal while serving with the 7th btn Green Howards in 1942 was published in the London Gazette on 24 September 1942. There was no individual citation. After Geoffrey received his officer's commission, he was transferred to the 5th Battalion East Yorkshire Regiment, which landed in Sicily on 9/10 July 1943.

Geoffrey Frederick Usher, age 25, was killed in action on the 14th July 1943 during the advance to hold the bridge at Primosole, Sicily. He received a Mention in Despatches, which was published posthumously in the London Gazette on 24 October 1943.

Geoffrey was buried in Catania War Cemetery Sicily grave reference II. A. 34.

Geoffrey is also commemorated on the following memorials.

- Bridlington School Second World War Roll of Honour.
- Bridlington War Memorial.
- St Mary (The Priory) Parish Church Roll of Honour.
- The Commonwealth War Graves Commission Website.

Chief Steward HECTOR THOROLD WADE

The Merchant Navy, Service No. not known

Hector Thorold Wade was born on the 11th may 1900, the son of Alfred and Mary Wade (nee Hall) of 20 Dale Street, Brighouse, Halifax. Hector joined the Merchant Navy and served in both World Wars and was awarded the WW1 Campaign Medal for merchant seamen. In January 1930 Hector Wade married a widow Winifred Johnson (nee Welch) at Hulme Manchester. During WW2 they lived at 37 Marton Avenue in Bridlington.

Hector Wade (find my past)

By 1941 Hector was Chief Steward on the British cargo ship MV *Dunkwa*. MV *Dunkwa* displaced 4,752 tons and was built in 1927 by A. McMillan & Son Ltd, Dumbarton for its owner the Elder Dempster Lines Ltd of Liverpool. On the 6 May 1941 *Dunkwa* was sailing from Glasgow to Opobo, Nigeria with a cargo of 3248 tons of general cargo and 868 tons of government stores. She was part of convoy OB-310, but this had been dispersed and *Dunkwa* was alone. At 17.17 hours the *Dunkwa* (Master John William Andrew), was hit aft by one stern torpedo from U-103 and sank within 8 minutes 216 miles west-northwest of Freetown. Five crew members and three gunners were lost. The Germans noticed that the 39 survivors were in one overcrowded lifeboat, so they righted a swamped lifeboat and provided water to the survivors. The master, 37 crew members and one gunner were picked up by the *Polydorus* and landed at Oban.

Unfortunately 40 year old Chief Steward Hector Thorold Wade was one of the five crew members killed. Hector has no known grave and is commemorated on Panel 36 of the Merchant Navy Memorial at Tower Hill, London. He is also commemorated on the following memorials:

- Bridlington War Memorial.
- St Mary (The Priory) Parish Church Roll of Honour.
- The Commonwealth War Graves Commission Website.

Note. U-103 was sunk by bombs on 15 April 1945 at Kiel.

Flying Officer (Flight Engineer) PHILIP WADSWORTH

The Royal Air Force, Service No. 53497, Bridlington School Old Boy

Philip Wadsworth was born in the December quarter of 1921 the son of Tom and Mona Kathleen May Wadsworth (nee Usher) of 55 Victoria Road, Driffield. Both of his parents were schoolteachers and Phillip came to Bridlington School in 1932 and left in 1937. Phillip was a talented organist and after leaving school he became an Apprentice at the RAF Technical School at Halton in Buckinghamshire.

In 1942 Philip married Margaret Annie Brundle and after their marriage they lived at 18 York Road in Driffield.

Philip Wadsworth (Bridlington School)

On the outbreak of war he volunteered for aircrew duties and was promoted to Sergeant before joining 156 Squadron. 156 Squadron re-formed in 1942 and by April 1944 it was a Pathfinder squadron stationed at Upwood, Cambridgeshire, and operating Avro Lancaster heavy bombers. Philip Wadsworth had already flown a complete tour of 30 sorties with 103 Squadron, Bomber Command. His promotion from Pilot Officer to Flying Officer was gazetted posthumously. Flying Officer (Flight Engineer) Philip Wadsworth was killed in action on the 28th April 1944 aged 22. His aircraft, Lancaster III ND409 (GT-S), took off as part of a force of 323 aircraft on a mission to bomb factories at Friedrichshafen, Germany. The aircraft was shot down by a night fighter and crashed into a wooded area about 1 km north of Neuhausen. There were no survivors and another 17 aircraft were lost that night. Philip Wadsworth was buried in Durnbach War Cemetery Bayern Germany collective grave reference 4.D.1-7. In 1992 his son, the Reverend Michael P. Wadsworth, published *'They Led the Way, the Story of Pathfinder Squadron 156'* in memory of his father and other squadron members. Philip did not live in Bridlington and is not recorded on the War Memorial or the Priory Roll of Honour but he is commemorated on the following memorials.

- Bridlington School Second World War Roll of Honour.
- The Commonwealth War Graves Commission Website.

CHARLES HENRY WAINWRIGHT

Civilian

Charles Henry Wainwright was born in the September quarter of 1880 at Wakefield the son of Joe and Annie Louisa Wainwright (nee Platts). In the 1901 census Charles was a hosier's assistant living in Scarborough. In the December quarter of 1904 Charles married Gertrude Elizabeth Ibberson at Scarborough and by 1911 they were living in Barrow-in-Furness.

Charles Wainwright (L Wainwright)

In 1914 Charles and Gertrude moved to Bridlington and Charles became a manager of the gent's outfitting department of Messrs Carlton's until 1935 when he went into business on his own as a gent's outfitter at 83 Hilderthorpe Road. On the 11 July 1940, a lone enemy aircraft on a hit and run raid, dropped a stick of high explosive bombs between Bridlington Railway Station and Hilderthorpe Road. Charles and Gertrude Wainwright were both killed along with two other civilians. A gunner in the Royal Artillery was also killed and another civilian was fatally injured and died later. This bombing raid devastated Hilderthorpe Road and the adjacent areas.

Charles and his wife Gertrude were a popular and well respected couple and they were buried together in Bridlington Cemetery on the 15 July 1940, grave ref V295.

Hilderthorpe Road (Bridlington Local Studies Library)

Charles is commemorated on the following memorials:

- Bridlington War Memorial.
- St Mary (the Priory) Parish Church Roll of Honour.
- The Commonwealth War Graves Commission website (Civilian War Dead).

GERTRUDE ELIZABETH WAINWRIGHT

Civilian

Gertrude Elizabeth was born on the 28th August 1881 in Sheffield, the daughter of Walter and Charlotte Ibberson (nee Milner). In the 1901 census Gertrude's mother Charlotte was a lodging house keeper at 26 Blenheim Terrace Scarborough, Gertrude age 19 was at the same address. In the December quarter of 1904 Gertrude married Charles Henry Wainwright at Scarborough and by 1911 they were living in Barrow-in-Furness. In 1914 Charles and Gertrude moved to Bridlington where Charles became a manager of the gent's outfitting department of Messrs Carlton's.

Gertrude Wainwright (L Wainwright)

In 1935 Charles went into business on his own as a gent's outfitter at 83 Hilderthorpe Road. On the 11 July 1940, a lone enemy aircraft on a hit and run raid, dropped a stick of high explosive bombs between Bridlington Railway Station and Hilderthorpe Road. Charles and Gertrude Wainwright were both killed along with two other civilians. A gunner in the Royal Artillery was also killed and another civilian was fatally injured and died later.

The Wainwrights shop window (L Wainwright)

Charles and Gertrude Wainwright were buried together in Bridlington Cemetery on the 15 July 1940, grave ref V295. Gertrude Elizabeth Wainwright is also commemorated on the following memorials:

- Bridlington War Memorial.
- St Mary (the Priory) Parish Church Roll of Honour.
- The Commonwealth War Graves Commission website (Civilian War Dead).

Royal Marine ALAN G. WAITES

The Royal Marines, Service No. PLY/X 3640

Alan G. Waites was born in the December quarter of 1921 at North Dalton, (Driffield registration District), Alan was the son of Ernest and Clara Elizabeth Waites (nee Smith), of 50 St. Johns Walk, Bridlington. Alan was educated at Speeton School and after leaving school was employed by Mr. Rodmell (Butchers) of Bridlington.

In September 1939 Alan joined the Royal Marines (sea service) and in May 1941 was serving on HMS. *Gloucester* (C62) one of the second group of three ships of the "Town" class of light cruisers. She was commissioned on 31 January 1939 and saw heavy service in the early years of World War II. The ship was deployed to the Indian Ocean and later South Africa before joining Vice Admiral Cunningham's Mediterranean fleet in 1940.

HMS *Gloucester* (Luis Photos))

Gloucester formed part of a naval force acting against German military transports to Crete, with some success. On 22 May 1941, while in the Kithera Channel, about 14 miles north of Crete, she was attacked by German Stuka dive bombers and sank, having sustained at least four heavy bomb hits and three near-misses. Of the 807 men aboard at the time of her sinking, 722 died and only 85 survived. Her sinking is considered to be one of Britain's worst wartime naval disasters.

Among those lost was 21 year old Royal Marine Alan G Waites. Alan has no known grave and is commemorated on Panel 60, Column 1, of the Plymouth Naval Memorial and on the following memorials:

- Bridlington War Memorial.
- St Mary (The Priory) Parish Church Roll of Honour.
- The Commonwealth War Graves Commission Website.

Able Seaman WALTER WAITES

The Royal Navy, Service No. C/JX 132210

Walter Waites was born in 1912, the son of Charles and Rose Anna Waites (nee Garnham) of Hunmanby Road, Bridlington. Before he enlisted Walter lived at 52 Pinfold Street, Bridlington.

Walter served in the Royal Navy and died on the 10th January 1941 when HMS *Gallant* was damaged by a mine.

HMS *Gallant* (H 59) was a G Class destroyer built by A. Stephen & Sons Ltd. Glasgow, Scotland and commissioned in 1936. During Operation Excess, *Gallant* struck a mine at 0834 hours on 10 January 1941 about 25 nautical miles south-west of Pantelleria. The mine detonated her forward magazine.

HMS *Gallant* (Wikipedia)

The explosion blew the bow off the ship, killing 65 and injuring 15 more of her crew. Her sister ship *Griffin* rescued most of the survivors and the destroyer HMS *Mohawk* towed her stern-first to Malta. At Malta she was beached in Grand harbour below Floriana. She was destroyed there during an air raid on 5 April 1942 and declared a constructive total loss. *Gallant* was finally sunk as a blockship at St. Paul's Bay in September 1943.

One of the 65 crew members killed on the 10 January 1941 was Royal Marine Walter Waites. Walter has no known grave and is commemorated on Panel Reference: 44, 1. of the Chatham Naval Memorial. He is also commemorated on the following memorials:

- Bridlington War Memorial.
- St Mary (The Priory) Parish Church Roll of Honour.
- The Commonwealth War Graves Commission Website.

Lance Corporal BERNARD WALKER

The Royal Army Service Corps, Service No. S/7663125

Bernard Walker was born in the March quarter of 1918, the last of 6 children of David and Maria Walker (nee Lydon) of 129 Clumber Street, Hull. Before his enlistment Bernard lived at 10 St. Cuthberts Road, Bridlington.

In WW2 Bernard was a Lance Corporal, serving in the Royal Army Service Corps (RASC) at the H.Q. Singapore Fortress, Miscellaneous Supply Depot. Japanese troops landed in the western sector of Singapore early on 9 February 1942. On the 13th February heavy bombing attacks, continued followed by incessant artillery barrages that made many of the depot position untenable and they were abandoned and the survivors moved to new defensive positions. Unfortunately 25 year old Bernard Walker was killed in action on the 13th February1942 just two days before Singapore finally surrendered.

Bernard Walker is commemorated on Column 99 of the Singapore Memorial that stands within the Kranji War Cemetery and bears the names of over 24,000 casualties of the Commonwealth land and air forces who have no known grave.

The Singapore Memorial (CWGC)

Bernard Walker is also commemorated on the following memorials:
- Bridlington War Memorial.
- St Mary (The Priory) Parish Church Roll of Honour.
- The Commonwealth War Graves Commission Website.

Captain COLIN MALCOLM WALKER

The York and Lancaster Regiment, Service No: 113393
Bridlington School Old Boy

Colin Malcolm Walker was born in the March quarter of 1918 registered in Ecclesall Bierlow. Colin was the son of Charles Matthew and Doris Ida Walker (nee Ponsford) of Whirlow, Sheffield. His father was a wholesale stationer and Colin came to Bridlington School in 1928 where he excelled in Tennis and was a contestant in the Yorkshire Schoolboys' Championships. Colin left the School in 1934.

Colin Walker (Bridlington School)

In the September quarter of 1941 Colin married Muriel Mary (Betty) Pratt of Dore, near Sheffield and after their marriage they lived at 467 Whirlowdale Road in Sheffield.

During WW2 Colin Malcolm Walker served with the 6th Battalion (Territorial Army) of the York and Lancaster Regiment. The 6th Battalion formed in 1939 as a duplicate of the Hallamshire Battalion. It served in the 138th Brigade throughout the war and saw action in France and Flanders in 1940. In March 1943 it was serving in the 46th (North Midland and West Riding) Division.

Captain Colin Malcolm Walker was killed in action on the 30th March 1943 aged 25, during the offensive to break through the Mareth Line and was buried in Tabarka Ras Rajel War Cemetery Tunisia, grave reference LA-6.

Tabarka Ras Rajel War Cemetery (CWGC)

Colin did not live in Bridlington and is not recorded on the War Memorial or the Priory Roll of Honour but he is commemorated on the following memorials.

- Bridlington School Second World War Roll of Honour.
- The Commonwealth War Graves Commission Website.

HARRY WALKER

Not Identified

A Harry Walker is commemorated on the following memorial:

- Christ Church Roll of Honour.

When the Bridlington War Memorial Committee were requesting names and details for the WW2 tablets, the Town Clerk sent a letter to the Reverend N. A. Vesey, formerly of Christ Church but now at the Rectory in Whitby, asking for background information on the name Harry Walker on the Christ Church Plaque. The Reverend replied on the 24 January 1950 that he had no information on Harry Walker, he had been given the name and he 'felt bound to include it'.

The outcome was that without any details of his arm of service, date of death and association with Bridlington the name of Harry Walker could not be recorded on the Bridlington War Memorial or St Mary (The Priory) Parish Church Roll of Honour.

There are 95 Harry and 95 Harold Walkers recorded on the CWGC and without any clues as to his identity it has proved impossible to date for the authors to identify the Harry Walker named on the Christ Church Plaque.

RONALD WARD

Not Identified

A Ronald Ward is commemorated on the following memorials:
- Bridlington War Memorial.
- St Mary (The Priory) Parish Church Roll of Honour.

There are 314 Ronald Wards recorded on the CWGC and it has proved impossible so far with any degree of certainty to find the identity of the Ronald Ward who is recorded on these Bridlington Memorials. His name was submitted to the Bridlington War Memorial Committee by a Miss K. Ward of Jubilee Avenue in Bridlington

A Kathleen Mary Ward was the daughter of Mr. and Mrs. Fred Ward of 16 Hazelmere Avenue in Bridlington. She was the Bridlington Cotton Carnival Queen in 1930 and the Bridlington Carnival Queen in 1931 but it has proved impossible to link her to a Ronald Ward.

The authors have looked at these possibilities:

1) A Ronald Ward born in Bridlington in the March quarter of 1924 with the mothers maiden name of Smith. There is a Malton marriage of a John Ward to a Gertrude Smith but no further details have been found.

2) Private Ronald Ward of the Argyll and Sutherland Highlanders. Service No. 3322912, killed in Action aged 29 on the 17 August 1944 while serving with the 7 battalion. Buried in Banneville-la-Campagne War Cemetery Calvados France grave reference VI. A. 15.
His will gives probate to John Ward farmer of Broxa Scarborough.

The CWGC and the Argyll and Sutherland Highlanders roll of honour website both give the age of 29 so this is not the Ronald Ward born in Bridlington in 1924.

If this proves to be the correct Ronald Ward then his connection to Bridlington or to a K. Ward of Jubilee Avenue is currently unknown.

WILFRED GEORGE WARDILL

Civilian, Bridlington School Old Boy

Wilfred was born in the March quarter of 1892 registered in Bridlington. He was the son of Frederick and Elizabeth Hannah Wardill (nee Jackson) of Cottesmore House, Bridlington. His father Frederick was a Surgeon / Dentist and the family lived at 9 Prospect Street in the 1901 and 1911 census and at 5 Prospect Street in 1921. Wilfred George Wardill came to Bridlington School in 1903 and left in 1909 and he was one of five brothers who attended the School, namely Joseph, Frederick, Harold, Cecil and Wilfred George Wardill.

Wilfred Wardill (Bridlington School)

By 1911 Wilfred was a boarder at 11 Luys Road Luton and was employed as an Engineer Fitter for a motor car manufacturer.

During the First World War Wilfred served in one of the `Hull Pals' battalions of the East Yorkshire Regiment. In 1925 Wilfred married Gwendolyn Rhoda Butcher; the marriage was registered in Luton district.

By 1942 Wilfred and Gwendolyn were living at 16, Brantwood Road Luton, Bedfordshire where Wilfred was a travelling salesman in dental equipment. On the 13 January 1942 Wilfred was on business in Lowestoft when at about 4.47 p.m. a cloud-skimming Dornier Do217 dropped four 500 kg high explosive bombs onto London Road. 50 year old Wilfred was killed at London Road North, a total of 54 people were killed in this, and another raid which took place around the same time.

Wilfred was buried in a cemetery in Lowestoft, Suffolk and was commemorated on a memorial chair in Bridlington School. Wilfred did not live in Bridlington so he is not recorded on the War Memorial or the Priory Roll of Honour but he is commemorated on the following memorials.
- Bridlington School Second World War Roll of Honour.
- Commonwealth War Graves Commission Website (Civilian War Dead).

DOROTHY GRACE WATSON

Civilian

Dorothy was born in 1896, the daughter of William and Eliza Copleston (nee Musk). She married James William Watson, the son of James and Elizabeth Watson of Walton Avenue Holland Street in Hull on the 25th February 1933 registered at Sculcoates.

Before WW2 Dorothy and James were running Foley's Cafe and Restaurant at 13 Prince Street, they shared the living accommodation there with Walter and Evelyn Parkin (nee Foley).

On the 23rd August 1940, Dorothy (44) and her husband James (40), who was serving in the Royal Air Force but was home on leave at the time, were both killed in an air raid attack on Bridlington Harbour. The third of four bombs wrecked Foley's Cafe in Prince Street and killed James & Dorothy Watson and two other civilians.

Foley's Café (Bridlington Local Studies Library)

Dorothy and James Watson were buried together in Bridlington Cemetery on the 27 Aug 1940, grave ref X69 in a simultaneous funeral with Evelyn Parker (nee Foley).

Dorothy Grace Watson is commemorated on the following memorials:

- Bridlington War Memorial.
- St Mary (the Priory) Parish Church Roll of Honour.
- Commonwealth War Graves Commission Website (Civilian War Dead).

Aircraftman 1st Class JAMES WILLIAM WATSON

The Royal Air Force, Service No: 168771

James William Watson was born on the 16th April 1900, the son of James and Elizabeth Watson of Walton Avenue Holland Street in Hull. After leaving school James became a clerk and was called up for war service when he was 18. On the 17th May 1918 he joined the Royal Air Force where he became an aircraft rigger and served until discharged on the 30th April 1920. James married Dorothy Grace Coplestone, the daughter of W C and Eliza Coplestone on the 25th February 1933 registered at Sculcoates. Before WW2 Dorothy and James were running Foley's Cafe and Restaurant at 13 Prince Street, they shared the living accommodation there with Walter and Evelyn Parkin (nee Foley). James was a popular member of the St John of Bridlington lodge 4434 of Freemasons and a former chief steward. With the war clouds gathering James rejoined the RAF as a class E reservist on the 3rd April 1939.

On the 23rd August 1940, Dorothy, age 44, and her husband James, age 40, who was home on leave at the time, were both killed in an air raid attack on Bridlington Harbour. The third of four bombs wrecked Foley's Cafe in Prince Street and killed James & Dorothy Watson and two other civilians.

James and Dorothy Watson were buried together in Bridlington Cemetery on the 27 Aug 1940, grave ref X69 in a simultaneous funeral with Evelyn Parker (nee Foley).

The grave of James and Dorothy Watson
(C Bonnett)

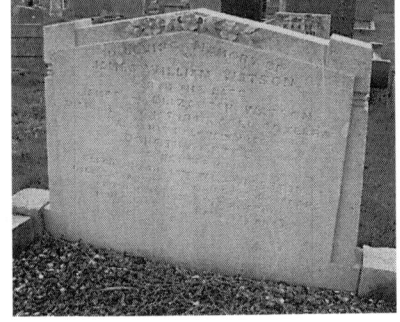

James William Watson is also commemorated on the following memorials:

- Bridlington War Memorial.
- St Mary (the Priory) Parish Church Roll of Honour.
- Commonwealth War Graves Commission Website.

The Bridlington Roll of Honour for the Second World War

Leading Seaman MAURICE GUYLEE WEBB

The Royal Navy, Service No. LT/JX 253526

Maurice Guylee Webb was born on the 10th May 1914 registered in Doncaster. He was the youngest son of Frank and Florence Webb (nee Guylee) of 27 St. Aidan Road Bridlington. Maurice was a server at Emmanuel Church and before joining the Royal Navy in November 1940 Maurice was in business with his brother Frank as a gentleman's outfitters.

In the September quarter of 1941 Maurice married Betty Pentith of London Colney Hertfordshire. After their marriage they lived at 9 Byass Avenue in Bridlington.

Maurice Guylee Webb (ww2 talk.com)

Maurice G Webb was serving with the Royal Naval Patrol Service and in 1945 he was one of the crew of Harbour Defence Motor Launch (HDML} 1336, (ML1336). 486 HDMLs were constructed during the war. They were 72 feet (22 m.) long, displaced 54 tons and were powered by two Gardner 8L3 marine engines of 152 bhp each. Speed was 12.5 knots and they had a complement of 2 officers, 2 petty officers and 8 ratings. Typical armament was twin 20mm Oerlikons, twin Vickers K machine guns and six depth charges. HDML 1336 was built by Nichol (Durban, South Africa) and commissioned on the 30th September 1944.

Maurice Guylee Webb died of drowning from HDML 1336 on Tuesday 20th March 1945 age 30. Maurice has no known grave and he is commemorated on Panel 17, Column 1 of the Lowestoft Naval Memorial. He is also commemorated on the following memorials:

- Bridlington War Memorial.
- St Mary (the Priory) Parish Church Roll of Honour.
- Christ Church Roll of Honour.
- Commonwealth War Graves Commission Website.

Note fellow crewman Alan Leathley died of drowning on the same day and was buried in Diego Suarez, Madagascar.

Sergeant HAROLD WHITAKER

The Royal Air Force, Service No. 1379266

Harold Whitaker was born in Bridlington in the September quarter of 1920 the son of Hugh Legatt and Alice Whitaker (nee Sewter) of 14 Melbourne Avenue, Bridlington. Harold's father Hugh Legatt Whitaker died in 1925 and his mother later married Henry Sunley and they all lived together at 18 Baptist Place, Bridlington.

Harold was educated at Oxford Street, Burlington and St Georges schools and played football for the Thursday Rovers Amateur Football Club (AFC). Before he joined the RAF he was employed by R Allan & Co. Ltd and then worked at the Britannia Hotel in Bridlington.

Harold joined the Royal Air Force and was assigned to the Royal Air Force Volunteer Reserve where he rose to the rank of Sergeant. In 1941 Harold was serving as a rear gunner in a detachment of 40 Squadron operating Wellington twin engine bombers in Malta. 40 Squadron operated from RAF Wyton and converted to Vickers Wellingtons from its original in Bristol Blenheim Mk IV in late 1940. It operated a detachment in Malta from October 1941 and the squadron moved there in February 1942.

21 year old Harold Whitaker died on the 25th November 1941 during night operations from Malta to Benghazi. He is commemorated on Panel 2, Column 2 of the Malta Memorial just outside the main entrance to Valletta. The Malta Memorial commemorates almost 2,300 airmen who lost their lives during the Second World War whilst serving with the Commonwealth Air Forces and who have no known grave.

Malta Memorial (CWGC)

Sergeant Harold Whitaker RAFVR is also commemorated on the following memorials:

- Bridlington War Memorial.
- St Mary (the Priory) Parish Church Roll of Honour.
- Commonwealth War Graves Commission Website.

Private WILLIAM WHITE

The East Yorkshire Regiment (The Duke of Yorks Own)
Service No: 4336135

William White was born in the June quarter of 1902 at Dalton Holme East Yorkshire, the son of Fredrick and Sarah Elizabeth White (nee Thurlow). In 1911 the family were living at 42 North Street in Bridlington and his father Fredrick was employed as a Horse Groom.

William enlisted in the Army on the 4th August 1919 and married Ida Fox in the June quarter of 1925, registered in Bridlington. After their marriage they lived at 23 St. Chad Road in Bridlington.

During WW2 William served with the 2nd Battalion of the East Yorkshire Regiment. The 2nd Batalion was a 'regular' battalion and posted to Palestine in 1937. On the outbreak of WW2 it was in Plymouth as part of the 8th Infantry Brigade, 3rd Infantry Division. In 1940 it went to France as part of the BEF and was one of the last Battalions to be evacuated from Dunkirk. After Dunkirk, the battalion and division spent many years on home defence, anticipating a German invasion and preparing defences on the south coast of England.

Private William White died on the 16th January 1942 age 39, at Raywell Sanatorium, Cottingham which specialized in the treatment of chest infections such as TB.

William was buried in Bridlington Cemetery, grave reference W32.
His widow Ida White died in 1958 and was buried in the same grave.

William's grave in Bridlington Cemetery (C Bonnett)

William White is also commemorated on the following memorials:
- Bridlington War Memorial.
- St Mary (The Priory) Parish Church Roll of Honour.
- The Commonwealth War Graves Commission Website.

Sergeant (Pilot) GEORGE HENRY WHITMAN

The Royal Air Force, Service No. 1378967

George Henry Whitman was born in the September quarter of 1912 at Ipswich, the only son of Arthur William, a Building Society Secretary, and Minnie Whitman (nee Norton) of Foxhill Road, Ipswich.

George Henry was the husband of Muriel Florence Whitman (nee Railton) of 93 the Promenade in Bridlington whom he married at the Holy Trinity Church on the 10th June 1939. They lived at Flat 4, third floor, the Expanse Hotel in Bridlington and George worked as an Insurance Clerk for the Phoenix Insurance Company in Hull, He also played badminton and was a member of the Red Cross.

George joined the Royal Air Force in June 1940, volunteered for aircrew and was assigned to the Royal Air Force Volunteer Reserve. 29 year old George Henry Whitman was killed on the 30th April 1942 when his plane crashed after taking off at Helwan, Egypt.

His unit is not recorded on the CWGC and news of his death reached his family in Bridlington on the 2nd May 1942, the very day that his only son was born!

George H Whitman (family archive)

George H. Whitman was buried with full military honours in grave reference: 1. G. 18, in Heliopolis War Cemetery, Cairo, Egypt.

Heliopolis War Cemetery (CWGC)

Sergeant Pilot George Henry Whitman RAFVR is also commemorated on the following memorials.

- Bridlington War Memorial.
- St Mary (The Priory) Parish Church Roll of Honour.
- The Commonwealth War Graves Commission Website.

Aircraftman 1st Class (WOP) ARTHUR JOHN WHITTAKER

The Royal Air Force, Service No. not known, Bridlington School Old Boy

Arthur John Whittaker was born in 1916 the son of Irvin and Alice Whittaker (nee Bell) of Bradford. Arthur came to Bridlington School in 1927 and left in 1930 when his family moved to 14 Oakwell Avenue, Leeds. After leaving Arthur spent four years at Leeds Grammar School.

Arthur applied for the RAF College, Cranwell, but was rejected owing to defective eyesight but went on to join the RAF as an airman and became a wireless operator. In 1937 he was a member of the RAF Guard of Honour at the coronation of King George VI and Queen Elizabeth.

Arthur Whittaker (Bridlington School)

By 1939 Arthur was a wireless instructor with 148 Squadron. The Squadron had re-formed in 1937 and by 1939 it was a Group Pool Training Squadron stationed at Harwell, Berkshire and equipped with Vickers Wellington and Avro Anson aircraft. In the September quarter of 1939 Arthur married Dorothy P. Trudgill at Ipswich in Suffolk.

23 year old Arthur John Whittaker was killed in a flying accident on the 28th November 1939 when Avro Anson I N5084 (BS-?) crashed on Exmoor, about 15 miles west-south-west of Minehead, Somerset during a night cross-country training flight. There were no survivors and Arthur had been married for only five weeks when he was killed.

Aircraftman 1st Class (Wireless Operator) Arthur John Whittaker was buried in Ipswich New Cemetery, Suffolk, grave reference Section XH, Division 5, Grave 250. Arthur did not live in Bridlington so he is not recorded on the War Memorial or the Priory Roll of Honour but he is commemorated on the following memorials.

- Bridlington School Second World War Roll of Honour.
- The Commonwealth War Graves Commission Website.

EDITH WHITTAKER

Civilian

Edith Whittaker was born in the September quarter of 1882, registered in Bridlington, the youngest daughter of Theophilus and Elizabeth Hermon a well-known Old Town family.

Edith was a schoolteacher and taught at Hilderthorpe and Oxford Street infant's schools. She married a fellow teacher and Schoolmaster George Ernest Spencer Whittaker in the December quarter of 1906, registered at Bridlington. George was a Freemason and Edith became a well-known member of the Priory Church Mothers Union.

Edith lived with her husband at 3 Victoria Road Bridlington and was injured on the 15 February 1941, at Bridlington when their house was destroyed in an air raid.

Edith never recovered from her injuries and the shock of seeing their house destroyed left her with increasing health problems and she died at 4 Fifth Avenue on the 12 April 1941.

59 year old Edith Whittaker was buried in Bridlington Cemetery on the 16 April 1941, grave ref X129.

Edith's grave (C Bonnett)

Edith Whittaker is commemorated on the following memorials:

- Bridlington War Memorial.
- St Mary (the Priory) Parish Church Roll of Honour.
- Commonwealth War Graves Commission website (Civilian War Dead).

Note:
Edith's husband George Ernest Spencer Whittaker died on the 9 March 1950 and was buried in the same grave.

Staff Sergeant (Pilot) ERIC BRIAN WIKNER

The 1st Glider Pilot Regiment, Service No. 4393249
Bridlington School Old Boy

Eric Brian Wikner was born in the March quarter of 1920 the son of Rudolf Lancelot and Evelyn Mary Wikner (nee Casson) of 115 Cardigan Road, Bridlington. Eric came to Bridlington School in 1931 and left in 1935. On leaving School he worked in local government as an assistant to Mr. H. S. Stead Relieving Officer and then joined the Green Howards in December 1940.

Eric Wikner (Bridlington School)

Eric subsequently volunteered for the Glider Pilot Regiment and was accepted. The regiment maintained very high standards and an estimated nine out of ten candidates failed to qualify as pilots. The glider pilots were trained to fight as Infantry when they had delivered their troops. The Glider Pilot Regiment was part of the Army Air Corps that formed in 1941 and in July 1943 it was part of the 1st Air Landing Brigade of the 1st Airborne Division. On the 10th July 1943 the 1st Air Landing Brigade was part of the spearhead of the Allied invasion of Sicily. American Waco gliders were used and a combination of misdirected Allied anti-aircraft fire and inexperienced US glider tug pilots caused many gliders to be cast off early and most of them came down in the sea. Those gliders which managed to reach dry ground were scattered up to 25 miles from the Landing Zone. 23 year old Glider Pilot (Staff Sergeant) Eric Brian Wikner was killed in action during this operation and was buried in Syracuse War Cemetery in Sicily grave reference II.B.11 and is commemorated on the following memorials:

- Bridlington School Second World War Roll of Honour.
- Bridlington War Memorial.
- St Mary (The Priory) Parish Church Roll of Honour.
- The Commonwealth War Graves Commission Website.

Second Lieutenant PETER WILKINSON

The 6th Royal Tank Regiment (R.A.C), Service No.184237

Peter Wilkinson was born in Sculcoates in the September quarter of 1914 the son of Robert Stanley and Emilie Wilkinson (nee Richardson) of 7 Trafalgar Crescent Bridlington. Before enlistment Peter worked for the Commercial Union Insurance Company.

In WW2 Peter served in the Western Desert with the 6th Royal Tank Regiment.). In 1942 the 6RTR took part in the Gazala battles in which it suffered heavy losses. Second Lieutenant Peter Wilkinson was wounded in action and died of his wounds on the 10 June 1942 during the battle for the Knightsbridge 'box'.

6RTR War Diary, 10 June 1942, 0600 onwards.

*2 patrols of A Sqn sent out to our old position. Orders received from Bde for attack on tanks on ridge SW of Knightsbridge. 2nd Armd Bde attacking from NE. Regt has RHA in support. 1st RTR covering left flank. Regt moved off from leaguer area. Regt reached area West of un-named BIR 382409 and came under fire from enemy tanks and A/Tk guns. C Sqn on left, B Sqn on right, A Sqn watching flanks. C Sqn pushed forward to engage enemy tanks. One enemy tank set on fire. Heavy fire from 88mm Bty to left flank, 2 Grants knocked out. 1 Grant and 1 Honey knocked out and another enemy tank set on fire. Very heavy and accurate fire from 88's, caused Regt to withdraw slightly. Bty RHA gave support and engaged the enemy guns. Tank attack reported coming in on 1st RTR on left. C Sqn moved round quickly to give support. Patrol of A Sqn sent out to look at 2 burning Grants and try and locate crews, driven off by A/TK fire. Some crews of the tanks knocked out in the morning walked in and reported that Italian infantry had been sent to destroy the damaged tanks and presumably had captured Capt RS Kemp, 2Lt Williams and **2Lt Wilkinson (wounded)** and some of the crews. Remainder of the day was spent in this area, some slight shelling. After dark Regt withdrew and leaguered some 3 miles back. Losses 3 Grants, 2 Stuarts.*

Second Lieutenant Peter Wilkinson was buried in Knightsbridge War Cemetery, Acroma, Libya, grave reference 10. B. 15. Peter is also commemorated on the following memorials:

- Bridlington War Memorial.
- St Mary (The Priory) Parish Church Roll of Honour.
- Christ Church Roll of Honour.
- The Commonwealth War Graves Commission Website..

Sergeant CYRIL WILLBOURN

The Kenya Regiment (Territorial Force), Service No. LF12678
Bridlington School Old Boy

Cyril Willbourn was born in Bridlington in the September quarter of 1897. Cyril was the son of Isaac and of Jane (Jeanie) Willbourn (nee Haynes). His father was a registered school teacher and the family lived in Cambridge Street in 1901 and 1911 and later at 25 St. Johns Avenue in Bridlington. Cyril came to Bridlington School in 1909 and left in 1913. He was one of five brothers who all attended Bridlington School.

Cyril Willbourn (Bridlington School)

During the WW1 Cyril served as a Lieutenant in the East Yorkshire Regiment and about 1920 he joined another brother Arthur King Willbourn in coffee planting and gold prospecting in Kenya. Cyril is believed to have joined the King's African Rifles in 1939 and fought in the Abyssinian campaign of 1940-1941. However the CWGC only lists Sergeant Cyril Willbourn as serving in the Kenya Regiment (Territorial Force) during WW2. The Kenya Regiment (Territorial Force) was a Colonial Forces Regiment formed on 1 June 1936 from Europeans as mainly a training unit for officers who were subsequently posted to other regiments. Cyril Willbourn aged 45 died of Illness in a hospital in Nairobi, Kenya, on the 21st December 1942 and was buried in Gilgil War Cemetery, Kenya, grave reference E. 14. There was a Memorial Chair in Bridlington School and he is also commemorated on the following memorials:

- Bridlington School Second World War Roll of Honour.
- Bridlington War Memorial.
- St Mary (The Priory) Parish Church Roll of Honour.
- The Commonwealth War Graves Commission Website.

Cyril's elder brother Horace Willbourn (Bridlington School 1899-1905) was killed in action in 1918 while serving with the Duke of Wellington's Regiment and is included in the School Roll of Honour for WW1.

JESSIE TERESA WILLBOURN

Civilian

Jessie Teresa Willbourn (nee Cooper) was born in 1890 and married Eric Stewart Willbourn in the June quarter of 1919 at Bridlington Priory Church. They initially lived at 22 St. Johns Avenue Bridlington before going to the Federated Malay Straights.

On the 5th June 1933 they left Liverpool as 1st class passengers aboard the SS *Dardanus* for Penang, the Federated Malay Straights (FMS), where Eric would be working for the government as a geologist.

By 1942 when the Japanese invaded, Eric Stewart (Bill) Willbourn was Director Geological Surveys FMS at Batu Gajah, and 2 i/c of the FMSVF with the rank of Major and Jesse was an Ambulance driver.

Jesse Willbourn was evacuated from Singapore on the *'Giang Bee'* which was intercepted and sunk by a Japanese destroyer on the 13th February 1942. Jessie was not among the survivors and was presumed drowned. Some reports say their children Anthony and Elizabeth were evacuated with Jessie and died in the sinking but this is incorrect and both Anthony and Elizabeth Willbourn survived the war.

Her husband Eric became a POW in Singapore and eventually returned to Bridlington where he died in 1977 aged 88.

There is a Memorial Inscription (MI 151) on the 'Willbourn' headstone in the Priory Cemetery in Bridlington that states "Jessie Teresa Willbourn Lost at sea through enemy action 13th February 1942".
Her death is not recorded on the Commonwealth War Graves Commission Website (Civilian War Dead) but Jessie Teresa Willbourn is commemorated on the following memorials:

- Bridlington War Memorial
- St Mary (The Priory) Parish Church Roll of Honour.

Sapper ARTHUR WILLIAMSON

The Royal Australian Engineers, Service No.NX19016

Arthur Williamson was born in Bridlington in the September quarter of 1905 the second son of George and Margaret Williamson (nee Foster) of 24 Windsor Crescent in Bridlington. Arthur was educated at Hilderthorpe School and emigrated to Australia when he was 17. He returned to Bridlington three years later but after six months he returned to Queensland Australia.

Arthur was the husband of Agnes Veronica Williamson, an Australian girl whom he married In January 1940, they lived at Highgate Hill, Queensland, Australia.

In June 1940 Arthur volunteered to serve with the Australian Imperial Forces and was posted to the 2/6 Field Company, Royal Australian Engineers, as a sapper. The 2/6 formed at Bathurst New South Wales in 1940 and was later attached to the 7th Division, 2nd AIF. The 2/6 embarked from Sydney for the Middle East on the original 'Queen Mary' and changed ships in Bombay to the Dutch liner 'SS Slamat' and arrived in Egypt were it transferred with 7th Division to Palestine. In Palestine the division formed the backbone of the Allied invasion of Lebanon and Syria; with British, Indian and Free French forces defeating Vichy French land forces in the Middle East in June and July1941.

7th Aust. Division

35 year old Arthur Williamson died on the 27 June 1941 from wounds received in action during the battles for Damascus, Fort Khiam and adjacent villages. Arthur was buried in Khayat Beach War Cemetery Palestine, grave reference: A. H. 11. This cemetery was prepared in 1941 for the burial of service war dead in northern Palestine (now Israel). Arthur is also commemorated on the following memorials:

- Bridlington War Memorial.
- St Mary (The Priory) Parish Church Roll of Honour.
- Christ Church Roll of Honour.
- The Commonwealth War Graves Commission Website.

Master Sergeant HARRY WILLIS

The Royal Air Force, Service No. 971577, Bridlington School Old Boy

Harry Willis was born in the June quarter of 1920 registered in Scarborough. Harry was the son of Harry and Isabella Willis (nee Clark) of Filey. Harry came to Bridlington School in 1930 and left in 1936. He joined the RAF, volunteered for air crew training and was assigned to the RAFVR. Harry served with 235 Squadron that re-formed in 1939 and began the war in Fighter Command until it was transferred to Coastal Command in 1940. By March 1941 it was stationed at Bircham Newton, Norfolk equipped with Bristol Blenheim twin engine bombers.

Harry Willis (Bridlington School)

Harry Willis visited Bridlington School on the 13th March 1941. Only ten days later on the 23rd March 1941, 20 year old Master Sergeant Harry Willis was killed in action. His aircraft Blenheim DZ6085 (LA-D) took off as part of a flight of three aircraft on a 'Pirate' anti-shipping patrol off the Dutch coast. A convoy was sighted, which was bombed and the flight was then attacked by three Messerschmitt Bf109's which shot down two of the Blenheim's. Blenheim (LA-D), with its port engine on fire, crashed into the sea off Hoek van Holland. The aircraft was claimed by Oberleutnant P. Stolte of 3/JG1.

Harry Willis has no known grave and is commemorated on Panel 55 of the Royal Air Force Memorial at Runnymede in Surrey. Harry did not live in Bridlington so he is not recorded on the War Memorial or the Priory Roll of Honour but he is commemorated on the following memorials.

- Bridlington School Second World War Roll of Honour.
- The Commonwealth War Graves Commission Website.

Sergeant HARRY LEONARD WILSON

The Green Howards (Alexandra, Princess of Wales's Own Yorkshire Regiment), Service No. 4391424

Harry Leonard Wilson was born in the June quarter of 1914 (as Leonard H) the son of Harry and Mary Wilson (nee Jackson) of 6 Gilbert Street, Bridlington. Harry was educated at Moorfield School and after leaving school he was employed by Messrs. William Jackson in their Bridlington Store. Harry played football for the Thursday Rovers and had trials with Grimsby Town. In the March quarter of 1940 in Buckrose district Harry married Catherine Lucy Leddy. After their marriage they lived at 43 Blackburn Avenue in Bridlington.

Harry joined the 7th Battalion, the Green Howards in 1939. The 7th and 6th Battalion, Green Howards, together with the 5th Battalion, The East Yorkshire Regiment formed the 69th Infantry Brigade. Before leaving for France the Green Howards assembled in Bessingby Fields where many local people saw them depart. They fought during the Battle of France until evacuated from Dunkirk, one of those rescued being Harry Leonard Wilson. In April 1941 the 69th Brigade, as part of 50th (Northumbrian) Infantry Division, was dispatched to the Middle East via Cyprus, Iraq, Syria, Egypt and then into Libya as part of XIII Corps in the Eighth Army. In May 1942 they took part in the Battle of Gazala in the vicinity of Tobruk. The 'Gazala Line' was a series of occupied 'boxes' each of brigade strength set out across the desert. In late May 1942 The Afrika Korps attacked the Gazala Line. The 69th Brigade and the remaining units of 50th Northumbrian Division escaped by attacking west through the enemy lines then sweeping back east to the south of the enemy forces, eventually they reached the El Alamein line by 1 July.

28 year old Sergeant Harry Leonard Wilson was killed on the 5th June 1942 during the Gazala battle and was buried in Knightsbridge War Cemetery, Acroma, Libya, grave reference 1. F. 13-17. Harry is also commemorated on the following memorials:

- Bridlington War Memorial.
- St Mary (The Priory) Parish Church Roll of Honour.
- Christ Church Roll of Honour.
- The Commonwealth War Graves Commission Website.

Corporal HENRY WILSON

The Green Howards (Alexandra, Princess of Wales's Own Yorkshire Regiment), Service No. 4387496

Henry Wilson was born in the June quarter of 1913 the eldest son of Walter Edmond and Rose Helen Wilson (nee Brown) of 51 Eastgate North in Driffield. Henry's father Walter died in WW1 and was buried in All Saints Churchyard in Nafferton. Henry was a bell ringer at Christ Church in Bridlington and a member of the local company of the Church Lads Brigade. He was a joiner by trade having served his apprenticeship with Mr. E. Gray of Bridlington. In the March quarter of 1934 Henry married Gladys Ida King in Driffield, they had four children and lived at 18 Midway Avenue in Bridlington.

About 1930 Henry joined the 5th Battalion (TA) of The Green Howards, a typical pre-war Territorial Army infantry battalion recruited from volunteers willing to give up their time for military training. When WW2 began the TA mobilised and the 5th Green Howards became part of the 150th Infantry Brigade, 50th (Northumbrian) Division in the B.E.F. They were among the last British units off the beaches of Dunkirk and Henry Wilson was among those rescued. In April 1941 the 50th Division was dispatched to the Middle East via Cyprus. The 50th Division moved from Cyprus to Palestine from where the 150th Brigade was sent to the Western Desert while the rest of the division went to Iraq and Persia before they all joined up in February 1942. The 50th Division was put into the Gazala Line defences (a series of fortified positions known as 'boxes') with the 150th Brigade in the Got el Ualeb Box which was isolated from any mutual support.

30 year old Henry Wilson was killed in action on the 28th March 1942 while the 5th Green Howards were defending the Got el Ualeb a Box. He was buried in Knightsbridge War Cemetery, Acroma, Libya, grave reference 2. F. 11. He is commemorated on the following memorials:

- Bridlington War Memorial.
- St Mary (The Priory) Parish Church Roll of Honour.
- Christ Church Roll of Honour.
- The Commonwealth War Graves Commission Website.

Warrant Officer (RSM) STANLEY WILSON

The Green Howards (Alexandra, Princess of Wales's Own Yorkshire Regiment), Service No. 4391220, Bridlington School Old Boy

Stanley Wilson was born in the March quarter of 1908 the second son of Harry and Lily Wilson (nee Marson) of 1 Nelson Street and Ferndale Terrace in Bridlington. Stanley came to Bridlington School in 1920 and left in 1924. After leaving school he was in business with his father as a Poulterer in Bridge Street Bridlington. In the June quarter of 1933 Stanley married Edith Glentworth and they lived at 4 Greenside Flats, St. Oswalds Road in Bridlington.

Stanley Wilson (Bridlington School)

Stanley was one of the first recruits to the 7th Battalion, Green Howards in 1939. He served in France and Flanders and was evacuated from Dunkirk. In April 1941 the 7th Green Howards went to the Middle East as part of XIII Corps in the Eighth Army. They landed in Sicily on the 9th July 1943 on the first day of the Allied forces invasion.

Extract from the diary of George Beswick RAMC in WW2.

"On Saturday July 10th 1943 we landed at the village of Avola (Sicily) with the Green Howards. I was working in the operating theatre under Major Rogers. At noon we set up a theatre in the Village School and the first patient we got in was RSM Stanley Wilson from the Green Howards, he was also a Bridlington man who I knew quite well. As we were preparing him for surgery he died in our arms through his wounds"

George added in another article that he told Major Rogers he knew Stanley Wilson and asked if he could keep a few items to take back to Stanley's family, this George did when he arrived home on leave in January 1944. 35 year old Stanley Wilson was buried in Syracuse War Cemetery, grave reference II.F.8. A memorial service for Stanley was held at the Central Methodist Chapel, Bridlington on the 5th September 1943 and there was a Memorial Chair in Bridlington School and he is commemorated on the following memorials:
- Bridlington School Second World War Roll of Honour.
- Bridlington War Memorial.
- St Mary (The Priory) Parish Church Roll of Honour.
- The Commonwealth War Graves Commission Website.

Pilot Officer BASIL BAXTER WITTY

The Royal Air Force, Service No. 44069

Basil Baxter Witty was born in 1915 the only son of Basil Worsdale Witty and Elsie May Witty (nee Baxter) of 33 Newland Avenue Hull. His father was the owner of the electro plating firm of B. W. W. & Co. Ltd of Hull. Basil was educated at Hymers College in Hull and he became a member of Bridlington Rugby Club the family having moved to 'Netherlands', 7 Summerfield Road in Bridlington. Before he enlisted Basil's address was 9 Grasmere Drive, Tang Hall Lane, York but formerly of 64 St John's Walk Bridlington.

During WW2 Basil was a Royal Air Force Pilot Officer with No. 47 Squadron. 47 Squadron was re-formed at RAF Helwan in Egypt in 1920 as a day bomber squadron equipped with the DH.9 with the role of, policing in Sudan and to help survey and mark out the route of the Cairo to Baghdad air route, and to carry air mail along that route.

In 1927 the squadron moved to Khartoum and re-equipped with Fairey IIIF's and in 1936 with Vickers Vincent's. In 1939 the squadron started to operate the Vickers Wellesley and to counter Italian forces entering the war the squadron moved north to Erkowit and flew its first combat mission of the Second World War against Asmara airfield in Eritrea on 11 June 1940 and continued to bomb Italian forces in Eritrea and Ethiopia until they surrendered in May 1941.

Basil Baxter Witty was taken captive in Abyssinia and died of wounds in Addis Ababa hospital on the 12th December 1940 age 25. He was buried in Addis Ababa War Cemetery Ethiopia, grave reference 2.A.4.

Addis Ababa War Cemetery (CWGC)

Basil B. Witty is also commemorated on the following memorials:

- Bridlington War Memorial.
- St Mary (The Priory) Parish Church Roll of Honour.
- The Commonwealth War Graves Commission Website.

Sergeant (Pilot) GEORGE GREENLEY WITTY

The Royal Air Force, Service No. 565438, Bridlington School Old Boy

George Greenley Witty was born in the March quarter of 1914 the only son of Alfred and Selina Witty (nee Greenley) who lived in Speeton and Bridlington before moving to York. George came to Bridlington School in 1925 and while at the School he was a County Scholar and a School Prefect. George left the School in 1930.

George Witty (Bridlington School)

George was a pre-war Regular, having joined the RAF at the age of 17 shortly after leaving school. He volunteered for air crew training and was assigned to the RAFVR. During WW2 George served as a pilot with 87 fighter squadron that re-formed in 1937and by October 1939 it was equipped with Hawker Hurricane Mk I fighters and stationed at Merville in France as part of the Air Component of the BEF.

On the 5th October 1939 in order to enable French anti-aircraft gunners to identify the Hawker Hurricane more easily, the squadron, comprising twelve aircraft, undertook a demonstration flight over the Lille area.

Hurricane IIc (F Bull)

After the demonstration the squadron split into four flights of three for landing. George Witty, in Hurricane L1776 (IM), was seen to break away and crash near the Forest of Nieppe. He was killed instantly and was the first Bridlington School Old Boy to lose his life on active service in the Second World War. Sergeant (Pilot) George Greenley Witty aged 25 was buried in Merville Extension Cemetery: Nord, France, grave reference 3 A32A. There was a Memorial Chair in Bridlington School and he is also commemorated on the following memorials.

- Bridlington School Second World War Roll of Honour.
- Bridlington War Memorial.
- St Mary (The Priory) Parish Church Roll of Honour.
- The Commonwealth War Graves Commission Website.

Driver HARRY GILBOY WOOD

The Royal Army Service Corps, Service No. T/286493
Bridlington School Old Boy

Harry Gilboy Wood was born in Hull in the June quarter of 1906 the son of George Thomas and Ellen Wood (nee Gillboy). His father was a wood turner and the owner of the firm of J. Wood and Sons Hull. Harry came to Bridlington School in 1919 and left in 1922. His Father died in 1930 and control of the family timber business passed to Harry and his brother George. In the September quarter of 1931 Harry married Martha Mary Pennock the marriage being registered in Sculcoates.

Harry Wood (Bridlington School)

By WW2 Harry and Martha were living at 30 Kirklands Road in Hull where Harry was a timber merchant and a director of J. Wood and Sons Hull. In 1941 Harry volunteered and became a driver with the Royal Army Service Corps. His unit was attached to 155 Field Ambulance, Royal Army Medical Corps. 38 year old Harry Gilboy Wood was wounded by blast and died in a US Army Hospital in the Netherlands on the 15th December 1944. At the time his unit was operating with the 52nd Lowland Division (Mountain). This Scottish division had been trained in mountain warfare, but never operated in this role and landed in France in October 1944 as part of 21st Army Group.

Harry Gilboy Wood was buried in Venray War Cemetery, Limburg, The Netherlands, grave reference V.G.7.

Venray War Cemetery (CWGC)

Harry did not live in Bridlington so he is not recorded on the War Memorial or the Priory Roll of Honour but he is commemorated on the following memorials.

- Bridlington School Second World War Roll of Honour.
- The Commonwealth War Graves Commission Website.

JOHN WILLIAM WOODCOCK

Civilian

John William Woodcock was born in 1874 the son of Tom and Anne Woodcock (nee Lowson). He married Louisa Riseam in the September quarter of 1893, registered in Bridlington district.

John was a lifelong resident of Bridlington and set up as a baker and confectioner in the High Street until the First World War. Afterwards he became a Turf Commissioning Agent assisted by his sons Tom & William. He was also a good sportsman and a breeder of canaries and budgerigars.

On the 18 June 1941 an enemy aircraft dropped two 1,000 kg parachute mines on Bridlington, they exploded in Lamplugh Road and St. Anne's Road. John Woodcock and his wife were at home and one of the houses destroyed was their home at 'Gambier' in Lamplugh Road. The ARP team rescued Mrs. Woodcock who was trapped under the stairs but 68 year old John Woodcock was killed.

Bomb damage in Lamplugh Road (Bridlington Local Studies Library}

John William Woodcock was buried in Bridlington Cemetery on 21 June 1941, grave ref T42. His wife survived and died in April 1947 and was buried in the same grave.

John Woodcock's grave (C Bonnett)

John Woodcock is also commemorated on the following memorials:

- Bridlington War Memorial.
- St Mary (the Priory) Parish Church Roll of Honour.
- The Commonwealth War Graves Commission Website (Civilian War Dead).

Sergeant (Navigator) FRANK WRIGHT

The Royal Air Force, Service No. 1457557, Bridlington School Old Boy

Frank Wright was born in the September quarter of 1922 the son of Edward and Ethel Wright (nee Leighton) of Hull. He came to Bridlington School in 1933 and left in 1938. On leaving School Frank followed a commercial career. Frank joined the RAF, volunteered for air crew training and was assigned to the RAFVR. He became a Sergeant (Navigator) with 12 Squadron. In April 1944, 12 Squadron was part of 1 Group, Bomber Command operating the Avro Lancaster heavy bomber from Wlckenby Lincolnshire.

Frank Wright (Bridlington School)

On the 11th April 1944 Sergeant (Navigator) Frank Wright aged 21 was one of the crew of Lancaster III ND844 (PH-M) which took off at 11.22 p.m. as part of a force of 167 aircraft on an operation to bomb railway marshalling yards at Aulnoye, France. Lancaster III ND844 (PH-M) crashed at Sailly-Cambrai, Nord, France, about 5 km west-north-west of Cambrai. Only one crew member survived and another six aircraft were lost on this operation.

Frank Wright was buried in Cambrai (Route de Solesmes) Cemetery, Nord, France, grave reference 1.A.4.

Cambrai (Route de Solesmes) Cemetery (CWGC)

Frank Wright did not live in Bridlington so he is not recorded on the War Memorial or the Priory Roll of Honour but he is commemorated on the following memorials.

- Bridlington School Second World War Roll of Honour.
- The Commonwealth War Graves Commission Website.

Appendix

Appendix

C H CARTER and C H GARRETT

C H Carter appears on the Bridlington War Memorial
C H Garrett appears on the Priory Screens

About 1947 a typed list of names for the Bridlington War Memorial was produced by the Town Clerk's Office and on this list was Raymond Garrett. The list was passed to the Priory who in reply gave the Town Clerk a hand written list of names to be inscribed on the Priory Screens that were not on the typed list. Among the list of names was 'Carter Raymond'. Raymond Carter was duly added to the typed list.

In October 1949 The Town Clerk received a letter from Mr Webster on behalf of the Priory which gave additional details of some of the names and went on to say that Garrett was Chas Hy (Henry), The letter went on to say *"but when the screen was carved the Christian names of Carter and Garrett had been transposed and this would be corrected by Mr Thompson when he comes to do certain works"*. As a result of this letter the Town Hall final list of names for the WW2 memorial tablets had Raymond Noel Carter changed to C. H. Carter.

It appears that this letter was somewhat inaccurate and the changes to the Priory Screen consisted of leaving Raymond Carter and C H Garrett alone and adding a Raymond Garrett as a 'correction' on panel 9.

As a result of this confusion the Bridlington War Memorial ended up with a 'C H. Carter' and a 'Raymond Garrett' while the Priory Screen has a 'Raymond Carter' and a 'Raymond Garrett'.

Our research indicates that 'Raymond Carter' and 'Raymond Garrett' are the correct names. There is no 'C H Carter' on the CWGC and the only 'C H Garrett' on the CWGC has absolutely no connection to Bridlington!

(For reference the C H Garrett on the CWGC is Captain Charles Herbert Garrett, Royal Engineers, Service No. 65688 born in the Isle of Man in 1914 the son of Herbert Douglas and Emily Alison Garrett and the husband of Alice Mowitt Garrett. Charles and Alice lived at No.6 Lynedene Gardens, Cheadle Cheshire. Charles died on the Ipswitch to Norwich main road at Stoke Ash, Suffolk on the 11 Nov. 1940 age 26 and was buried in Cheadle and Gatley Cemetery, grave reference, Sec. A. Grave 28 - no connection to Bridlington has been found.)

Appendix

Gunner EDMUND REGINALD BEECROFT

The Royal Artillery, Service No. 2086946

Gunner Edmund Reginald Beecroft of The Royal Artillery was the soldier, unnamed at the time, who was killed on Wednesday the 21 August 1940 at the Britannia Hotel during an air raid on Bridlington.

20 year old Edmund was born on the 15 October 1919, the son of Edmund and Mabel Beecroft (nee Pindar) of Thornton, Bradford. Edmund was serving as a Constructional Engineer with the 397 Battery, 49 Searchlight Regiment (6th Battalion the West Yorkshire Regt.) when he was killed.

The Britannia Hotel
(Bridlington Local Studies Library)

The Yorkshire Post of 23rd August reported the death as follows:

> Mr and Mrs E Beecroft of Close Head House Thornton Bradford have been informed that their son gunner Edmund Reginald Beecroft (20) has been killed in England. Before being called up with his unit on the outbreak of war he was engaged as a draughtsman with Henry Barratt and Sons Ltd. structural engineers of Bradford. He was an old Bradford Grammar School boy. Gunner Beecroft was the man who with his Lewis Gun shot down a Junkers 88 during a daylight raid on Britain yesterday week. This plane was the first to be brought down by his unit

Why the identity of gunner Edmund Reginald Beecroft was not revealed when he was killed in Bridlington is not known. His death certificate clearly states he died at the Britannia Hotel but he is not recorded on any Bridlington memorial.

Edmund Reginald Beecroft was buried in Horsforth (St. James) Woodside Churchyard Horsforth Leeds and he is recorded on the CWGC website.

Lance Sergeant ERNEST ARTHUR FREDERICK PLUCK MM

The Durham Light Infantry, Service No. 6024842

Ernest Arthur Frederick Pluck was born in 1915 the only son of Frank and Maud Pluck of Dukes Head Street Lowestoft, Suffolk. Ernest moved to Bridlington and was employed for a number of years by Messr's Bradleys Clothiers and tailors until 1937 when he moved to Clacton-on-Sea Essex.

By 1942 Ernest was serving as a corporal with the Essex Regiment and on the 27th October 1942 Ernest Arthur Frederick Pluck married Dorothy Wright, the only daughter of Mr. & Mrs. Alfred Wright of 10 Palanza Terrace Bridlington. The marriage took place at Christ Church in Bridlington and after their marriage they lived with Dorothy's parents in Bridlington.

Ernest Pluck at a later unknown date transferred to the 1st Battalion (68th Light Infantry) of the Durham Light Infantry. At the time of his death in November 1944, Ernest was serving as a Lance Sergeant with the Durhams. The 1st Battalion DLI had returned to Italy where it joined the 10th Indian Infantry Brigade of the 10th Indian Infantry Division and by 19th May was back in the line north of Ortona. It transferred to the Tiber valley in June and fought toward the Gustav Line until September when it was transferred once more to the Adriatic coast and fought its way through the Gothic Line. Ernest was awarded the Military Medal with 'A' Company in October 1944 during an attack on Mont Spaccato near Cesena when he rescued four men under fire and set "a magnificent example to his men" (gazetted 26/05/1945).

On the 25th November 1944 during the crossing of the river Montone Ernest stepped on a German mine and lost both his feet. He died in hospital four days later on the 29th November and was buried in Cesena War Cemetery, grave reference VII E 8 19. Ernest's medals are currently in the DLI Museum (Medal Case 16 Display Group 2).

Lance Sergeant Ernest Arthur Frederick Pluck is not on any of the Bridlington WW2 memorials but he is recorded on the CWGC website.

Flight Lieutenant (Pilot) LESLIE GEORGE BULL DFC

The Royal Air Force, Service No. 43932

"Bridlington woman's husband shot by Germans". When Steve Adamson was researching for this book he came across the above headline in the Bridlington Free Press of 1944, suitably intrigued, a search on the internet produced a big surprise. The *'husband'* was Flight Lieutenant (Pilot) Leslie Bull and in 1944 he was involved in one of the most famous events of WW2, the 'Great Escape' from Stalag Luft III which was made into a 1962 Hollywood film of the same name starring Steve McQueen. Leslie Bull, also known as 'Johnny' Bull was one of the main tunnelers, and it is said that Steve McQueen's character in the movie is based on him.

On Sunday the 17th July 1938 Leslie George Bull of London had married Kathleen Mary Adeleine Organ of 46 Windsor Crescent Bridlington at the Roman Catholic Church of Our Lady and St. Peter in Bridlington. Leslie (Johnny) Bull was captured in November 1941 when he and his crew were forced to bail out over occupied France when the starboard airscrew fell off his 109 Squadron Wellington Mk IC (s/n T2565).

On the night of the 'Great Escape' in 1944 'Johnny' was 'escaper number 1', the first man to exit the tunnel. However, when he pushed the hatch open the tunnel was short of cover of the woods so he devised a signal rope from the trees to indicate no guards were looking that way. He stayed on the rope and became 'escaper no 12', 76 prisoners escaped but 73 were later recaptured including 'Johnny' Bull. Tragically on March 29th 1944 he was murdered by the Gestapo, one of 50 'escapers' shot on the direct and personal orders of Adolf Hitler. 'Johnny' was 27 years old.

When 'Johnny' was captured in 1941 his wife Kathleen, was expecting their first child and David was born without his father ever meeting him. At the time of writing Kathleen is still alive and living in New Zealand.

The cremated ashes of Leslie George Bull were buried in Poznan Old Garrison Cemetery Poland, grave reference 7. C. 1. He is commemorated on a WW2 plaque in the Church of St Mary and All Saints Dunsfold Surrey and on the CWGC website. He is not on any Bridlington memorial. After the war Gestapo officers associated with the murders were tried as war criminals, 13 were hanged and 17 received long prison sentences.

More Than Just A Name

Index
Name to Page

Name	Page		
ABELL Edwin Raymond	34	CHEETHAM Arnold Foster	68
AKESTER Alfred Harold	35	CHEETHAM Frank Alan	69
ALLAN William Stewart	36	CHIVERS Frank	70
ALLBUT John Frederick Brooke	37	CLARK George Ellis	71
ALTHAM Edwin John Thurston	38	CLARK Robert Ernest	72
ANDERSON Alfred William	39	CLARK John	73
ANDERSON Annie Maria	40	CLARKSON Arthur	74
ANDREWS John Norman	41	CLAXTON Leonard	75
ARKSEY Sidney Kenneth	42	COATES William Noel	76
ARMITAGE Eric Leonard	43	COLE Kenneth Gordon.	77
ASTON Derek Wilson	44	COLMAN Robert William	78
ATHRON Thomas Sydney	45	CONSTABLE Arthur Robert	79
ATKINSON John Joffre	46	COOPER John Dawson	80
AYRE Edward	47	COOPER Kenneth George	81
BAILEY Vincent Thomas	48	COPSEY Frederick	82
BAKER Harry	49	CORNELL George	83
BARNBY Richard Vivian	50	CORNELL Sydney	84
BARRON Walter Frederick	51	CRAMER Roland Montague	28
BARRON Louis Arthur	52	DACRE Arthur Kenneth	85
BATTYE Leslie	53	DARWEN Geoffrey George	86
BEECROFT George	54	DOBSON Geoffrey	87
BEECROFT Edmund Reginald	311	DONDER Otto D	25
BELL Arthur Lawrell	55	DOWSE Leonard	88
BEUTING Harald	25	DOWSE Wilfred Lawrence	89
BIHR Robert	25	DRISCOLL John Featherstone	90
BRAITHWAITE Thomas Henry	56	DUNKERLEY Eric	91
BREMNER Alexander	57	DYNES George Charles	92
BROWN Charles Ernest	58	EARNSHAW Dennis	93
BROWN Frank	59	EDWARDS George	94
BULL Leslie George	313	ELLIS Francis Gordon	95
BURGESS John William	60	ELLIS Fred	96
BUTCHER James A.	61	ELLIS John	97
CAMPBELL Malcolm Anderson	62	ELLISON John	98
CAPPLEMAN Derek	63	EMMERSON William	99
CARTER C H	310	EZARD Henry Stancliffe	100
CARTER George	64	FEATHERSTON Frank	101
CARTER Raymond Noel	65	FINNERTY Francis Joseph B.	102
CAWKILL William R	66	FIRMAN James G.	103
CHATTERTON Elsie Gertrude	67	FISCHER Burghard	28

Name	Page	Name	Page
FLETCHER Charles Henry	104	HEBDON Donovan	143
FLOWER Charles Frederick	105	HENNESKE Georg	28
FORBES Alec Edward	106	HERMON Herbert Cecil	144
FORSTER Thomas Atkin	107	HILDREW Clara Edith	145
FOSTER Harry	108	HILLS Cyril	146
FOWLER Norman Charles	109	HINCHLIFFE Denis Aubrey	147
FREEMAN David	110	HOBSON John Derrick	148
FREEMAN Ward	111	HODGSON Albert William	149
FRIEND Harry Lancelot	112	HOGARTH Kenneth Herbert	150
FUSSEY Gilbert	113	HOGGARD Tom Christopher	151
GANT John Lawrence	114	HOGGARD William Henry	152
GARBETT Leslie Percival	115	HOLDEN Gertrude	153
GARBUTT Peter Denis	116	HOLDERNESS Thomas Clive	154
GARRETT Charles Hy	310	HOLMES Arthur	155
GARRETT Raymond	117	HOPE Frederick William	156
GEE Arthur	118	HORNBY Aubrey Trevor	157
GEE Frederick Henry	119	HORSAMAN Granville	158
GIBB Geoffrey Robson	120	HOUGHTON James Donald	159
GIBSON Ronald Ernest	121	HOWES William Henry	160
GILBERT Frederick	122	HYLAND Molly	161
GILMOUR William Arthur	123	IRELAND George	162
GILSON John Wilson	124	JACKSON William	163
GIOVETTI Pietro Alfredo	125	JAMES Frank Stanley	164
GLAZIER Francis Brian	126	JAMESON Peter	24
GLEDHILL Sydney	127	JEFF John Ernest Phillip	165
GLENVILLE Patrick	128	JEFF Robert Voase	166
GOW Charles Henry	129	JEFFREY Alfred	167
GOW Ian Malcolm	130	JORDAN Arthur J	168
GRAINGER George Kenneth	131	JORDAN Mark	169
GRAF Ulrich	28	JORDAN Ronald Henry	170
GRAY Cyril	132	JULIAN John Philip Reginald	171
GRAY David Anthony	133	KELLY Vincent	172
GREENSIDES Alan Swann	134	KENNY William	173
GREGORY F W	135	KIRBY Arthur William	174
GRONEN Albert	28	KOSCIELNIAK Mieczyslaw	26
GUTHERLESS Ernest Victor	136	KRAUSE Heinz	29
HALSIG Paul	28	KURSCH Severin	25
HANTON Lucas Samuel	137	KWIECINSKI Josef	26
HARDEN George James	138	LAFON Christian Roger Michel	175
HARRISON Alan Bruce	139	LAMMING Malcolm Redfearn	176
HARTLEY Harold Edward	140	LEASON James William	177
HAWKINS Robert Kemplay	141	LEASON John William	178
HAWKSWORTH Richard W. A	142	LEDDY Joseph Patrick	179

The Bridlington Roll of Honour for the Second World War

LESNIAK Jan	26		PINDER Harry	220
LINDSAY Graham Douglas	180		PINKNEY George Olaf	221
LINSLEY John William	181		PLUCK Ernest A. Frederick	312
LISTER Brian John Barnett	182		POHL Robert	25
LOCKWOOD Charles Hellawell	183		POLLARD Francis Harold	222
LONGDEN George Henry	184		POTTER Dennis Kilvington	223
LUMB Arthur	185		POTTER Mabel	224
LYTH Sidney	186		POWLS Frank	225
MARTIN Edward F. Inkereield	187		PRAGER Walter	29
MARTINDALE Frank	188		PRZYWARRA Bruno	29
MARTINDALE Peter Drake	189		PURDON John Kirkwood	226
MASSEY Louis Patrick	190		PURDON Peter D Kirkwood	227
MAXWELL Stanley Maxwell	191		QUODT Wilhelm	25
McALLISTER James	192		REDDING Edward Stanley	228
McKIRDY David	193		RENNOLDSON Thomas	229
MEGSON George	194		RILEY Norah	230
MILLARD John Wilfred	195		RIPLEY Richard James	231
MILLS James Francis Dawson	196		ROBINSON Joseph	232
MILNER Charles	197		ROBSON John Henry	233
MITCHELL Harold	198		ROBSON Norman Cook	234
MOLLETT Richard Douglas	199		ROGERS Harold Dennis	235
MORRIS John William	200		ROGERS Percy	236
MURRAY Robert Maclean	201		ROMYN Ronald Hoskins	237
NAYLOR Claude Lambert	202		ROUNDING John Raymond	238
NEAL Albert Leslie	203		ROUTLEDGE George Elliott	239
NEEDLER George Stephenson	204		ROWLEY Joseph Peter	240
NEUMEYER Arnulf	25		RUSSELL Frank Lincoln	241
NEW Kenneth Eric	205		SAMPSON Joseph	242
NEWTON Jane	206		SANDERSON Gerald	243
NEWTON Thomas Arthur	207		SANGWIN Keith	244
NICHOLSON Agnes Annie	208		SAWDEN Charles	245
NICHOLSON Benjamin	209		SAWDON John Bennett	246
NICHOLSON Patrick James	210		SCHMIDT Erich	29
NIXON Stanley W	211		SCHONE Hermann	29
ORUM Sidney Nielsen	212		SHAW Esther	247
OXTOBY John Martin	213		SHAW John J.	248
PARISH Edward Grant	214		SHIPPEY Harry	249
PARKIN Evelyn	215		SIMPSON Bernard	250
PARKINSON William	216		SIMPSON Norman	251
PEACE Eric Henry	217		SIMPSON Stanley	252
PERKINS Percival George	218		SINZ Helmut	25
PETRY Gerhard	29		SLAUGHTER Henry James	253
PEXTON Harold Cass	219		SMITH Brian Arnold	254

SMITH Malcolm Boston	255	WIKNER Eric Brian	295
SMITH Paul Bostom	256	WILKINSON Peter	296
SMITH Robert	257	WILLBOURN Cyril	297
SPEAR Betty	258	WILLBOURN Jessie Teresa	298
STOREY George Alexander	259	WILLIAMSON Arthur	299
STUBBS Frank	260	WILLIS Harry	300
STURGEON Ernest	261	WILSON Harry Leonard	301
TAYLOR Eric	262	WILSON Henry	302
TEMPLE Charles Henry	263	WILSON Stanley	303
TEMPLE Edward Wilson	264	WITTY Basil Baxter	304
THACKERAY Edward Derek	265	WITTY George Greenley	305
THOMAS Ronald	266	WOOD Harry Gilboy	306
THOMPSON Arthur	267	WOODCOCK John William	307
THOMPSON Stanley William	268	WRIGHT Frank	308
THWAITES Eric Arthur	269	ZDUNEK Aleksander	26
TOWSE Christopher Danby	270		
TRUELOVE Arthur	271		
TURNER Peter Everatt	272		
TWIDDY Donald F.	273		
UNDERWOOD Ernest R.	274		
USHER Geoffrey Frederick	275		
WADE Hector Thorold	276		
WADEY James Joseph	28		
WADSWORTH Phillip	277		
WAINWRIGHT Charles Henry	278		
WAINWRIGHT Gertrude Elizabeth	279		
WAITES Allen G.	280		
WAITES Walter	281		
WALKER Bernard	282		
WALKER Colin Malcolm	283		
WALKER Harry	284		
WARD Ronald	285		
WARDILL Wilfred George	286		
WATSON Dorothy Grace	287		
WATSON James William	288		
WEBB Maurice Guylee	289		
WHITAKER Harold	290		
WHITE William	291		
WHITMAN George Henry	292		
WHITTAKER Arthur John	293		
WHITTAKER Edith	294		